THE ORIGINS OF SOCIALISM

Other Works by George Lichtheim

MARXISM: AN HISTORICAL AND CRITICAL STUDY

THE NEW EUROPE

MARXISM IN MODERN FRANCE

THE CONCEPT OF IDEOLOGY AND OTHER ESSAYS

George Lichtheim

The Origins of Socialism

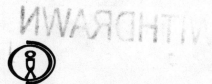

FREDERICK A. PRAEGER, *Publishers*
New York · Washington

BOOKS THAT MATTER

Published in the United States of America in 1969
by Frederick A. Praeger, Inc., Publishers
111 Fourth Avenue, New York, N.Y. 10003

© 1969 by Frederick A. Praeger, Inc.

Library of Congress Catalog Card Number: 69–10520

Printed in the United States of America

For Inna

Preface

The work now before the reader has assumed its peculiar and somewhat daunting shape in response to problems stemming from the fact that it is part of a larger project. Originally intended to serve as the opening section of a general history of socialism and communism, it has for technical reasons been brought to a halt in 1848: that is to say, at the moment when an autonomous socialist labor movement had begun to emerge in Europe from the matrix of the democratic revolution. The interaction between democracy and socialism (or communism) supplies one of the main themes, but it is also the reason why it has not been possible to execute the original project beyond a certain point in time. The explanation will, I believe, become clear to the reader as he considers the record of the six decades between the French Revolution and the upheaval of 1848. It is in part the story of a movement which had to emancipate itself from inherited illusions before it could attain a consciousness of its true nature. And when this clarification was effected, it became evident that socialism was not simply a radicalization of democracy, but something new and distinctive.

Because this is so, a brief analytical history of the socialist movement, from its beginnings to the present time, remains to be written, and it is in fact my intention to provide such an account at a later date. The purpose of the present work is different: to clarify the origins of socialism, both as a world-view and as the specific response of workers and intellectuals to the twofold upheaval of the French Revolution and the industrial revolution. This concentration upon the circumstances of the movement's difficult birth has the unwelcome consequence that nothing can be said about similar stirrings elsewhere in Europe. In particular, the reader will not encounter the founders of Russian Populism: Herzen, Bakunin, and Chernyshevsky. Justice, or at least a measure of reparation, will have to be rendered elsewhere to their angry shades.

There is a further difficulty which had better be faced at the outset. Just as a history of liberalism, or democracy, or both, does well to start in 1776 and to treat as crucial the period ranging from the American Revolution to 1848, so a history of socialism must begin with the French Revolution, for the simple reason that France was the cradle of "utopian socialism" and "utopian communism" alike. The latter, unlike the former, was from the start a plebeian or proletarian movement—a circumstance to which we shall have to return. But both currents stemmed from the great upheaval of 1789–99. Yet it was the industrial revolution in Britain which simultaneously created the material preconditions of modern capitalism and the labor movement; and it was the latter which became the principal vehicle of collectivist thought and practice, once liberal individualism and socialist (or communist) collectivism had been brought face to face. This interaction between the two major West European countries will furnish the theme before we set out to consider the third and final element of our triad—the Marxian synthesis.

So much for the external arrangement. The reader who wonders why he is not told more about the mature thought of Proudhon or Marx should bear in mind that these writers composed their major works after 1848. This is particularly true of Marx, who moreover was the guiding spirit behind the First International founded in 1864, the year of Lassalle's death and Proudhon's last significant public pronouncements. Similarly, it would be pointless to go into details about aspects of Proudhonism (or, for that matter, Blanquism) that point forward to the great catastrophe of the 1871 Paris Commune. I have dealt elsewhere with this subject and must be excused for neglecting it on the present occasion.

This having been said, it only remains to disclaim any intention beyond the obvious one of providing the student with a concise analysis of the subject and a critical introduction to the literature. For the most part, the discussion of technical points has been relegated to the Notes, whose dimensions have also been swelled by the attempt to cite as many sources as possible. It has not, of course, been possible to furnish an exhaustive list of even the secondary literature. Partly for this reason I have taken the liberty of dispensing with a Select Bibliography. There is always some embarrassment about deciding what should go into such a catalog, and it has seemed better not to try. The discerning reader who takes the trouble to consult the Notes will be guided to those writings which the author has found useful for his purpose, though by no means all of them.

It is habitual on these occasions to conclude with an expression of thanks to friends or colleagues who have lent their aid in the final stages of composition. I regret having to depart from this agreeable custom, but the fact is that, while I have discussed the subject for many years and on many occasions with a multitude of acquaintances, I am solely responsible for the conclusions reached in the present study. No part of it has been read in advance of publication by anyone, save Mrs. Elisabeth Sifton, whose editorial labors have rendered the manuscript fit for publication. In recording my gratitude for her unfailing tact and patience (not to mention the stylistic improvements due to her vigilance), I also wish to express my thanks to her for making me feel that the effort invested in this work has not been wholly wasted.

GEORGE LICHTHEIM

London
June 1968

Contents

THE ORIGINS OF SOCIALISM

Introduction:
The Socialist Vision

Socialist history is often written as the story of egalitarian strivings, as ancient perhaps as society itself, or as the record of intellectual systems spun by men reflecting upon the injustices of the social order and determined to set them right. At the other extreme, the term "socialism" is reserved for the class movement of the industrial proletariat, which made its entry on the world scene in the middle decades of the nineteenth century, and whose theorists then preferred to describe themselves as "communists." There is always some arbitrariness in the employment of concepts, but in dealing with a major political and ideological current one cannot disregard the manner in which it has defined itself. The significance of a doctrine, or the purpose of a movement, is revealed by the manner in which it differentiates itself from its surroundings. Hence if one knows that the term "socialism" made its first appearance around 1830 among the radical sects in Western Europe which had sprung from the French Revolution, one will be justified in supposing that its authors saw a connection between that great upheaval and the new social conflicts of the industrial age. It is not as though the concept were external to the activities of the early pioneers who gave currency to it. Whatever may be the case in other fields, the choice of political terminology is never accidental, nor is it without practical significance. Theory and practice are interwoven from the start. The invention of a new concept signifies a new way of looking at the world, and thus helps to constitute forms of social life which at a later stage are embodied in institutions. The first step counts, and in the case of socialism it was taken in an environment profoundly affected by the recent experience of the French Revolution.[1]

That experience was of two kinds. On the one hand, the Revolution had given rise to the first serious attempt to make political democracy a reality in a major European country. On the other hand, it had instituted, or at any rate legitimized, a social order that was profoundly individualist and quite deliberately weighted in favor of a minority of property owners, for whom alone the new creed of *laissez-faire* made sense, in that it corresponded to what they were actually doing. For the bulk of society, then made up of peasants and artisans, economic freedom—in the sense of an uncontrolled market in commodity values, operating in accordance with its own impersonal "laws"—held danger as much as promise. To the proletariat, already in existence on the eve of the industrial revolution in the shape of a mass of paupers deprived of "active" citizenship, this kind of freedom signified virtually nothing beyond the bare right to sell one's labor to the highest bidder. Economic liberalism thus conflicted with social democracy, unless it could be shown that all members of society stood an equal chance of attaining to ownership of property. Such an assertion was more plausible in the America of Jefferson and Jackson than in the France of the July Monarchy, or the England of the 1832 Reform Bill, whence the decisive impact of socialist doctrines in Western Europe and their relative failure to attract attention in the United States.

Beyond these immediate issues there lay the deeper problem of the moral legitimacy attaching to a social order which had proclaimed individual self-interest as its only guiding rule. The Anglo-French and more particularly the Scottish Enlightenment, whose literature had helped to prepare the ground for the political emancipation of civil (or bourgeois) society, was committed to a naïve doctrine of social harmony arising spontaneously through the liberation of private initiative. From about 1800, when revolutionary ardors began to cool, a reaction set in which at first took the form of romantic conservatism. The socialist challenge around 1830 thus represented a second stage in a process of disillusionment. Unlike the conservative critics of early liberalism, those writers who a generation later called themselves socialists (or in some cases communists) had no desire to return to an earlier age. What they did was to combine the rationalist faith in science and industry with a radical critique of the new individualism.[2]

It is important to distinguish this theme from the analysis of the fully developed capitalist system which later became the special concern of the Marxian school. Although Marx and his associates had their roots in the romantic socialism of the pre-1848 period, which (like the entire romantic movement) went out of fashion in the 1850's, Marxism represented a conscious break with the "utopian" creed of the first generation of pioneers. That generation reacted to the new social environment in a manner determined by modes of thought proper to a pre-industrial culture. In particular, it showed an inclination to identify the critique of capitalism as a system of production with the rejection of industrialism as such. There was also a good deal of confusion over the role of science and in particular a tendency to dismiss economic reasoning as "abstract," by comparison with the greater concreteness of historical or literary perception. Lastly, the industrial revolution and the French Revolution were conflated into a single phenomenon: a challenge to what was sometimes described as a Christian social order.

In all these respects 1848 was a watershed. It marked off one age from another—not because the *Communist Manifesto* was published in that stormy year, but because in Britain this period witnessed the defeat of Chartism and the consolidation of Victorian society. We shall have occasion to revert to these circumstances. What matters here is to single out their relevance for the emerging socialist movement. Once more it has to be stressed that the theoretical content of socialism cannot be divorced from the circumstances of its birth, as though it were a timeless protest against inequality or injustice which accidentally took on flesh at one particular moment. What was intended from the first was the assertion that a particular social order was possible and desirable. This order was visualized in different ways, but it excluded the uncontrolled ownership of the new means of production by a class of wealthy proprietors. It also implied a criticism of the Benthamite faith in rational self-interest, though not of utilitarianism as such (if simply understood as a criterion for legislation designed to promote individual and collective welfare). On all these counts, the socialist movement from the start defined itself as a critique of liberalism which yet conserved the prime heritage of the

Enlightenment: the commitment to personal liberty and rationality. Socialism, in the minds of its adherents, presented itself as a creed transcending the battle-cries of the parties who had confronted each other in the course of the French Revolution.[3]

The three-cornered struggle between conservative, liberal, and socialist ideas and movements during these decades must be seen both in its uniqueness and for the light it sheds on later situations and other environments. The precise circumstances of the age were of course never reproduced. History being irreversible, it was not possible for other civilizations to undergo once more the peculiar birth-trauma of modern Western society. Once the memory of 1789 and 1793 had faded, the social conflicts arising from the impact of the new mode of production were no longer viewed through the distorting lens of polemics between Jacobins and anti-Jacobins, republicans and royalists, rationalists and defenders of established religion. The formative years of the socialist movement —broadly speaking 1815 to 1848—coincided with the aftermath of the French Revolution and the political passions it had aroused. The character of the movement was marked by these experiences, hence the relationship of socialism to democracy was inevitably viewed in the light of the political convulsions France and Europe had recently undergone. Yet on theoretical grounds it might have been argued that there was no necessary connection between the two. The industrial revolution, after all, had started in England around 1760, and there seemed to be no obvious reason why the economic changes it was causing should be brought into relationship with the political convulsions on the Continent. The vision of a single upheaval embracing all these phenomena, plus the American Revolution and the anti-slavery movement, came well after the event, and its authors included aristocratic conservatives like Tocqueville, or moderate liberals like John Stuart Mill, as well as radicals like Marx. By 1848, when this phase was over, theorists belonging to all three schools had more or less established the terms of discourse for the remainder of the century, but the first generation of socialists had to make their way unaided. Moreover, unlike the still dominant conservative forces in state and society, or the rising liberal school with its hold over the propertied and educated middle class, these early socialists lacked institutional backing and a recognized "constituency." The labor movement was still in its infancy. Its relationship to the emerging socialist critique of bourgeois society had to be clarified, and this task occupied an entire generation. Indeed down to 1848 this was the first order of business for socialists or communists (as the more radical critics of private property came to be called). Theoretical refinements such as the Marxian analysis of capitalism came later. The immediate issue was quite simply the nature of the new social order which by 1830 had emerged from the turmoil of political and economic change.

Yet the historical approach must not be pushed to the point of identifying the content of the new socialist doctrines with the circumstances under which they first saw the light. It is undoubtedly the case that the socialist movement, as it came into being around 1830, bore the imprint of the dual revolution. At the same time, the specific novelty of socialism lay in the fact that it differentiated itself from the much more widespread democratic radicalism of the period by stressing the idea of cooperation (or alternatively of public regulation) and disputing the claims of private ownership. This marked a line of division between democrats and socialists, although the former could and did manifest some concern over issues such as pauperism and the condition of the working class. The "social question" introduced a cleavage between the socialist school and those democratic radicals who contended that all men stood to benefit from private enterprise. The belief that there was nothing intrinsically wrong with private ownership was just what distinguished one party from the other. In this sense the term "social democratic," which became fashionable after 1848 (and more particularly after 1864), veiled an ambiguity, albeit those who adopted it thought of themselves as (democratic) socialists. In any case, whether they were democrats or not, socialist critics of capitalism defined themselves not simply by deploring the condition of the laboring poor, but by rejecting the claims of economic liberalism.[4]

England and France being the twin birth-places of the new movement, it was inevitable that national differences should enter into the understanding of what the term socialism signified, for not all those who employed it were committed to the revolutionary ideas which its French adherents had taken over from the men of 1789 and 1793. In France, Jacobinism for many years remained the dominant mode of thought among what was coming to be known as "the Left," even though some prominent French socialists were critical of this tradition. To the British it was a foreign import, and Robert Owen's followers in particular tended to disparage it. The association of socialism with democracy took time to establish itself; that of socialism with republicanism (let alone atheism) was far from obvious, at any rate to radicals outside France. There were good reasons for this, not least the existence of a Christian socialist current which for historical reasons was more important in England than on the Continent. The notion that socialist conclusions could be derived from religious precepts made an obvious appeal to philanthropists stemming from the middle class, even though the bulk of that class was firmly on the side of economic *laissez-faire*. There were also a few socialist sympathizers among the aristocracy, who perhaps disliked the new individualism chiefly because it was subversive of the kind of ordered hierarchical community in which they believed. However this may be, the frontiers between conservatism and socialism remained fluid for some time—at any rate in England, less so on the Continent. Though the churches in all countries generally sided with authority, it appeared possible that a pacific and reformist kind of socialism might obtain the tacit blessing if not of the hierarchy, at any rate of significant numbers of the laity. Something of the sort actually occurred in England at a later stage, in the 1890's, when the growth of the labor movement reflected itself in the spread of socialist ideas among Evangelical Dissenters disappointed with liberalism. By that time, however, socialism as a doctrine was already fully formed, and the attitudes it encouraged, although tinged with religious sentiment, were subversive of the social teachings which the churches had traditionally made their own.[5]

Teachings of this kind, although never hostile to private ownership as such, implied a certain degree of resistance to the unrestrained pursuit of private gain, over and above what was termed a reasonable remuneration for an individual's labor (which of course included the labor of the merchant or manufacturer). Difficult to apply in practice, such attitudes nonetheless formed a barrier to that intensive concentration on the production of material wealth which was the precondition of economic growth. Hence in part the ideological resistance which the full-blown ideology of economic liberalism encountered in Catholic countries. Hence also the importance that Calvinism possessed for the entrepreneurial middle class, once Calvin's followers had come to terms with the new spirit. It is perhaps well to remember that European capitalism antedated the Reformation. Still, Protestant ideology was clearly helpful at some critical phases. Much later, after socialism had formulated its critique of bourgeois society, the Calvinist accommodation to the new industrial order became the target of rueful self-criticism. The authors of such critical reflections commonly treated the medieval "satisfaction of wants" doctrine, proper to a society of small commodity producers, as the standard by which to judge the conditions of their own times. Popular among craftsmen who were beginning to be dispossessed by the industrial revolution, this form of anti-capitalism lost ground when modern socialism, with its implicit acceptance of the new industrial order, appeared on the scene.[6]

This was the negative side of the matter. But the religious tradition could likewise be employed to legitimize the longing for a communal way of life, and the belief that men had in fact once lived in a genuine community before their ancient ways were uprooted. If all men were in principle equal—and this had always been affirmed in religious teaching, albeit with qualifications which safely removed the dangerous sting from this proposition—was it not right and just that their basic needs should receive equal attention? In the past, such demands had been dismissed as impractical, but now that the industrial revolution, by unleashing the forces of production, had opened new vistas of wealth-creation, it became difficult to argue that equal satisfaction of material wants, though perhaps praiseworthy, was in practice unattainable. If society was potentially so much richer than had always been supposed, why should not all reasonable material needs be met in accordance with simple moral criteria? And if the prevailing social organization stood in the way, why should it not be transformed—peacefully if possible, less peacefully if the propertied class offered resistance? These awkward suggestions could not be dismissed once it was seen that general welfare was in fact practicable—had indeed become so precisely owing to the industrial upheaval which the bourgeois revolution had got under way. In so far as the religious inheritance comported an egalitarian bias, it was possible to assert that a measure of equality could and should be translated into practice; not merely, as before, in small isolated communities, but in relation to the whole of society. And this was precisely what the "utopian" schools of socialism between 1815 and 1848 undertook to do.[7]

We are thus faced with the paradox that the same religious tradition which implicitly condemned the pursuit of material gain also encouraged the quest for greater equality, and to that extent made it respectable for socialists to demand that the new wealth should be equitably shared. This is perhaps no more than to say that in an environment profoundly conditioned by a millennium of Christian teaching such demands (as well as the doctrines of opposing schools) were necessarily framed in terms inherited from the past. As we shall see, this was not uniformly so. The socialist vision could also support itself with arguments drawn from the naturalist and materialist doctrines of the eighteenth century. This particular tradition was stronger in France than in England, but it permeated the movement in both countries. Conceptually, socialism in its origins is an Anglo-French creation, although its classical formulation was only achieved by Marx with the help of German philosophy. This threefold movement involving the three principal countries of Western Europe is the theme to which we shall have to give our attention.

But before venturing upon our main topic, something will have to be said about the precursors—above all Rousseau and the presocialist current of thought and feeling which stemmed from him. We shall of course encounter his pupils as we approach the first part of our triad, but what of the man himself? And what of the philosophical legacy which lay at the back of his thinking and of much besides—the Natural Law tradition? One cannot hope to reconstruct the entire intellectual history of the period, but it really is impossible to understand either the French Revolution or the early socialists unless one possesses some awareness of the challenge which the new liberal individualism represented to older ways of life. At the ideological level, which concerns us here, the challenge evoked a variety of responses, from Tory romanticism and Catholic paternalism to the primitive "communism" of writers like Mably and Morelly, who were Rousseau's contemporaries and perhaps his rivals. However, Rousseau's response is the best known, and it is also the one which in the short run had the most profound political impact. Where then does he stand and how shall we classify him?[8]

So as not to burden this introductory discussion with technicalities which have no place here, I shall resist the temptation to say something about the connection between Natural Law philosophy and the labor theory of value. The topic will engage our attention when we come to Ricardo and his school. But Natural Law itself cannot be ignored. It played its part in validating both the American and the French revolutions. It was subjected to destructive criticism by Hegel, and, as we shall see, Marx had the greatest difficulty in reconciling the Hegelian approach with the Natural Law tradition still alive and at work in the socialist and communist doctrines he encountered during his transition from Germany to France, and from philosophy to politics. On these grounds alone it is important to ask how far Rousseau was responsible for the faith of the early French socialists and/or communists. (The distinction between these terms will be cleared up later.) But there is more to it than historical exegesis: we are still, at the present day, faced with some of the unsolved problems inherited from an age when it was held that a socialist critique of liberal individualism, or of bourgeois society (which from the sociologist's viewpoint amounts to the same), must take a stand upon the most ancient of philosophical issues: is there such a thing as a definable "human nature," and if there is, what is it? And does it provide a yardstick whereby to judge existing social institutions? The Stoic philosophers of antiquity had one answer to this question, and so did medieval Christianity, albeit a different one, rooted not in the Stoics but in Plato and Aristotle. Rousseau too had an answer (or thought he had one), and his Jacobin pupils put his doctrines to the test of experience. When the result failed to come up to their expectations, two different reactions were possible. The failure could be blamed upon particular political errors (or particular social classes). Alternatively, the Rousseauist inheritance could be abandoned altogether. On the whole, the French socialists tended toward the first solution, the Germans toward the second. (Marx, as we shall see, tried to synthesize the two.) And the British? Ostensibly they abandoned philosophical speculation in favor of an approach rooted in their own traditional empiricism: the utilitarian doctrine, with its stress upon practical consequences and the "greatest happiness" of the greatest number. But utilitarianism was itself derived from Natural Law, even though Bentham and James Mill might be unaware of the fact! There is no getting away from it: both the liberal school and its socialist critics held certain moral assumptions in common. Had they not done so, there could not have been any significant debate between them, or between both and the conservatives who clung to the older religious standpoint.[9]

Where precisely does Rousseau stand in the matter? To cut a long story short, he substantially adopted the Natural Law doctrine in its original Stoic form; that is to say, he affirmed that men are sociable *by nature* and possess an inborn inclination to do good to their fellow-men. Secondly, he asserted that there had once been a primitive age when a moral code based upon uncorrupted human nature was actually operative. And thirdly, he held that the code could not be made to work under the conditions prevalent in the society of his own age, but *might* recover its original purpose if that society were purified. Natural man, following his spontaneous inclination, is sociable and benevolent; it is civilization which is evil. This did not signify that a return to a hypothetical state of nature was literally possible. It *did* mean that institutions should be judged in terms of what they had done, or might do, to natural man as such.

What does this have to do with socialism or communism? Rousseau—unlike Morelly and Mably—did not preach the community of goods, but he did assert that the fall from the original state of equality had been precipitated by the introduction of private property. This notion, however, was also held by Enlightenment thinkers such as Helvétius and Diderot who were resigned to the thought that a price had to be paid for civilization. Rousseau's importance lies in his insistence that the re-creation of an egalitarian social order is possible, although he never managed to explain precisely how an uncorrupted society could be established by the corrupted individuals composing the actual world of men. The way out—so far as he felt able to indicate a practical approach to the legislator confronted with the problem of instituting an egalitarian order—lay in appealing to the "general will" of the community, as distinct from the sum of particular wills. But—and it is this which made him a precursor of socialism—*the general will operates only in a society with equal distribution of property* (*or with socialized property*). Thus we seem to have a circle: the regeneration of society demands an appeal to the general will, but in a corrupt world the general will is inoperative. This circularity, however, is not a problem for the philosopher, whose duty it is simply to state the truth as he sees it. The truth as Rousseau saw it was that for practical purposes an egalitarian social order could only be introduced under exceptional circumstances. When pressed, the example he gave was Corsica—the birthplace of Bonaparte, who in his youth became a fervent Rousseauist but progressively lost his enthusiasm for Rousseau as he grew older and acquired personal power.

All this, however, pertained to the domain of the legislator. It did not disprove the truth intuitively seized upon by Rousseau: the truth that, by Natural Law standards, society was corrupt. There was a tension between "is" and "ought." What, then, could men do? According to Rousseau, they had only to trust their inborn moral sense, and society might yet be regenerated.[10]

That this was not in fact a sufficient answer to the question how a new social order might be created by a deliberate act of will became evident in the course of the French Revolution. The reaction to this disillusionment in turn produced, among other things, a renewed emphasis upon the study of concrete historical circumstances, as against Natural Law speculation about the nature of man or the remote origins of civilization. This emphasis is very marked in Hegel—especially the later and more conservative Hegel, who yet retained some of his youthful enthusiasm for the *ideals* of the French Revolution (as distinct from its actual outcome). We are thus brought to the threshold of our theme, for reasons having to do both with the immediate impact of the upheaval and the relevance of Rousseau for the next generation of Europeans. That generation witnessed a debate between conservative traditionalists, liberal individualists, and socialist collectivists faced with a triumphant bourgeois society and the overwhelming reality of the new industrial technology. In what follows, these developments are treated not precisely in the order in which they arose (for the industrial revolution was already under way when the political explosion occurred in France) but rather in the order in which they presented themselves to the minds of the participants. We therefore begin with France, and with the emergence of primitive socialism and communism from the crucible of the great Revolution.

PART ONE

Heirs of the French Revolution

1. The Egalitarians

No study of socialist origins can attempt to resume, however briefly, the events of the period or the political cleavages to which they gave rise. On the other hand, it would evidently be futile to discuss the radicals of the period in terms of their ideas only. The historian is confronted with the turmoil of the years between 1789 and 1799, when the first attempt was made to introduce democracy in France. One cannot speak of the egalitarian movement without invoking the names of Babeuf and Darthé, who went to the guillotine in May 1797. But how is their so-called Conspiracy of the Equals to be described without letting in a mass of circumstantial detail about the France of those years? The mere fact that Babeuf's principal successor, Buonarroti, an Italian-born Frenchman by naturalization, was briefly Bonaparte's colleague, and in 1796 still advised him on Italian affairs, is enough to inspire a wealth of reflections upon the theme that liberalism, republicanism, communism, and Bonapartism were all born at the same time. But it is just this which makes it impossible to go beyond the mere enunciation of these topics.[1]

One might devote entire pages to the biography of François-Noël Babeuf (1760–97) or the career of Buonarroti and still fail to do justice to the endless complications of the bloodstained scene upon which the Babouvists made their brief appearance, during the interval between the fall of Robespierre in 1794 and Bonaparte's seizure of power in 1799. And having done so, one would still be at a loss to account for the fact that Buonarroti became the teacher of Auguste Blanqui and, through him, a fountainhead of that part of the revolutionary tradition which is summed up in the term "dictatorship." For these underground filiations are comprehensible only when one takes into account the conspiratorial sects of

17

the Restoration period (1815–30), the republican risings following the July Revolution of 1830, and the subsequent conversion of
some among the conspirators to a primitive form of socialism or
communism. All this is part of the turbulent history of the age
and needs to be borne in mind in trying to assess the peculiar
mental and moral atmosphere in which that generation of men
lived and moved. But in an analytical account of socialism these
circumstances must simply be taken for granted. With one important proviso, however: the events are to be regarded not as a
"background" to the evolution of doctrines, but rather as the
crucible in which the ideas, programs, manifestos, and other overt
manifestations of thinking and feeling were formed. The passions
that inspired the actors were not external to the movement of
thought. French socialism was revolutionary from the very beginning, just as English socialism was reformist from the hour of
its birth. The decisive difference lay in the fact that the French
Revolution had taught men to think in terms of seizing power.
Even the least violent among the French socialists of the 1840's,
even Louis Blanc and his followers, were committed to assumptions about the political process which across the Channel were
entertained only as a matter of academic speculation.

We are thus obliged to make an arbitrary choice in restricting
ourselves to themes that fall under the general heading of intellectual history. This expository device is to be regarded as a kind of
shorthand, the full text (which cannot be supplied) being the
political history of the age. To be sure, even the latter is no more
than an abstraction if viewed against the full reality of an irre-
coverable past. Not even the most dramatic account can do more
than conjure up a pale wraithlike representation of the actual
spectacle as it once unfolded upon a scene now gone forever. Historical thought, like all thought, operates at a remove. It seizes
upon spoken or written utterances which once possessed something
of the magical quality pulsating in those evanescent figures, causing
them to speak and act in ways that left an enduring mark on the
hearts and minds of their contemporaries. At a further remove,
even the individual writings and their authors disappear from view.
What remains are general terms—liberty, equality, and so on. Yet

we know that these concepts can be turned into symbols and as such have power over men's minds. The Tricolor, the Marseillaise, the Red Flag, the International—these images have behind them a reality of toil and strife, of suffering long endured and passions deeply repressed, suddenly exploding into historical action, "real" action, as we say. The symbols mediate between the concepts and the individuals who seize upon them as expressions of their emotions: following the flag, marching to the chant of the battle hymn. Yet in the sort of account that must of necessity prevail where ideas and programs are in question, the symbols, and the passions they evoke, are absent. We are left with the "gray on gray" of textbook history.

This is said by way of warning, not in order to apologize for the lack of descriptive detail. Intellectual history is inevitably confined to one particular dimension of reality. All one can do is try to remember what the conceptual shorthand stands for, to recall the painful emergence of these intellectual images from their blood-stained environment. Thus, in speaking of the Babouvist conspiracy, we may remind ourselves that Babeuf and Sylvain Maréchal had been stirred in their youth by the writings of Rousseau. Alternatively, we may search the *Discourse on Inequality* and the *Social Contract* for the first faint stirrings of what would later be termed communist ideas. But we do not suppose that the writings of Rousseau, or those of Meslier,[2] Mably,[3] or Morelly,[4] hold the key to an understanding of left-wing Jacobinism or of Babouvism. These short-lived political movements refract the concrete experiences of disillusioned radicals, who from about 1795 onward reacted violently to the discovery that the Revolution and the Republic had not introduced social equality or done away with material poverty. The life stories of the individuals concerned enter into the political drama of the period: the fall of the Jacobin regime in 1794, the establishment of the Directory as the first executive government of a bourgeois Republic in 1795, and the abortive revolt in 1795–96 of radical extremists who aimed at a terrorist dictatorship, a general confiscation of wealth, and the establishment of an egalitarian commonwealth. This was the birth trauma of French communism and of the nascent French proletariat, but we cannot deal with it here beyond the bare mention of a few names. It must be enough to indicate the precise moment when communism, as a definite political and ideological current, makes its first appearance. We shall then see what it is that differentiates communists from socialists, and how the terms "socialism," "communism," and "anarchism" come to stand both for general ideas and for particular episodes. Once this has been grasped, the later history of the concepts is seen to reflect a set of problems that were already present, albeit in a more primitive form, when the storm of the Revolution burst upon France.[5]

The reason why 1795–96 marks such a crucial watershed can be clearly stated: down to that moment, the egalitarian drive to do away with poverty or with the distinction between rich and poor citizens had still been held within the accepted framework of personal ownership. Even the extremists guillotined by Robespierre a few months before his own fall in July 1794 were not communists in the modern sense of the term. They might favor the proscription of the rich and the seizure of their property for the benefit of poorer citizens, but such notions were commonplace among radical democrats of the age, and if put into practice they would scarcely have resulted in more than a generalization of poverty. What lay behind such slogans was not the vision of a new social order but the defensive reaction of an old one. The Parisian *sans-culottes* were for the most part independent artisans, though they also included salaried workers, more or less steadily employed. Their aim, insofar as they possessed one, was a state of affairs in which all men would individually own a few tools, a plot of land, or a workshop—just enough to support a family. For practical purposes this had been the aim of Rousseau and his followers, for all their occasional (and rather irrelevant) railings against private property as the prehistoric source of all evil. To the extent that they pursued an egalitarian vision based on the equal distribution of individual ownership, even the most extreme and terroristic among the radicals who backed the government of the Montagne and the Jacobin Club in 1793–94 were still moving within the orbit of what communists would later call bourgeois democracy. This is not to deny that there was a profound social cleavage between these plebeians and the middle-class democrats who followed the lead of

Robespierre and the Jacobin Club. But this cleavage did not at first affect their joint commitment to the Rousseauist ideal of a society in which all Frenchmen would be free and equal—that is, active citizens and owners of property. Plebeian discontent was held in bounds by the conviction that private property *could* be shared equally and that the Republic had been instituted for the purpose of effecting such a share-out. As long as such beliefs were held by those vaguely known as "the poor," their growing dissatisfaction with the bourgeois Republic could not yet be labelled "communist."[6]

The Conspiracy of the Equals marked, then, the dividing line between Rousseauist democracy and communism. The line was crossed by radical democrats who had come to believe that the consumption (if not as yet the production) of material goods must be regulated by the community on the basis of strict equality. From this moment onward there were two parties on the "Left": democrats and communists. Or rather three, for as we shall see in the next chapter, the first socialists took an intermediate position, although this was not at the start clearly perceived by all concerned.

Babouvism thus enters history as an abortive rising of the nascent urban proletariat against a bourgeois regime, at a moment when the bourgeoisie (or a section of it) was itself revolutionary and moreover had just won the backing of the newly enfranchised peasantry (and consequently of the army, which was mostly made up of peasants and led by officers drawn from the middle class). This alone is enough to characterize the plebeian insurrection as hopeless. The conspiratorial details do not concern us. The importance of Babouvism lies in the fact that it foreshadowed the themes of the later communist movement, after an industrial working class had come into being. Babeuf's (or rather Sylvain Maréchal's) *Manifeste des Égaux* of 1796 is the first communist document, in that it fuses the traditional demand for equality with the revolutionary spirit released by the events of 1789 and 1793. "The people" are to seize power, do away with class distinctions, and institute a commonwealth in which there will be neither rich nor poor.[7]

Whether or not the future order was seen as stateless as well as classless, the immediate aim was the establishment of a dictatorship and the intensification of terrorism. In this respect Babeuf and his associates appear as the precursors of nineteenth-century radicals like Blanqui and, at a remove, of the Russian revolutionary Populists of the 1860's and 1870's whose heritage was subsequently assumed by the Bolsheviks. The extreme wing of the French Revolution may thus be said to have given birth to a set of notions which, while never successfully pursued in France, were destined to become politically effective in Russia. The crucial factor is the belief that the abolition of poverty demands a temporary dictatorship which will dispossess the rich, who are also the effective holders of power. The dictatorship will be exercised in the name of the people (or the proletariat), and it will come to an end when its enemies have been forcibly removed or otherwise rendered harmless. This is what "communism" signified to the followers of Babeuf and Sylvain Maréchal, and it is this understanding of the term which was transmitted, by way of Buonarroti, to Blanqui and ultimately to his followers among the leaders of the 1871 Paris Commune, who made a brief and abortive attempt to put the scheme into practice.

One must not suppose that the distinction between communism and radical democracy was clearly apparent to Babeuf and his companions, though they were conscious of some difference from the other adherents of the democratic 1793 Constitution with whom they were briefly allied in 1795–96. Ideologically, both groups were committed to some form of Rousseauism, but the future communists were beginning to draw radical conclusions from the demand for a limitation upon the claims of private ownership. Politically, they were held together by the common struggle against the Directory and the inegalitarian Constitution of 1795 which limited the right to vote, thereby in effect excluding the urban working class from citizenship. In the short run, these circumstances counted for more than Babeuf's commitment to a form of communism which in practice would have signified little more than the levelling of incomes. There was as yet no thought of socializing the means of production, which were all in the hands of small producers. The "communist" aspect of the whole scheme was barely perceptible to the government or the public, and 'in the ensuing trial Babeuf and his associates appeared simply as associates of rebellious "Jacobins," "Maratists," and other "terrorists" accused of conspiring to restore by force of arms the dictatorship of a faction supported by the *sans-culottes*.

None of this is surprising when one considers that in the France of the 1790's the term "property" signified above all ownership of land. There was no question of socializing large-scale industry, for none existed. Social radicalism could only take the form of legislating for a redistribution of privately owned wealth. When applied to farm property, this would normally lead to the assertion that the land should periodically be redivided, that is, parcelled out equally among all the inhabitants, to be held by them individually. Insofar as such notions were then current, they had been outlawed by the Convention, which on March 18, 1793, decreed the death penalty for advocates of what was then known as the "agrarian law." Like so much else at the time (e.g., Babeuf's adopted *prénom* "Gracchus") this was a classical reminiscence, for it was commonly supposed that any extremism would take the form it had once assumed in Greece or Rome. There is some evidence that Babeuf, whose background was one of rural poverty and agitation for radical land reform, had advanced beyond these primitive notions, but the matter was never put to the test. In respect of the urban proletariat—and the Babouvist conspiracy was after all an urban affair—"communism" could only signify the confiscation of private wealth belonging to "the rich," that is, in practice to the bourgeoisie which had recently won control of the government and the parliamentary assemblies. In the circumstances it is hardly surprising that the discovery of the conspiracy alarmed the middle class, since its aim appeared to be the re-establishment of terrorism and a general "soak the rich" policy; but by itself this did not amount to communism in the modern sense.[8]

In so far as genuine communism enters Babeuf's rather primitive system of ideas, it does so by way of his concern for ending the misery of the poor, a term under which he includes indifferently both urban and rural paupers. His notions on the subject are expounded at somewhat tedious length in a programmatic letter to

Charles Germain of July 28, 1795, which may be regarded as the summary of his mature political views.[9] Starting from the familiar eighteenth-century doctrine that Nature intended men to be equal, he employs a few Natural Law propositions to underpin a fairly drastic system of legislation designed to expropriate the rich and prevent the re-emergence of inequality. This is to be done (after the preliminary leveling) by attaching every man to the employment or occupation he knows best, collecting the products of his labor in a central store owned by the community, and distributing the fruits of toil on a strictly egalitarian basis to the associated producers. Wages are to be equal, and no account is to be taken of differences in skill or of claims based on superior talent or intelligence. (This last point is developed at some length in another document, the *Manifeste des Plébéiens,* composed in the following year, where reference is made to the practical experience gathered in this form of administration by the armies of the Republic—an interesting anticipation of the notion of "armies of labor" which was to figure briefly in the early stages of the Russian Revolution.) It is not clear whether the egalitarian system of distribution is to rest on a genuine "communism of production," for which in any case the time was hardly ripe. There are some indications that Babeuf did not favor the subdivision of peasant property implicit in the then current notions of periodic agrarian redistribution, but he can hardly be said to have worked out an alternative model of communal or cooperative farming, though there are some passing remarks about the advantages of such a system.[10]

The later development of Babouvism is linked with the name of Buonarroti, whose personality and record are somewhat less shadowy and better documented. Philippe Michel Buonarroti (1761–1837), who for some reason called himself Filippo Michelangelo Buonarroti, survived the catastrophe of the abortive rising and the furious official persecution of 1796–97, which claimed many of his associates. While Babeuf and Darthé perished on the scaffold (as had the Robespierrists and the Hébertists before them), Buonarroti escaped with banishment and spent the remaining four decades of his long life transmitting the Babouvist inheritance to the secret societies which flourished in Western Europe before and after the Revolution of 1830. Did he hand on the heritage intact? It seems probable that the original body of ideas underwent a sea change as the workers' movement became more important, while peasant rebellion retained its relevance in Spain and Italy (and subsequently in Poland and Russia) rather than in France. In this sense Buonarroti is a link between the democratic and the socialist movements or, if one prefers it, between the French Revolution and the European risings of 1848. The conspiratorial aspect remained, and was inherited by Blanqui, whose ascetic figure dominates the secret history of the following age. On the other hand, the terrorist note is progressively muted, though it does not disappear altogether. On its organizational side, Blanquism probably owed as much to the Charbonnerie (the French branch of the secret society based in Italy and known as the Carbonari) as to Buonarroti's example. It can be argued that Blanqui's understanding of "communism" was substantially related to the Babouvist tradition, as was his fanatical patriotism, his dislike of international organizations, and his indifference to the slowly developing labor movement in industrially more advanced countries. On all these counts he appears as a transitional figure and as Buonarroti's legitimate heir, if not his disciple in a precise biographical sense. At one stage, in 1832, both men adhered to one of the secret societies, the Amis du Peuple. It is not clear when and where they met, but Buonarroti mentions Blanqui in his correspondence.[11]

Whether or not there was an "apostolic succession" (of which the Blanquist tradition has conserved some pious memories), Blanquism may be said to embody the chief elements of what has been called "Jacobin communism"—possibly a misnomer, save in so far as Blanqui is sometimes credited (wrongly, it seems) with having coined the term "dictatorship of the proletariat."[12] Before turning to these matters, it will be convenient to deal with the other socialist and communist schools of the 1830's.

2. *The Utopians*

It was remarked above that the terms "socialism" and "communism" from the start translated different attitudes toward the society that emerged from the turmoil of the Revolution. If in what follows we deal first with the so-called utopian schools of French socialism, principally the Saint-Simonians and the Fourierists, this arrangement is not to be understood as signifying that the concept of socialism relates exclusively to their peculiar doctrines. At a later stage we shall encounter other variants (notably the anarcho-socialism of Proudhon) which clearly belong to the same general stream while displaying quite distinct characteristics. The relevant point is that in all these cases we have to do with writers who entertained no sympathy for Jacobinism and stood aloof from the radical-democratic sects described in the previous section. The egalitarian current was not the only one, and it was possible to develop a critique of bourgeois society with the help of assumptions quite different from those of Babeuf and his communist progeny.

Let it also be borne in mind that we are dealing with socialists, not simply with people who were critical of *laissez-faire* or alarmed by the spectacle of pauperism. The dividing line admittedly is fluid, for the socialist school was constituted by way of incessant arguments among critics of the new economics. These included men like Sismondi, who should perhaps be described as a left-wing liberal; and unorthodox Catholics like Lamennais, who combined attachment to republican democracy with romantic leanings obscurely pointing in the direction of what was later styled Christian socialism. For our purpose, critics such as these may be disregarded, and this for two reasons: they had little influence; and their practical proposals led away from the central issue brought into prominence by the Saint-Simonians after 1830, when socialism

26

at last achieved public recognition and a measure of political relevance. That issue was social control of the new industrial economy, not merely the furtherance of equality or the alleviation of pauperism. There were indeed some prominent former Saint-Simonians who adhered to an undogmatic kind of Christianity, e.g., Pierre Leroux, but they were root-and-branch socialists, not simply "social reformers." We are therefore justified in disregarding the occasional heretics within the liberal or the Catholic camp, with the obvious proviso that their existence introduced a certain unrest among people unaffected by socialism (let alone communism) properly so described. In terms of intellectual history, these outsiders may safely be called Rousseauists. That is to say, they belonged to the past. Insofar as their writings issued in practical policy recommendations, they reduced themselves to variations on the familiar theme that all citizens (not merely the rich) *ought* to become owners of (private) property.[1]

We therefore begin, in the conventional manner, with the true utopians—Etienne Cabet (1788–1856) and Charles Fourier (1772–1837)—before turning to the Saint-Simonian school. Of the two, Cabet, although the author of a genuine Utopia, the *Voyage en Icarie,* was less interesting as a writer, though far more energetic and enterprising as an individual. His literary futurama has affinities to such later specimens of the genre as William Morris's *News from Nowhere* and Edward Bellamy's *Looking Backward.* It is communist, not merely socialist: the communist slogan "to each according to his needs" (an inheritance from the Babouvists, of whom Cabet for other reasons was critical, though he knew and admired Buonarroti) appeared on the frontispiece of his book. Moreover, Icaria was conceived, at any rate ideally and in principle, on a national scale, with a system of government on authoritarian lines. It is noteworthy that in outlining his model state, Cabet showed himself to be neither a pure agrarian nor a mere associationist like Owen, whom he personally admired but criticized for spending too much energy on the promotion of small model communities. Yet the only practical attempt to institute an "Icarian" settlement took a markedly Owenite form. It was made in the United States in 1848–49, and Cabet can thus claim the merit of having introduced communism to America, albeit on a small scale. A first experiment in Texas having misfired, the locale was transferred to a former Mormon center at Nauvoo, Illinois. There Cabet himself took charge, having left France after the failure of the 1848 revolution. A second and more successful settlement (at Corning, Iowa) lasted until 1895. The story of these experiments is perhaps less relevant than the fact that they represented a departure from the original spirit of Cabet's work, which was meant to possess national importance for France and indeed universal significance for mankind.

In a biographical study of prominent figures among the early French socialists and communists, Cabet would merit more than the passing reference here accorded him. For one thing, he was in his own person an important link between the Jacobinism of the secret societies and the new working-class movement, having started his political life, as did so many other republicans of the period who later turned to socialism, in the Charbonnerie during the Restoration. It was quite in accordance with the spirit of this organization that Cabet should have taken part in the July Revolution of 1830 which placed Louis Philippe on the throne and been rewarded for his activities by being made *procureur-général* in Corsica for a brief period, as well as entering the Chamber of Deputies in 1831. But thereafter his radical republicanism soon carried him beyond the bounds of legality and of the July Monarchy in general. His paper, *Le Populaire,* was suppressed and he himself in 1834 exiled for five years. In England, where he spent his enforced leisure, he came under the influence of Owen and witnessed the first great upsurge of an independent trade-union movement. This was an eye-opener, and by the time he returned to France in 1839 he had become a "communist"; that is to say, he had grafted the new Owenite principles of industrial organization onto the old Jacobin-Babouvist stem. His utopian novel (published pseudonymously at the end of 1839) is the record of this intellectual fusion. It made him famous and brought him a following among the Parisian workers. It also introduced a certain tension between his long-range aims and his short-run political activities, which terminated with his participation in the democratic movement following the February revolution in 1848. For it was only after the disappointment of his hopes with the bloody suppression of the June insurrection in Paris that he exiled himself to the United States—voluntarily this time and for good. The only advice he was able to give his adherents by then was to follow his example and emigrate.[2]

There is thus a distinction to be made between Cabetism as an offshoot of Jacobinism, and Icarianism as a system of utopian communism. In respect of the latter, Cabet resembled some of the later American and Australian radicals who likewise sought a solution for European problems on non-European soil. Viewed simply as a blueprint, his *Voyage en Icarie* was thoroughly utopian, though he differed from Owen in advocating a radical form of communism, and from Fourier in planning his imaginary Icaria on a national scale, with industry supporting a population of a million. (The actual settlement never exceeded 1,500.) As a social philosopher Cabet belongs to the eighteenth-century tradition associated with Mably and Morelly: egalitarianism in his eyes signified the application of Natural Law ethics. Morelly (unlike Mably) had regarded communism as a practical proposition, and Cabet took the same view. Also like Morelly he held that there are certain universally true propositions about human nature which, once understood, can lead to only one conclusion: that by going back to "nature" (i.e., to the pre-capitalist order of things) men will go back to their own "true" nature. This is a Stoic rather than a Christian doctrine. There is a further point to be made: Cabet, by profession a middle-class lawyer, was dead serious about equality. His imaginary Icaria (unlike the real Icaria, which represented a compromise) was to exclude private property and every conceivable form of social inequality, down to differences of clothing. All citizens were to give their labor to the community on equal terms, draw from a central storehouse whatever they needed (but no more), and be dressed alike. Elected officials, subject to recall, would draw up annual production plans and delegate their execution to groups of citizens, while the instruments of production would belong to the collectivity. There was to be equality between the sexes, but the family was to be retained as the basic unit of

society and the father recognized as its head—an evident inconsistency. For the rest, life was to be simple, though a few (strictly
censored) newspapers would be permitted and there might be a
rudimentary form of public life (no electioneering and no party
politics). All in all, it is a fairly austere vision of utopia, as befits
an admirer of Thomas More.[3]

In dealing with Cabet we have run ahead of the historical se-
quence, since as a promoter of rationalist social utopias he had
been anticipated by Fourier. The justification lies in Cabet's role
as an intermediary between the Jacobin-Babouvist tradition and
the emerging communist movement. This is made explicit in his
1841 pamphlets *Comment je suis communiste* and *Mon Credo
communiste,* where he appeals to the principles of 1789 and 1793
for the foundation of his radical egalitarianism. Implicitly his own
intellectual descent from Babeuf and Maréchal appears in his
Histoire populaire de la Révolution française de 1789 à 1830, the
fruit of his London exile. His progression from radical democracy
to communism had been facilitated by his stay in England, but the
basic motivation of his thinking was derived from the revolutionary
impulse that had carried Babeuf and his associates beyond Robes-
pierrism. One is thus justified in saying that Babouvism was the
direct ancestor of "communism," while "socialism" (understood
as the reorganization of society to take account of the industrial
revolution) could and did assume a variety of different forms.
What distinguished the early "communists" was just this particular
ancestry and the cast of mind that went with it, notwithstanding
Cabet's respect for Christianity in general and Thomas More in
particular. The identification of communism with atheism belongs
to the post-1848 era.

For all his importance as a precursor, Cabet is a less interesting
figure than Fourier, at any rate to the collector of intellectual
curiosities. The trouble with Fourier indeed is that he is almost
too interesting. In what follows, the more bizarre aspects of his
career and his system must unfortunately be sacrificed to the
exigencies of space and the need to present as clear a picture as
possible of the intellectual climate in which Fourierist socialism
flourished for a period.[4]

François-Marie-Charles Fourier (1772–1837) shares with Cabet and Saint-Simon the distinction of having pioneered the early French socialist movement. There the resemblance ends. Fourier had come upon the scene after Saint-Simon and before Cabet, but in other respects he is difficult to classify. This is not merely because as an individual he was eccentric even by the tolerant standards of his age. The truth is that his writings exhibit an idiosyncratic strain (to put it mildly) which sets him apart. Saint-Simon may at times have appeared slightly deranged to those around him, but on the whole he corresponded to a fairly familiar type: the *déclassé* grand seigneur with a bee in his bonnet. As for that energetic lawyer-politician, conspirator, party leader, and organizer Etienne Cabet, no one ever questioned his sanity. Fourier is a different case. With the best will, the reader of his works cannot altogether discard the impression that the dreamer in him on occasion ventured beyond the merely fantastic. At the same time he is clearly among the most original of the early socialists, and even some of his more bizarre ideas have turned out to possess a kernel of sense. If the unrestrained fertility of his imagination at times suggests an unconscious parody of Swift (with a literal intent lacking in the author of the voyage to Laputa), it also produced astonishing insights into the human condition, anticipating the discoveries of later and more pedestrian writers. Who but Fourier would have conceived the anti-lion, that queer beast which was to take the place of the present carnivore? Who but Fourier, on the other hand, would have seen (in 1820) that instinctual repression is a major source of unhappiness and social strain? If he is to be ridiculed for his grotesque fancies, he must also be given credit for his flashes of illumination.[5]

The fancies are certainly startling enough. They have been dissected at length by his detractors, including some modern historians in whose eyes the socialist tradition appears compromised by the eccentricity of a writer whom Marx (and more especially Engels) valued for his brilliant pamphleteering and his sardonic view of the commercial frauds practiced by the business community of his age. Fourier, a self-taught thinker with a knack for projecting elaborate systems from his rather scanty knowledge of the natural sciences, did his cause some harm by associating socialism in the eyes of the public with his private cosmology. But it is not apparent that these quaint notions are related to his Rousseauist conviction that the human race had somehow taken the wrong turning when it embarked upon the adventure of modern civilization.[6] Does it really matter that he believed the stars to be animated beings like ourselves, or that he credited the planets with an androgynous nature (although he also suspected them of having intercourse with each other)? In what way are his very interesting observations on human nature discredited by his belief that the moon was once a lady called Phoebe, and that her death caused the Flood reported in the Old Testament? These and other fantasies, too numerous and grotesque to be listed here, surely point to nothing more alarming than a hidden vein of poetry for which he had found no suitable outlet. They should not be allowed to take precedence over his prophetic warning that real progress was something other than the mechanical confection of instruments for destroying human happiness.[7]

Still, the reader who may want to satisfy his curiosity about Fourier's peculiar system of natural philosophy is entitled to know that it is most fully expounded in his first major work, entitled *Théorie des quatre mouvements et des destinées générales,* which appeared in 1808 and (in the words of a modern author) "was professedly published in Leipzig, for the sufficient reason that it had, of course, no connection with Leipzig."[8] This tends to make Fourier seem even more eccentric than he really was. A provincial tradesman by origin (he was born in Besançon, the son of a wealthy cloth merchant, but lost his patrimony during the Revolution, when he also narrowly escaped being executed at Lyon in 1793 for participation in an anti-Jacobin rising), Fourier was totally unknown in 1808, and it was not unreasonable that he should have launched his first important work under fictitious auspices. The practice was common enough. What is perhaps more to the point is that a later version was set in type at Lyon by a young printer named Pierre-Joseph Proudhon, himself destined to become the author of important works of socialist theory. These founders of the movement became acquainted with each other in a rather more haphazard fashion than was customary later on.[9]

The originality of Fourier is an aspect of this state of affairs. It would not be accurate to say that he invented the first socialist system, since Saint-Simon preceded him. But he was the first writer of his time to place the critique of bourgeois society (or civilization, as he called it) in the context of a materialist doctrine of human nature. In this respect his descent from Rousseau is obvious. But Rousseau had identified the desirable social order (or anyway the order that was practically possible under modern conditions) with the promotion of an essentially bourgeois form of equality: he was close enough to his native Switzerland to believe that the independent farmer or artisan could and should become the foundation of democracy. Fourier had seen too much of early capitalism to regard popular sovereignty in the Rousseauist sense as a panacea—this quite apart from the fact that his personal experiences during the Revolution had filled him with hostility to Jacobin concepts of popular rule. In a sense he may be said to have become a socialist because he had no faith in democracy. This is important for an understanding of his complex relationship with the Saint-Simonians, whom he accused of plagiarism and with whom his followers conducted a lively debate in the 1830's. Like Saint-Simon he saw in the system of economic *laissez-faire* the poisoned fruit of the Revolution.

The common factor underlying all this early socialist theorizing in France was a growing perception that the bourgeoisie had been the principal beneficiary of the great upheaval and that its social hegemony was concealed by the newly fashionable verbiage of the liberal economists. Fourier's originality lay in the fact that he joined these insights to a homespun philosophy which made bourgeois civilization appear the predestined outcome of a fundamental departure from the true norms of social life. This perversion, in his view, was rooted in ignorance of the permanent needs of human nature. The "laws" of this nature, discovered at last and set out in systematic form, were the true foundation of the ideal human order, an order concording both with nature and with the will of God (for Fourier was no atheist). It was only by making proper use of natural human desires and capacities that one could hope to arrive at the right social organization. Then why had this not been done before? Because no one had thought of it! Fourier (who after all had been born in 1772) was enough of a rationalist to believe that the truth had only to be stated for reasonable men to act on it. It was this rationalist assumption, as much as his personal naïveté, that led him to expect salvation from some wealthy philanthropist who might be persuaded to adopt and propagate his system.

Setting aside the oddities of the founder, what of the system itself, in so far as Fourier felt able to sketch it out? In contradistinction to the Saint-Simonian blueprint, Fourier's model was communal rather than industrial and technocratic. He had no use for large-scale industry and no faith in the beneficial effects of technical progress. A true Rousseauist, he thought in terms of the small agricultural community, though unlike Rousseau's immediate followers he had no illusions about the sturdy yeoman farmer. People were to live in associations—the famous *phalanstères*—and perform all work in common. They were also to be housed in common, though there was to be privacy for those who desired it, and special rewards were to be given for managerial or technical skill (a sharp departure from the radical egalitarianism of the communists). Personal life and private property were to be preserved within the context of the phalanstery, an association open to investors of share-capital! These provisions make it plain why Fourier cannot be described as a communist. He is the ancestor of all those forms of socialism which seek to combine a minimum of public regulation with a maximum of individual freedom.

How is the *phalanstère* to be set up, and on what principle is the work to be shared out? First of all, the organization is to be voluntary and in no way subject to state control or subsidy. Next, it is to be based on skilled agriculture—or rather horticulture, stock-breeding, and poultry-farming—and the products will largely be consumed by the members themselves (a guarantee of their quality). They will include an ample variety of vegetables (notably salads, of which Fourier was perhaps inordinately fond). Trade with the outside world or with other communal settlements will be at a minimum. The members will engage in a variety of manual occupations, will periodically shift from one to another, so as to avoid the boredom of excessive specialization, and will have the free choice of what they intend to do, attaching themselves to such occupational groups as correspond to their requirements and to the general plan. Ideally, the typical phalanstery is to have 1,600 to 1,800 members, so as to cater to all possible tastes and temperaments, and to supply each individual with a suitable partner of the opposite sex. It is also to make provision for a varied cultural life. Who will do the dirty work? Here Fourier, with a veritable stroke of genius, solves a problem that has baffled many organizers of similar projects. One has only to watch children at play, he points out, to realize that they enjoy dirtying themselves and, moreover, have a natural tendency to assemble in groups or "hordes." The solution then is to make use of their natural aptitudes by letting them do the repair work, the scavenging, and all the other unpleasant jobs from which adults tend to shy away. Since Fourier can never leave well enough alone and has a tedious habit of elaborating his ideas, he engages in some rather tiresome stuff about age-groups and the best way of organizing the "little hordes"; he also goes into unnecessary detail about the nursing of infants (he was a bachelor), and about sex. Regarding this latter topic, indeed, he lands himself in a difficulty, for while he does not explicitly dispense with permanent ties, he says enough about free love and reciprocal infidelity (not to mention the woman's right to choose her partner or partners) to make it seem dubious whether under his system the family could survive. He was indeed a radical feminist (the first and not the least influential of that breed) and an advocate of complete equality between the sexes. He was also unsympathetic to the institution of marriage, as being conducive to egotism and social atomization. Marriage binds people to each other, and Fourier considers that their sympathies should not be thus limited to a narrow circle. It is also unfair to woman, relegates her unjustly to the status of housekeeper, and interferes with the proper development of her natural talents. On all these counts Fourier is a precursor of modern notions, just as he is far ahead of his time on the subject of education and the sympathy due to children. His *phalanstère* was to have been the laboratory of entirely new relations between the sexes and between parents and children. It was perhaps this aspect of his teaching that caused the greatest scandal. Even Marx and Engels felt bound to pour some water into this heady wine, though Engels at least may be said to have been a practicing Fourierist, at any rate in the sense that he consistently dispensed with formal marriage ties.[10] Fourier's radical critique of marriage was a novelty, and while it caused some unease, it also won him support from writers concerned to promote feminine emancipation. His anatomy of adultery, lengthily catalogued as part of his general social satire, was psychologically acute and gained him the plaudits of no less a connoisseur than Balzac, then engaged on the earlier sections of the *Comédie humaine*. It also furnished a rich theme for that influential branch of socialist literature which flourished under the July Monarchy: the sentimental indictment of bourgeois heartlessness when confronted with the sufferings of the poor, the weak, and the oppressed. In this respect Fourier was the founder of a tradition which increasingly made socialism synonymous with humanitarian sentiment. If no major works of art emerged from the school, the general effect of its teaching was to confirm the association of socialism with philanthropy which the Saint-Simonians had already initiated. Sympathy for criminals, prostitutes, and other outcasts of society became a standard theme of socialist writing. This too is part of Fourier's heritage and perhaps in the long run not the least important.[11]

Like the remainder of Fourier's system, the detailed organization of the phalanstery rests on the assumption that all basic human needs and desires are compatible with each other. A conflict-free society is possible, given the proper institutional framework and avoidance of needless repressions, sexual or social. Here Fourier assigns special prominence to the enslavement of woman by man. He is the ancestor of the notion that the subjection of woman is part of a process whereby the relatively free and equal, albeit primitive, culture of tribal society has been transformed into the class society of recorded history, with its political oppression, its social inequalities, and its authoritarian religious and moral doctrines. Fourier's own system of "guarantism" (not to mention

the higher stage of "harmonism," when people will live in phalansteries and will enjoy complete social and sexual freedom) is
operative only on the Rousseauist assumption that social conflict is
unnecessary. "Guarantism" signifies that everyone will be assured
of work and a livelihood. Even so, people will have to toil, and
some of the toil will be unpleasant, but Fourier does not envisage
compulsion, whether economic or political. His distinction between
the earlier guarantism and the later "associative" stage (the highest
phase of which is "harmonism") evidently corresponds to the subsequent Marxian discrimination between "socialism" and "communism." But Fourier does not see economic scarcity as a constitutive
factor of the earlier socialist stage, and it is not altogether clear
how the work-shy are to be dealt with.[12]

Woman's emancipation is an aspect of the slow progress toward
"harmonism" by way of "guarantism." It finds its completion in
the phalanstery, where personal relations will have attained a degree of freedom such that the monogamous family will in practice
have dissolved (though this does not exclude permanent unions
formed by those who wish them). For the intermediate stage between "civilization" and "association," Fourier lays down the general principle that progress is to be measured by the degree of
woman's freedom from oppression. "The change in an historical
epoch can always be determined by the progress of woman toward
freedom, because in the relation of woman to man, of the weak to
the strong, the victory of human nature over brutality is most evident. The degree of feminine emancipation is the natural measure
of general emancipation."[13]

The general presupposition of the system is the concept of history as a necessary progression from "savagery" via "civilization"
(both "preharmonic") toward "harmony," by way of "guarantism"
or "sociantism." The material precondition of this progress is the
harnessing of nature. Once this has been done, only ignorance can
prevent men from bringing their desires into harmony with the
material and spiritual satisfactions open to them. War, poverty,
oppression, and the forcible restraining of the passions are unnecessary evils. "Civilization" has hitherto worsened the lot of
men, instead of improving it, as the Encyclopedists had thought.

So far from being the ultimate fulfilment of men's hopes, it is a mere stage on the road to that social harmony which corresponds to the universal harmony willed by God or Nature (the distinction is not very clear). Underlying the laws of the physical universe Fourier discerns a general principle of mutual attraction. Newton had specified its operation in the astronomical sphere. Fourier believes he has extended it to the world of human affairs. Our passions, rightly regarded, will set us on the road toward the attainment of social and individual bliss. It is mankind's destiny to climb upward through a succession of stages until this final harmony has been attained.

The secret of Fourier's popular appeal, once the wall of silent disapproval had been breached, should by now be plain: his work formed part of the general stream of romanticism. It is an agreeable paradox that this should have been the legacy of a crotchety old gentleman who rarely troubled to communicate with other people save through his writings. If one cares, one may relate these personal circumstances to the rather similar environment in which some of the most bizarre (and in the long run most influential) creations of literary romanticism took shape in Germany. At the back of both there lay the ancient legacy of a type of speculation to which the title "natural philosophy" had once been given and which was still designated in such terms by German writers of the period, some of whom were making quite important advances in medicine and biology. All this is part of the spiritual climate of the age, an age that ended in 1848, when romanticism died on the barricades, to be succeeded by the colder climate of positivist science and "scientific" socialism. Among the important socialists of the period, Marx and Proudhon may be said to have bridged this gulf, whereas Fourier belongs wholly to the era of romanticism and utopianism.[14]

3. *The Saint-Simonians*

Claude-Henri de Rouvroy de Saint-Simon (1760–1825) stands at the watershed dividing the eighteenth century from the nineteenth or—if one prefers it—the age of the French Revolution from the era of nascent industrialism and democracy. Chronologically he comes before Fourier, let alone Cabet, and in a purely narrative account of the early French socialists his proper place would be at the beginning. But here we are concerned with the school of thought he founded, rather than with his person, and this imposes a different order. For although Saint-Simonism and Fourierism emerged as coherent doctrines almost simultaneously around 1830, the Saint-Simonist school had a deeper impact upon the nascent socialist movement in other countries—notably across the Rhine, where it impinged directly upon Marx and his predecessors. Since we shall be encountering them as we near the crucial date of 1848, there is something to be said for placing Saint-Simonism in a perspective slightly different from that proper to the Fourierist school. This is the justification for considering Saint-Simon together with the movement he started and which survived him, although in important respects he and his followers represented quite different attitudes. It has indeed been questioned whether Saint-Simon was a socialist at all, even though he anticipated most of the themes destined to achieve prominence in socialist literature from the 1830's onward. He is in this sense a transitional figure, and in speaking of Saint-Simonism one is really referring to a doctrine or a set of attitudes which his disciples—principally Barthélemy-Prosper Enfantin, Saint-Amand Bazard, and Pierre Leroux—worked out after the master had left the scene.[1]

None of this diminishes the spell cast by the personality of Henri de Saint-Simon. The trouble is rather that one cannot give an adequate account of his career without losing the thread of a

narrative mainly intended to bring out the permanent features of
the school he founded. An eighteenth-century grand seigneur who
survived the Revolution and helped to launch the early socialist
movement is already something of a prodigy. But Saint-Simon also
involved himself in French and European politics; in canalization
and the banking system; in the founding of the sociological tradition (through Comte, who for some years was his secretary); in
the origins of Marxism (by way of the "left Hegelians" whom he
influenced and from whom Marx obtained his first rudimentary
notions about contemporary history); and even in the reform of
Christianity. He was both a precursor of Europeanism and the
ancestor of the "technocratic" faith which in our days has become
the doctrine of self-styled socialists in charge of newly independent countries in Asia, Africa, and Latin America. All told, Saint-
Simonism has probably done more to shape our world than any
other socialist school except the Marxian (which took over some
of the Saint-Simonist inheritance). It is a remarkable paradox that
all these innovations should have originated with a writer who
claimed lineal descent from Charlemagne and who has been described as "the last gentleman of France and the first of its socialists." When it is added that at the age of nineteen he fought
in the American War of Independence; that the French Revolution found him renouncing his title (and speculating in Church
property) under the name of Citizen Bonhomme; or that in 1802
he proposed to Madame de Staël (unsuccessfully) and simultaneously offered his services and his advice to Napoleon (also without
success), it becomes plain why historians have found him fascinating—and why in a study of the socialist movement we must regretfully refrain from pursuing to the full the opportunities presented
to his biographers.

But let us nonetheless try to record the major stations of his
journey. Born in Paris on October 17, 1760, he belonged to a col-
lateral branch of the family of his namesake, the Duke who au-
thored the *Memoirs* on the Court of Louis XIV. In 1779 he sailed
for America with his regiment to take part in the war (not as a
volunteer, but as a regular officer), saw action in a number of en-
gagements and distinguished himself at Yorktown, becoming a

member of the Society of Cincinnatus in recognition of his services. Switching from the army to the navy, he was on board the
French flagship in the disastrous naval action at St. Kitts in April
1782, was struck by a cannon-ball, but survived and was taken
prisoner and interned by the British in Jamaica. On his release he
traveled to Mexico where he presented to the Spanish Viceroy
his first great engineering project, a scheme for a transoceanic
canal through Lake Nicaragua. Further unsuccessful canal projects
in Spain, and an abortive scheme for driving the British out of
India with the aid of the Dutch, were followed by his involvement
in the French Revolution. From the politics proper to a liberal
aristocrat he rapidly gravitated to republicanism, surrendered his
title, assumed the democratic style of Citizen Bonhomme, presided at revolutionary meetings, took charge of the National Guard
in his locality, but also speculated in real estate with money originally lent him by a German diplomat in Spain, and for a time became the owner of a considerable fortune. Vast enterprises were
linked with his name—it was even rumored that he had made a
bid for Notre Dame de Paris! As a friend of the Dantonists and
the associate of wealthy Parisian bankers and speculators, he attracted the unfavorable attention of Robespierre, a circumstance
that led to his arrest in November 1793 and very nearly cost him
his head. Having survived the Terror, he rose to wealth and
prominence under the more tolerant rule of the Directory, for a
while playing host to a brilliant circle of scientists and artists, whom
he helped financially and who introduced him to the latest intellectual fashions. This was followed by financial ruin, a brief and
disastrous marriage, and travels to England and to Switzerland
(where he met Madame de Staël). From Geneva in 1802–3 he
issued the first of his numerous manifestoes, the *Lettres d'un
habitant de Genève à ses contemporains,* of which he sent a copy
to Bonaparte, recently become First Consul. Spurned by the future
Emperor and increasingly short of funds, he solicited help from his
friends in Paris, obtained a very minor employment, and for years
was supported by one of his former servants who rescued him
when he was ill and penniless. Increasingly lonely and embittered,
he nonetheless poured out a stream of projects for the reorganiza-

tion of the sciences, but received no encouragement and suffered severe depressions and breakdowns. These landed him briefly in the insane asylum at Charenton, where, like his contemporary, the Marquis de Sade, he was treated by the celebrated Dr. Pinel. In 1815 he obtained official employment during the Hundred Days following Napoleon's return from Elba, but lost it after Waterloo and the Restoration of the Bourbons. This final setback, however, also proved a turning-point. In the Paris of the Restoration era he became a member of an influential circle of liberal-minded bankers, economists, and publicists, including J. B. Say and others. A liberal opposition against the Bourbons was beginning to form, and Saint-Simon for a while became its spokesman. This was also the time when, together with the youthful Augustin Thierry (later to achieve fame as a historian), he wrote a pamphlet entitled *De la Réorganisation de la société européenne* advocating alliance between France and England as the centerpiece of a European federation. The idea of the "liberal alliance" (from the 1830's on a constant theme of liberal journalism in London and Paris) originated with Saint-Simon. When in 1860, under the far from liberal reign of Napoleon III, the former Saint-Simonian Michel Chevalier signed the Cobden-Chevalier commercial treaty abolishing protective duties on trade between France and England, an important plank in the early liberal program had at last found fulfilment.[2]

For a brief period, then, Saint-Simon virtually functioned as an unofficial propagandist for the liberal bourgeoisie which had grown up under Napoleon, had begun to acquire political weight and experience under the constitutional monarchy established in 1815, and was quietly working toward its political triumph in 1830, when the Orléans family displaced the Bourbons in the revolution that brought Louis Philippe to the throne. Yet by 1830 Saint-Simon's disciples (the master having departed from the scene in 1825) had given birth to the new and subversive creed of socialism and were soon to conflict with the "bourgeois Monarchy" founded by Saint-Simon's old friends (the great banker Laffitte among them). What had happened in the interval to bring about this realignment? In itself the emergence of a radical protest movement was not surprising, for the July Revolution of 1830 had not satisfied the aims of the republican intellectuals or the workers. It was natural enough that the followers of Blanqui and Buonarroti should take to the barricades once more in 1832 or that radicals like Cabet should dissociate themselves from the Orléanist regime, for the "bourgeois Monarchy" of Louis Philippe was anything but democratic: the vote remained the privilege of a propertied minority, even though the franchise was extended to a larger section of the middle class. Thus the normal reaction of republican radicals was to press for full democracy. The emergence of a socialist movement led by Saint-Simon's disciples, on the other hand, seems mysterious at first sight, the more so since Saint-Simon himself was contemptuous of democracy and quite willing to let political power lie with bankers and industrialists. What was it in his doctrine that emboldened his followers to strike out along quite new and unexpected paths?

The conventional reply is that the more radical of these men—notably Bazard and Leroux—altered the meaning of his message when they addressed themselves to the working class. This is true enough, but one has to ask how they could do so in the name of their recently departed master. The explanation must be that Saint-Simon's own message was sufficiently ambiguous to permit socialist deductions to be drawn from it by men who were so disposed. The disposition existed in the group of radical young intellectuals who around 1830 began to form themselves into a political movement preaching the new gospel, and they were able to draw upon the spiritual testament of their recently departed teacher. At some point during the concluding decade of his life, Saint-Simon unwittingly crossed the line separating liberalism from socialism. He never realized what he had done—indeed he went on addressing himself to those whom he called "the industrials" (*les industriels*), a term under which he comprised entrepreneurs and workers alike. The "industrial society" of the future he painted in colors very agreeable to the new class of private enterprisers, for he had no use for state control and some of his most effective polemics in the 1820's were directed against the deadweight represented by a swollen bureaucracy. Even his somewhat fanciful vision of a virtually stateless future had nothing frightening about it so far as the industrialists were concerned. It might have struck them as utopian, but in some ways it echoed their own longings. On all these counts, Saint-Simon's status as the inspirer of the principal socialist school in the France of the 1830's must appear paradoxical.[3]

In part the explanation clearly has to do with the inordinate political timidity of the French bourgeoisie under the Bourbon Restoration. The bankers and industrialists who financed Saint-Simon's publications in 1815, and for a few years thereafter, disliked his criticism of the Church, were alarmed by his disdain for the Crown, and dropped him cold when he ran into trouble with the authorities for having advocated (as they saw it) the removal of the entire governing class in a tract suggesting that the aristocracy, the clergy, and the principal officers of state were parasites on the body politic. It was Saint-Simon's misfortune that this particular piece of writing, the famous "Parabole," appeared shortly before the assassination in February 1820 of the Duke of Berry: a pure coincidence which almost landed him in prison, though in the end he was acquitted. The "Parabole" itself—an amusing *jeu d'esprit* suggesting that France could easily survive the loss of the old nobility, plus the hierarchies of Church and state—did not go beyond the bounds of what might be called democratic radicalism. Moreover, Saint-Simon was careful to explain that while kings, nobles, and ministers could be spared, bankers and industrialists on the contrary were just as indispensable as scientists and artists. This ought to have reassured the wealthy supporters who had taken him up, but he had already lost their favor when in Volume III of his periodical *L'Industrie* (written in cooperation with Comte in 1817–18) he implicitly attacked the Church by advocating what he called "terrestrial morals." There was, moreover, a dangerous hint in his "Vues sur la propriété et la législation" (Volume IV of *L'Industrie*) that the constitution of property was "the real basis of the social edifice," the implication being that the social order was subject to change and that the status of property might be revised. His banker friends judged his views to be "destructive of all social order and incompatible with liberty," and withdrew their support from the publication of *L'Industrie*. Saint-

Simon's brief role as the apostle of the bourgeoisie thus came to an end (as did Comte's position as his secretary).[4]

It is important to be clear about the issue involved in this repudiation of Saint-Simon by the men who were the leaders of the liberal opposition under the Restoration and the core of the ruling class under the Orléanist regime of 1830–48. On the face of it there was nothing in the essays published in *L'Industrie* or in *L'Organisateur* that challenged the social pre-eminence of the *haute bourgeoisie*. Saint-Simon had gone out of his way to give pride of place not only to the industrial entrepreneurs but to the bankers, upon whom he bestowed the flattering title of *industriels généraux*, a designation intended to convey the sense that the controllers of monetary credit were destined to become the "generalists" of the new social order. This surely was all they could have desired. And yet Saint-Simon alarmed them, for the decisive criterion he chose in sketching the new industrial society was not, as they would have wished, the familiar term "property" but, rather, the new-fangled concept of "production." The line he drew separated producers from nonproducers, and while he extolled what he called the "industrial class," his *producteurs* were not necessarily men of property. They might or might not be. They could also be scientists (or writers, like Saint-Simon himself). They did not, indeed, include the laboring poor. (It was left for his disciples to take this step.) But the concept of "production" was too elastic for the taste of men who had only recently acquired secure title to their possessions and for whom property was the decisive criterion. In their eyes, Saint-Simon, by making production the test of social usefulness, had inverted the hierarchy of bourgeois values.[5]

What Saint-Simon himself thought he was doing is clear enough: he was convinced that he had grasped the logic of the new industrial system that was beginning to emerge from the old agricultural and mercantile society of Europe. His pro-British inclinations fitted this perspective, since they enabled him to treat England as the natural and predestined ally of a modernized industrial France. In this respect he was in the tradition of the French Enlightenment, notably as typified by Voltaire and Montesquieu, who even then had looked to England, with its comparatively free institutions, as the model to be followed. Like Benjamin Constant and other liberals of his age, he had come to dislike militarism and to extol the blessings of commerce. With his faith in the future, Saint-Simon stood at the opposite pole from the followers of Rousseau, with their social pessimism, their yearning for the simple life, and their cult of the honest farmer or artisan. The new age held no terrors for him. A liberal grand seigneur could hardly fail to admire the British, and for the rest Saint-Simon had been thoroughly bitten by the scientific bug: another inheritance from that part of the Enlightenment which during the Revolution was embodied by the luckless Condorcet and his more fortunate successors, the scientists and *idéologues* of the Institut de France. If one treats Saint-Simon as the ancestor of technocracy, one must also grant that he embodied that strand of the rationalist tradition which went with anticlericalism, faith in science, and hope for the future. As a social thinker he occupies the watershed between liberalism and socialism. The question to which school he "really" belongs cannot be answered, even though his more radical disciples claimed him for socialism. His own position remained ambiguous to the end. It is clear enough that he did not think in terms of an incipient antagonism between *entrepreneurs* and workers: their interests, he thought, were identical; it was left to Comte, many years later, to pronounce dogmatically that bourgeois property relations were sacrosanct—Saint-Simon himself was silent on the issue. It was only after his death that his pupils, moving in opposite directions, gave birth almost simultaneously to the socialist system embodied in the 1830 *Exposition de la doctrine de Saint-Simon* and to its conservative-authoritarian counterpart, Comte's *Philosophie Positive*.

The ambiguities—or, if one prefers it, the latent contradictions —inherent in Saint-Simon's own standpoint are evident enough in retrospect but were hidden from his view. Consider his unembarrassed treatment of the concept of social class in one of his last writings, the *Catéchisme des industriels* (1823):

Q. What rank should the industrials occupy in society?
A. The industrial class should occupy the first rank, because it is

the most important of all; because it can do without the others, while none of the others can do without it; because it exists by its own force, by its personal labors. The other classes ought to work for it because they are its creatures and because it maintains their existence; in a word, everything being done by industry, everything should be done for it.

Q. What rank do the industrials occupy in society?

A. The industrial class, in the present social organization, is constituted the last of all. The social order still accords more consideration to secondary labors, and even to idleness, than to the most important labors and those of the most urgent usefulness.

This is followed, a little further on, by the statement that, to satisfy the public good, one must "entrust to the most important industrials the task of directing the public fortune; for the most important industrials are most interested in the maintenance of tranquility . . . in economy of public expenditure . . . in restricting arbitrary power; lastly, of all members of society, it is they who have given proof of the greatest capacity for positive administration." It is plain enough from this catalog of virtues that the men Saint-Simon was thinking of were those newly emergent "captains of industry" whose rise to power so fascinated (and appalled) his contemporary Balzac. To employ contemporary language, one may say he was naïve enough to hold that corporation presidents should run the government.[6]

The Saint-Simonian hierarchy is crowned by the bankers, notably the great banking houses in Paris, who from their central location are best able to coordinate the activities of the various industries. This notion made an appeal to the youthful financiers who attached themselves to Saint-Simon in the closing years of his life, and after his departure it inspired them to undertake some of the more grandiose enterprises in the history of European·railway-building and canalization, notably during the reign of Napoleon III (himself in his early days a Saint-Simonian fellow-traveller of sorts). The Crédit Mobilier, founded by the Pereire brothers as an industrial investment bank, certainly owed something to this inspiration, for while its eventual failure can perhaps be blamed on unfavorable circumstances, the idea behind it—a financial center to plan transport systems and public utilities—was

clearly of Saint-Simonian origin. Even so it seems a trifle extravagant to suggest that the Saint-Simonians "succeeded in changing
the economic structure of the Continental countries into something
quite different from the English type of competitive capitalism."[7]

In the 1820's, when Saint-Simon drafted the *Système industriel*
and the *Catéchisme des industriels* (not to mention his last and
most famous work, *Le Nouveau Christianisme*), all this still lay in
the future. How were the producers to gain political power? Saint-
Simon was not too clear about the answer, but ready enough to
envisage a momentous upheaval:

> The producers are not interested in whether they are pillaged by one
> class or another. It is clear that the struggle must in the end be-
> come one between the whole mass of the parasites and the whole
> mass of the producers. . . . This question must be decided as soon
> as it is put directly and plainly, considering the immense superiority
> in power of the producers over the non-producers.[8]

In this passage the "producers" are seen to constitute the great
bulk of society, while elsewhere they are identified with the *industriels*, i.e., *entrepreneurs* and scientists. Saint-Simon was not a
systematic thinker, and it is useless to inquire just what exactly
the term *producteur* meant to him. Probably he did not know himself. What is certain is that he envisaged a confrontation which
would give power to those engaged in some form of industrial
production. To employ Marxian terminology, he thought in terms
of a "bourgeois revolution," though this is not how he would have
put it. The upheaval of July 1830, which drove the aristocracy
from power and installed a government of bankers, should have
been to the taste of his disciples. Why did it disappoint them so
soon, and what was it that induced them to identify industrialism
with socialism?

It is no use going to *Le Nouveau Christianisme* (1825) for an
answer, for while this celebrated tract started the Saint-Simonians
off on the road to becoming a quasi-religious sect with a regenera-
tive message for mankind, it cannot be said to contain anything
specifically socialist. Its denunciation of Catholicism, as an antiquated and useless religion proper to the Middle Ages, was in the

rationalist tradition. As has rightly been remarked, the social order of which the New Christianity was to be the moral principle was envisaged by Saint-Simon in terms quite compatible with capitalism and the "profit motive." There was nothing here of which bankers and industrialists need have been afraid. *Le Nouveau Christianisme* belongs to that part of the Saint-Simonian inheritance which later issued in the mysticism of Enfantin and his associates. This phase may be said to have commenced in December 1829, when the disciples constituted themselves as a "church" under the sacerdotal authority of Bazard and Enfantin (thereby losing the support of another early follower, Buchez). The story of Enfantin's later career as an apostle of feminine emancipation cannot be related here, nor can we pursue his quarrel with Bazard and Chevalier or the peregrinations of the sect to the Orient in search of the redemptive Great Mother. This bizarre episode is associated with the name of Emile Barrault, who with Enfantin in 1831 launched a crusade for feminine emancipation along Fourierist lines and perhaps under the influence of Fourier's writings. Enfantin's and Barrault's unrestrained eroticism led to a schism and the departure of the more level-headed members of the sect. Barrault seems to have uncorked the vision of a coming reconciliation of man and woman, spirit and flesh, which would also reconcile Occident and Orient. Hence the journey to the East to locate the Great Mother who was to redeem mankind: for the *Femme-Messie,* or *Mère Suprème,* was to be an Oriental Jewess, according to a vision vouchsafed to Barrault (who believed her to be in Constantinople, while others thought to find her on the banks of the Nile). The practical outcome of this singular venture was the building of the Suez Canal by Ferdinand de Lesseps in the 1860's, following the miscarriage of an earlier attempt by Enfantin which cost the lives of a few Saint-Simonians unused to the Egyptian climate. The story is fascinating, but somewhat tangential to our theme. As a religious sect Saint-Simonism came to birth after Saint-Simon's death, but then the same applies to other historic movements associated with a founder whose doctrines serve as the starting-point for developments unforeseen in his lifetime. The fact itself is not extraordinary. What is remarkable about the Saint-Simonians is that they responded to the social conflict inaugurated by the July Revolution of 1830. If ever a group of intellectuals arrived on the scene at a moment ideally suited for the propagation of a new faith, it was the disciples of Henri de Saint-Simon.

The group had constituted itself as a formal association within a month of the master's death, and it promptly launched a new journal, *Le Producteur,* which lasted from October 1825 to November 1826. Edited by Olinde Rodrigues, it numbered among its contributors both members of the inner circle and sympathizers like Comte, who soon withdrew. At about the same time, *Le Globe,* founded by Pierre Leroux in 1824, gradually moved away from conventional liberalism, though it was only in 1831 that Leroux identified himself with the socialist cause. A former typographer, he understood the working class and its problems, and this was presumably a factor in causing him to side with the more radical spirits when socialists split from liberals after July 1830. In the interval Saint-Simon's followers had gradually traversed the distance from "industrialism" to socialism, and by 1830 they were able to present the first coherent statement of the new creed, the *Exposition de la doctrine de Saint-Simon:* a two-volume condensation of public lectures delivered in 1828–30 by Enfantin, Bazard, Abel Transon, Jules Lechevalier, and others. The *Exposition* is one of the landmarks in the history of socialism, and its long-run influence has been immense.[9]

What distinguished the writings assembled in *Le Producteur* and the *Exposition* from Saint-Simon's own essays was the gradual radicalization of the master's teachings, to the point where the institution of private ownership was seen to be incompatible with the optimal functioning of the new industrial system. The assault on bourgeois property as such lay hidden behind criticism of one of its aspects: inheritance. As the Saint-Simonians saw it, a new principle had entered the world—namely, the possibility of creating boundless wealth through the scientific exploitation of technology; but its operation was blocked by the "constitution of property, the transmission of wealth by inheritance within the family." Now this arrangement, like all other social forms, was subject to change. The proper solution lay in "the transfer to the state, which will become an *association of workers,* of the right of inheritance which today is confined to members of the family. The privileges of birth, which have already received so many heavy blows in so many respects, must disappear entirely."[10] The term "privileges of birth," familiar to Frenchmen since 1789, hid an innovation: what was at stake was private property. But here there lurked a danger, for the principle of family inheritance was as important to the peasantry as it was to the bourgeoisie. Abel Transon, who expressed himself on the subject in another Saint-Simonian publication, the (second) *Organisateur,* attempted to meet the difficulty by distinguishing between bourgeois property and property owned by peasants and craftsmen. His approach anticipates some of the formulations familiar from later socialist literature:

> As the owner of land and capital, the bourgeois disposes of these at will, and does not place them in the hands of the workers, except on condition that he receive a premium from the price of their work, a premium that will support him and his family. Whether a direct heir of the man of conquest, or an emancipated son of the peasantry, this difference in origin merges into the common character I have just described.[11]

This may be seen as a first attempt to formulate an exploitation theory by drawing an analogy between feudal and bourgeois property. The public was already familiar with the stock arguments against landlordism, and it was natural that the emerging socialist school should seek to classify bourgeois property as a sub-species of the kind of "absentee ownership" commonly associated with the nobility: a stratum that had recently been dispossessed (and then compensated by the Restoration government). As for the bourgeoisie, it was notorious that a sizable part of its recent wealth was due to real-estate speculation during the stormy decade following the upheaval of 1789. Saint-Simonian propaganda after 1830 spared neither the old nobility nor the new bourgeoisie, thus transcending the precepts (though not perhaps the tacit aims) of the school's founder. However shaky the economic logic of the argument, the issue had been brought into the open: private property, in its bourgeois-capitalist form, was no longer sacrosanct. At this point the liberals drew back. *Le Producteur* numbered among its early

contributors prominent liberals like the economist Adolphe Blanqui (brother of the famous conspirator) and Armand Carrel, later
to become a saint of republicanism. Carrel had at one stage defended the Saint-Simonians against the attacks of doctrinaire liberals such as Stendhal and Benjamin Constant, but neither he nor
Adolphe Blanqui felt able to support the new socialist heresy.[12]

Socialism was thus defined as an economic doctrine which drew
an unflattering contrast between the "bourgeois" and the "industrials." The distinction had been latent in Saint-Simon's utterances,
but it was left to his followers to spell it out. The central concept
gradually developed between 1826 and 1829 (possibly under the
influence of Sismondi's *Nouveaux principes d'économie politique,*
a new edition of which had appeared in 1826) was that land and
capital were mere instruments of labor, held in trust by private
owners whose duty it was to place these means of production at the
disposal of the workers. If they failed in this duty or if they
monopolized the fruits of technical progress, they were acting in
an antisocial manner and must be dispossessed. More was at stake
than mere economic rationality—what the economists would later
call the "optimal allocation of resources." The incipient socialist
critique of bourgeois liberalism undercut the arguments employed
by the defenders of a private-enterprise economy in which the
means of production were the monopoly of the wealthy. It asserted that this arrangement was *immoral.* Concretely, Bazard in
the lectures later assembled in the *Exposition* condemned what
he was the first to term "the exploitation of man by man":

> If, as we proclaim, mankind is moving toward a state in which all
> individuals will be classed according to their capacities and re-
> munerated according to their work, it is evident that the right of
> property, as it exists, must be abolished, because, by giving to a
> certain class of men the chance to live on the labor of others and in
> complete idleness, it preserves the exploitation of one part of the
> population, the most useful one, that which works and produces, in
> favor of those who only destroy.[13]

This social arrangement, on the other hand, is the source of that
"decentralized decision-making" (as liberal apologists were to call

it) which results in general planlessness and, through the confused gropings of the individuals, seeks to satisfy society's basic
needs. In its place the Saint-Simonians propose to install a system
of central regulation. The economy will no longer be left to the
whims of irresponsible owners:

> A *social* institution is charged with these functions which today are
> so badly performed; it is the *depository* of all the instruments of
> production; it presides over the exploitation of all the material re-
> sources; from its vantage point it has a comprehensive view of the
> whole which enables it to perceive at one and the same time all
> parts of the industrial workshop.[14]

This "social institution," logically enough, is the banking system
—not as presently constituted, i.e., left in private hands, but properly coordinated and crowned by a central bank which is to serve
as the supreme planning body:

> The social institution of the future will direct all industries in the
> interest of the whole society, and especially of the peaceful laborers.
> We call this institution provisionally the general banking system,
> while entering all reservations against the too narrow interpretation
> which one might give to this term.
>   The system will include in the first instance a central bank which
> constitutes the government in the material sphere; this bank will
> become the depository of all wealth, of the entire productive fund,
> of all the instruments of production, in short of everything that
> today makes up the mass of private property.[15]

It was only in February 1832 that Leroux's journal, *Le
Globe,* coined the term *socialisme,* but the *Exposition* of 1830 and
the preceding public lectures on which it was based had already
familiarized the public with the central tenets of the new faith:
public ownership and the abolition of social inequality. This went
considerably beyond Saint-Simon's own proclaimed intentions, as
did the school's increasing absorption in topics such as feminine
emancipation, or the improvement of the lot of paupers, lunatics,
and criminals. The fusion of these themes (recently popularized
by an upsurge of romantic and quasi-religious sentiment) with
radical social criticism was not indeed peculiar to the Saint-

Simonians: it had been anticipated by Fourier. But the Saint-Simonian school abandoned Fourier's personal eccentricities, and the propagators of the doctrine included both scientists and men of letters. Their sudden impact upon the educated public in France, and generally in Western Europe, had the effect of a bomb explosion.

By the time the *Exposition* was ready for publication, the lectures on which it was based had clarified the social content of the new doctrine sufficiently for no one to be able to mistake it either for ordinary romanticism or for conventional liberalism. The Saint-Simonians did take over the vocabulary of the Romantic school and its appeal to the passions, but they transmuted these sentiments into something very different from the familiar Catholic idealization of the past—specifically the prerevolutionary past, when France (in the opinion of the traditionalists) had possessed an "organic" constitution later wrecked by the Jacobins. Down to 1830, this kind of Romantic organicism represented a conservative reaction against the Revolution, against its rationalism, its faith in progress, even its neoclassical style in the arts. The Royalist and Catholic cause after 1815 was so deeply integrated with this Romantic current that even an instinctive radical like Balzac felt obliged to take the anti-liberal side. His masters—de Maistre, Bonald, Chateaubriand—had to some extent restored the prestige of the Church. Starting from there, the more demagogic Royalists could easily sound an anti-bourgeois note. It was only necessary to identify liberalism with selfishness and money-grubbing, a theme in which Balzac excelled. The originality of the Saint-Simonian movement lay in the fact that it combined the Romantic yearning for harmony with a prophetic vision transcending the quarrel between bourgeois liberals and Catholic conservatives. Saint-Simon's *Nouveau Christianisme* had effected the original fusion, and by 1830 the Saint-Simonian "religion"—the term was employed in deadly earnest—released an emotional torrent that swept thousands of men and women off their feet. Here, all of a sudden, there was a new vision of man no longer dull and rationalistic, but sentimental and passionate. The synthesis operated at every level: intellectual, moral, political, metaphysical. Socialism was a *faith*

—that was the great discovery the Saint-Simonians had made! It was the "new Christianity," and it would emancipate those whom the old religion had left in chains—above all woman and the proletariat![16]

There was, as we have seen, an economic core to the argument, but it was not this that appealed to the public, and indeed it did not at first attract a great deal of attention. Of the seventeen lectures forming the first half of the *Exposition,* only three or four dealt predominantly with economics. On the whole, Saint-Simonism was still conceived as a creed of social and moral regeneration. However, since Bazard delivered most of these lectures (the editing of his notes for the *Exposition* was mainly the work of Carnot), the finished work came to have a logical coherence noticeably absent from Enfantin's and Barrault's subsequent campaign for feminine emancipation, free love, and the unchaining of the passions. It is necessary to bear in mind that Saint-Simonism meant different things at different stages of the movement. Its origins, as noted before, already concealed a latent tension between the positivism of Comte and the religious mysticism of Enfantin. For a time these differences were submerged by the commonly felt urge to spread the new social gospel. After 1830, when socialists split from liberals, Enfantin and his associates fused socialism with feminism and romanticism. On the other hand, the influence of Leroux, who in 1830 threw the *Globe* open to the socialists, worked in the direction of greater sobriety. These dissensions do not concern us, and neither does the bizarre episode at Christmas 1829 when Olinde Rodrigues, amidst scenes of religious enthusiasm, consecrated Enfantin and Bazard as the two *Pères Suprèmes* of the new Church. It is credibly reported that at some of the early apostolic sessions the disciples saw visions of Christ, suffered hysterical seizures, or found themselves suddenly possessed of the gift of tongues. All this, and a great deal besides, forms part of the mental climate of the epoch and helps to explain the impact of the new socialist creed upon a public recently disoriented by the decline of institutional religion and the spread of the new Romantic faith. But fascinating though they are, these circumstances do not help one to grasp the theoretical content of the new doctrine. At most they make it easier to understand how a group of young men around 1830 was able to effect a breakthrough into a new social and intellectual dimension.[17]

The subsequent fortunes of the movement, in the interval between the upheavals of 1830 and 1848, form part of the general history of France during these troubled years. By 1848, when the first great proletarian uprising of modern times occurred in the streets of Paris, Saint-Simonism as an organized school was dead, and its former adherents had scattered, some of the more prominent survivors ending as highly successful, if somewhat eccentric, pioneers of industrial and financial capitalism. The seed they had sown was harvested by others, Proudhon and Marx among them. The connection admittedly cannot be easily traced, for the personal divergencies resulted in theoretical disputes. Still, it is a point of some importance that Leroux, having parted company with Enfantin and the other Saint-Simonians and founded his own organ, the *Revue encyclopédique*, in 1833 brought the term "socialism" into general currency through an essay on the theme *De l'individualisme et du socialisme*.

Leroux, who lived until 1871 and whose writings, notably *De l'égalité* (1838) and *De l'humanité* (1840), were influential in the propagation of socialist ideas, is clearly a figure of some consequence. Nor can one overlook George Sand, the novelist and feminist, who became a fervent admirer of Leroux and who was prominent in the literary movement leading from the Romanticism and Byronism of the 1830's to the socialism of the 1840's. On the other hand, too much has perhaps been made of Enfantin, whose colorful personality and bizarre career has an irresistible fascination for the historian, but whose contribution to socialist theory was considerably less important than that of Bazard. Enfantin's contemporaries already asked how it had been possible for an exalted visionary of his kind to cast a spell over men like Michel Chevalier, a mining engineer destined to win fame as an economist, railway promoter, and chief negotiator of the Anglo-French commercial treaty of 1860; Henri Fournel, a director of the Creusot iron works; Talabot, Clapeyron, Flachat—the men who constructed France's first rail network; and last but not least Ferdinand de Lesseps. The answer perhaps is that in the nineteenth century a romantic imagination was needed to keep pace with the industrial revolution—at any rate in France, where the bourgeoisie was slow to lend its support to the first *industriels* and where socialists were needed to pioneer capitalism.

If one may ignore the quasi-religious aspect of Saint-Simonism, while remembering that it was this which chiefly attracted the curiosity of the public and also gained the school the esteem of influential literary figures, there remains the sociological core of the doctrine. This has two aspects: a theory of the industrial revolution as the harbinger of a new society; and a critique of social inequality. The point where they come together is indicated by the celebrated phrase that the exploitation of man must and will give place to the exploitation of nature. The political doctrine follows from this. It can be summarized in these terms: the French Revolution liberated the bourgeois; the time has now come to liberate the proletarian. Private property stands in the way. It is not to be abolished (the Saint-Simonians are not in the egalitarian tradition of Babeuf), but converted—from an absolute right into a social function alterable at will. *Society* takes precedence over the individual. To be exact, society is perceived no longer as a mere assemblage of free and equal individuals, but as a concrete totality with problems and tensions not reducible to the interplay of private interests in the market place (including the market of ideas). In this manner the socialist critique of liberalism revives the Rousseauist concept of a human community antedating the rise of modern bourgeois civilization. In their own fashion the Romantics had already sounded this note, but most of them tended to sympathize with the conservative idealization of the past, a past hopelessly shattered by the industrial revolution. In its socialist version, the Romantic vision is projected upon the future: the lost community of values will be restored at a higher level. This had been the message of Fourier. What the Saint-Simonians did was to proclaim the imminence of a revolution that would inaugurate the golden age.[18]

Yet the conflict between the dominant liberal viewpoint and the nascent socialist critique also had a different aspect: it induced a generation of socialists to underrate the permanent importance of those conquests of the Revolution which liberalism had particularly made its own—principally the attainment of personal freedom. Since liberalism was increasingly turning into a veiled apology of capitalism, it was tempting to denounce the one as well as the other. From the idea of the social order as a reality antedating the recent unfettering of individual appetites, it was a short step to the conclusion that a return to communal values entailed a revival of hierarchical and authoritarian forms of rule. Saint-Simon had already toyed with such notions when he sketched out his model of a society held in balance by the satisfaction of human desires and interests. These desires were conceived as unequal and not reducible to a common denominator: men had different needs, and the legislator must take account of this circumstance, instead of vainly seeking to institute a social order allegedly based on what all had in common. In this respect Saint-Simon was not so very far removed from Bonald and de Maistre, the theorists of the counterrevolution. The more authoritarian among his followers— Comte above all—continued this anti-liberal tradition of thought. After 1830, when socialists parted company with their liberal allies, the temptation to take up the conservative battle-cry and to represent socialism as a return to an age of unquestioned authority was resisted only with considerable difficulty. On the whole, most socialists conserved the libertarian heritage and even added to it, e.g., by taking up the cause of feminine emancipation. But there were sufficient back-slidings and ambiguities to make socialism suspect to republican democrats who had no intention of surrendering the conquests of the Revolution. The "republican socialism" of the 1840's, which we shall encounter in the next chapter, was an attempt to close this gap. It was partly successful and thus enabled the socialists in 1848 to take the lead in the struggle for democracy; but an uncertainty remained which opponents were not slow to exploit. A further generation had to pass before socialism shed its vestigial hankering for political shortcuts incompatible with republican liberty. The curious role of the Saint-Simonians in the reign of Napoleon III (1852–70) is not unconnected with this ambiance.[19]

At the philosophical level, the conflict between libertarian and authoritarian interpretations of the new world-view was extensively discussed in the 1830's and 1840's, with libertarianism gradually asserting itself, as one would expect from a debate largely confined to the intelligentsia. It is a commonplace that French literary life during this period was profoundly marked by Saint-Simonism, though some important writers—notably Balzac—remained unaffected by it.[20] Outside France, Thomas Carlyle and John Stuart Mill counted as influential sympathizers, the former representing the authoritarian, the latter the libertarian aspect of the new doctrine. In Germany, Saint-Simonism was spread by the poets of the "Young Germany" school; more importantly, it reached the left-wing Hegelians—above all, the greatest of them, Marx. As a secularized form of religious commitment to the cause of the oppressed, it possessed an appeal denied to scientific positivism (and to the positivist version of Marxism brought into fashion, in the second half of the century, by Engels and Kautsky). The appeal, one may fairly say, was an aspect of the Romantic revolt in its original, humanist, and philanthropic form which antedated the aristocratic and elitist philosophy of later writers such as Nietzsche. Romanticism as interpreted by the early socialists stood for emancipation—not least the emancipation of woman (and therefore of that part of human nature which had been sacrificed on the Altar of Reason). In the words of a modern historian:

> Simultaneously the Saint-Simonians, Fourier, and Auguste Comte made a momentous discovery. They came to realize that women, one half of humanity, with their unique capacity for feeling, tenderness, and passion, had been suppressed for centuries because the Judeo-Christian tradition had identified them with evil, with the flesh, and with the grosser parts of human nature. The Saint-Simonian proclamation of the emancipation of women, Fourier's masterful depictions of their real needs and wants, and Comte's idealization of his beloved angel, broke not only with Catholicism but with the eighteenth-century tradition of many *philosophes,* who even in their most expansive moods had regarded women as either frivolous or lesser human beings.[21]

4. The Socialism of the 1840's

Some Preliminary Remarks

As one advances from the minor watershed of 1830 to the great divide of 1848, it becomes apparent that the rise of socialism during this period cannot be described, even in the barest outline, without taking account of the nascent workers' movement. But something else becomes evident too, namely that 1848 was a stage on the road to 1871 and the Paris Commune. Yet it was during the interval that primacy within the socialist movement slipped away from France, as did the political leadership of Western Europe. The change is symbolized by the intellectual system that bears the name of Marx: a synthesis of German, French, and English theorizing during the antecedent era that terminated in 1848.

Many of the later dissensions had their roots in different national reactions to what occurred in 1848. There is a further difficulty: Proudhon, like Marx, began his career as a socialist theorist in the 1840's but continued to develop his views until his death in 1865. Much of his later work indeed represents a reaction against the romantic illusions which died on the barricades in 1848. Yet Proudhonism as a movement points forward to the even greater catastrophe of May 1871, when the Paris Commune was drowned in blood. One is thus obliged to introduce a somewhat artificial *caesura* in treating 1848 as the terminal point in the story of pre-Marxian socialism. So far as France is concerned, this chapter really ends in 1871. Taking 1848 as the provisional signpost is a consequence of the need to pull the strands of the argument together so as to identify the various national traditions which went into the formation of European socialism.

In relation to French history, some additional justification can be drawn from the very real continuity linking the crises of 1830 and 1848. The continuity was personal as well as social and ideological. When Louis Philippe in February 1848 suddenly vacated the throne he had assumed in July 1830, the personnel of the Orléanist regime, and of the various liberal or republican opposition groups, consisted largely of men who had won their spurs during, or shortly after, the 1830 upheaval. The same applies to the socialists, whether they were reformists like Louis Blanc or revolutionary conspirators like Blanqui. It also applies to those former Saint-Simonians or Fourierists who in the meantime had gained a reputation as theorists of social change. All the doctrines developed after 1830 met their challenge in 1848. None stood the test. Orléanists, republicans, and socialists alike tried their hand at the government of France or at the reform of society, and all alike failed. When the dust had settled, these ancient parties or sects had disappeared, leaving the field clear for new and more momentous forces: Bonapartism, anarcho-syndicalism (at first in its Proudhonist form), and finally Marxism, although the decisive victory of Marx over Proudhon (and Blanqui) had to await the even greater debacle of 1871.[1]

The other preliminary remark concerns the French working class between 1830 and 1848. It is unfortunately impossible here to go beyond the bare statement that these were the years when a primitive labor movement took shape as a spontaneous reaction against the new environment of the industrial revolution. The resulting conflicts were something quite different from the frequent popular insurrections of the eighteenth century, which were typically directed against food shortages in the countryside or in the towns. Food riots had been an important factor during the stormy decade of the 1790's. Held down by the reorganized state apparatus between 1800 and 1830, they burst out afresh after that date, but now it was no longer a disorganized urban crowd that rioted briefly before being dispersed: the newly formed industrial proletariat had begun to replace the plebeian *sans-culottes* whom Babeuf tried to mobilize in 1796; and the chief weapon of this new working class was no longer the old-fashioned riot, but the strike. More ancient forms of combat did not indeed vanish overnight, especially since the rather formless protest movements after 1830 soon led to clashes with the authorities, if only because strikes were still illegal. The greatest outburst of the period, the strike of the weavers at Lyon in April 1834, climaxed in an attempted insurrection. Like its predecessor in November 1831 it involved men and women who were literally starving and whom only extreme misery had goaded into revolt. The movement in fact was in its origins purely spontaneous. The association of such instinctive rebellions with republicanism, and later with socialism, took time and followed from the gradual realization that the government always sided with the employers.[2]

Blanqui

Socialism around 1830 signified either Fourier or Saint-Simon, but there was also the Babouvist tradition as represented by Buonarroti, while by the end of the decade Cabet had introduced his own variant of utopianism. There is no need to revert to Cabet —though his name came up frequently in 1848, when to the Paris workers (and to the frightened bourgeoisie) he was the symbol of "communism"—but one cannot ignore Blanqui, the leader in the transition from neo-Jacobin militancy to proletarian revolt. At the other extreme, politically speaking, the historian encounters Louis Blanc, who in 1848 was destined to cut a tragicomic figure as a member of the shortlived Provisional Government. Blanqui the eternal conspirator and Louis Blanc the luckless reformer embody two contrasting aspects of socialism in the 1840's. Yet they also have something in common: it was in part due to both men that the republican faith amalgamated with the new socialist creed. Originally the two had been distinct. For Saint-Simon and Fourier, as we have seen, the failure of Jacobinism furnished the starting-point for their critique of Rousseau's philosophy, and Saint-Simon had gone very far in repudiating democracy altogether. Nor had his followers altogether abandoned his outlook by the time the 1830 upheaval caught them unawares. The subsequent fusion of radical republicanism with the workers' movement passed them by. For some years, indeed, the socialists trailed in the wake of

Buonarroti's followers, who were active in promoting armed risings against the Orléanist regime, while socialism was still identified in the public mind with propaganda for peaceful reform. At some stage between 1830 and 1840 this situation changed, though Blanc and Blanqui continued to stand for very different versions of "republican socialism," the former being a democrat, the latter an adherent of minority dictatorship. But in inquiring why and how democracy and socialism fused after 1830, doctrinal study is no great help. The new synthesis was spurred by the political conflicts of the period: above all by the popular rebellions after 1830—notably the events of April 1834, when the republican secret societies in Paris took to the barricades in sympathy with the Lyon strikers.

This union of two forces—rebellious workers on the one hand, armed republicans on the other—produced the phenomenon soon to be known as Blanquism. It is well to bear in mind that Blanqui was a left-wing Jacobin before he became a "communist." He belongs to the egalitarian tradition associated with Babeuf. As one approaches the rising of 1848, the various currents on the political map tend to converge, and their separate identities reduce themselves to personal and ideological differences between a handful of party leaders. Of these Blanqui, if not the most important, was certainly the most colorful, and there is some justification in starting with him. There is also the advantage that the theoretical part of his message need not detain us for long. Blanquism as a political tradition, even as an organized party, was to endure until the very end of the century, but here we are concerned only with its founder and with the immediate circumstances which made this type of "republican socialism" a political force in the 1830's and 1840's.[3]

Let us further note that the revolts of the Lyon workers in 1831 and 1834 had for their echo the Paris risings of 1832 and 1834, and that the Société des Droits de l'Homme, in which Blanqui played an active role, was dissolved after the suppression of the 1834 insurrection. This is as good a way as any to approach Blanquism as a political phenomenon. It only needs to be added that the leaders of the 1834 insurrection in Paris chose for their platform the declaration Robespierre had presented to the National Convention in June 1793—the date of the Jacobin seizure of power following an uprising in Paris. This, then, was the model. But what was good enough for Buonarroti (who died in 1837) did not altogether satisfy Blanqui, in whose person a new generation had arrived upon the scene. The Société des Droits de l'Homme was succeeded by the Société des Saisons (earlier known as the Société des Familles, from its organizational structure based on small secret groups). This change of name corresponded to a gradual radicalization which in the end obliterated the dividing line between democracy and communism. Blanqui's name may stand for this transition, although it had been initiated by Buonarroti and helped along by others (notably Armand Barbès, founder of the Société des Familles, a rich and romantic Creole whom Proudhon was to describe as the "Bayard" of democracy). What came to be known as Blanquism was just this: the notion of a popular insurrection, organized and led by the secret societies, and resulting in the establishment of a popular dictatorship which would dispossess the rich and inaugurate the reign of equality. This "communist" aspect of Blanquism repelled the orthodox republicans, who otherwise had no objection to armed risings or temporary dictatorship; while its terrorist visage alarmed those democratic socialists who were beginning to assemble behind Louis Blanc.

Of Louis-Auguste Blanqui (1805–81) himself, we may note that he was the son of a Girondist who had played an active role in the Revolution, had thereafter (like many others) entered Napoleon's service, and had eventually lost his employment at the Bourbon Restoration in 1815. The son joined the Charbonnerie in 1822 at the age of seventeen, took part in the July uprising of 1830 while a journalist on Pierre Leroux's *Globe* (then just about to turn socialist), was wounded during the fighting, joined the Amis du Peuple, plunged into conspiracy, was active in all the subsequent insurrections against the July Monarchy, and, in 1839, together with Barbès, came close to pulling off an armed *coup d'état* in Paris—an enterprise that cost him eight years in prison (largely spent on the island fortress of Mont Saint Michel) until very nearly the eve of the February revolution in 1848. His activities during that momentous year concern the historian of French democracy. Here we must attempt to give a brief summary of what may be termed the doctrinal content of Blanquism.[4]

Blanqui's general standpoint was a development of French eighteenth century rationalism and materialism, as represented by Diderot, Holbach, Helvétius, La Mettrie, and others. He had no use for deism and even less for organized religion: an attitude very different from that of Comte, whom he disliked and whose indifference to the propagation of atheism he ascribed to cowardice and social conformism. Blanqui's radical humanism and materialism (nourished on the classics as well as on the Encyclopedists) place him in the tradition of Hébert and Babeuf—the extreme democratic wing during the great Revolution—and left a permanent imprint upon that section of the French workers' movement which was eventually taken over by the Communist Party. In the 1830's and 1840's such attitudes were still confined to the radical intelligentsia, and it was the latter rather than the embryonic labor movement that furnished the cadres of Blanquism.

What separated Blanqui, then and later, from ordinary radical republicans who otherwise shared his general outlook—men like Clemenceau, who began his political career in the 1860's as a Blanquist—was his commitment to socialism or, as he preferred to call it, communism. What did he mean by this term? Certainly not what Marx meant, although the two men thought well of each other, and their followers after 1870 gradually learned to cooperate. Nor did Blanqui have much use for the utopianism of Cabet or the "mutualism" of Proudhon (his principal rival in the 1850's and 1860's). In his eyes they were doctrinaires who spent their time disputing over what the distant future might be like. Cabetism and Proudhonism, he said on one occasion, "stand by a river bank, quarrelling over whether the field on the other side is wheat or rye. Let us cross and see."[5]

This activist note supplies the key to what was to become the distinguishing features of Blanqui's political life: his extreme voluntarism, impatience with theorizing, and exaltation of revolutionary violence. This attitude went with veneration for the classical style in literature and for the revolutionary tradition of 1793, with its conscious adaptation of Roman models. Blanqui differed from the socialists of the period (i.e., followers of Fourier and Saint-Simon), among others, in that he had no sympathy for the Romantic movement—an attitude shared by his orthodox republican contemporary Armand Carrel and by the neo-Jacobins in general. There is a characteristic story about Blanqui bursting into Mlle. de Montgolfier's salon during the July 1830 streetfighting, covered with blood and blackened with powder, crashing his rifle on the floor and shouting triumphantly, "The Romantics are finished!" But this attitude belonged to the intellectual ambiance of the period, an ambiance shared by other radicals who differed from Blanqui on the issue of communism. It is the latter that concerns us.[6]

In this context it is not particularly relevant that Blanqui had taken over from the Saint-Simonians and Fourier a vague belief in "association" and a profound loathing for liberal economics (as propagated by, among others, his brother Adolphe). Nor does it matter that he interspersed his economic tracts with moralistic railings against the taking of interest or the nefarious influence of bank credit and paper money. These quirks were not peculiar to him, any more than was his curious notion that the population of France consisted of 30 million "proletarians" ruled by a handful of exploiters. Such beliefs had their roots in a democratic populism which in his time was still flourishing and which he never quite managed to outgrow. Proudhon and his anarcho-syndicalist progeny, who in other respects differed sharply from Blanqui, were weighed down by similar remnants of a tradition that in mid-nineteenth-century France was still very much alive.[7]

In so far as Blanqui can be termed a socialist, he merits this title for one reason only: he believed that capitalism as an economic system was inherently unstable and due to be replaced by some form of cooperative association. The details of the latter he left unclear and refused to engage in debate about them. For the rest, he held that under capitalism the expansion of productive capacity only resulted in widening the gap between production and consumption, thereby provoking constant crises. As an economist (if he can be called one) Blanqui must be classed among the under-consumptionists. It was his firm belief that the uncontrolled operation of a market economy could only lead to growing extremes of wealth and poverty. The central mainspring of the system he saw in the exaction of interest by capital-owners, which caused goods to be priced at more than the purchasers could afford to lay out. This implied that commodities were uniformly sold above their (labor-created) values: a naïve misconception which Marx later took pains to demolish, though with little success so far as the Blanquists were concerned.

Since Blanqui believed that the capitalists kept going by overcharging the consumers (rather than by exploiting the producers), he looked forward to a money-less economy in which the producers would exchange their goods at their exact cost value. The details he left blank, contenting himself with the statement that communism was to be regarded as "the final form of association." Of greater relevance for the development of the socialist movement in France was his insistence upon the need for temporary dictatorship, though not (as is sometimes said) a "proletarian dictatorship." This latter term he did not employ, although it appears in a document signed by some of his followers together with Marx and Engels in 1850. It seems to have been the contribution of Marx.[8]

What rendered Blanquism crucial to the development of the revolutionary movement in France were the techniques of conspiracy and armed insurrection, and the idea of a brief interim dictatorship of "true republicans." This last had greater relevance than Blanqui's definition of communism or his rather elementary critique of capitalist economics. His emotional identification with the proletariat (by which he meant "the toilers," that is, all those who worked with their hands) was of importance in enabling his followers after 1871 to make the transition to Marxian socialism. But Blanqui himself was not a communist in the Marxian sense. He did not hold that the wage-earning industrial working class was the class of the future and the privileged vehicle of the revolution, believing rather that a vanguard of professional revolutionaries (though he did not employ this term) should seize power on behalf of the oppressed and impoverished majority. It was this vision which made him an ancestor of Russian "Jacobins" such as Peter Tkachev, who handed the conspiratorial and elitist faith on to Lenin. In the France of the 1830's and 1840's, such views could be regarded only as an extreme form of that democratic radicalism which sought to combine the tradition of 1793 with the new concept of loyalty to the proletariat.

Flora Tristan and Victor Considérant

In the dialectic of the revolutionary movement under the July Monarchy, Blanqui and Louis Blanc stand at opposite poles: the former continuing the tradition of Babeuf and Buonarroti; the latter (with Leroux, Buchez, and Pecqueur) anticipating the mature democratic socialism of the future. Meanwhile on the horizon there already looms the "father of anarchy," Proudhon, while in the background that busy mole Etienne Cabet can be dimly seen at work undermining the foundations of the social order. Dark planets circling the dying sun of the July Monarchy, whose exhaustion they converted into spiritual energy, these theorists of revolution caught the imagination of contemporaries and historians alike. Yet the France of the 1830's and 1840's also contained a host of lesser figures—heirs of Saint-Simon and Fourier, founders of phalansteries and apostles of liberated womanhood, romantic novelists like George Sand and militant feminists like Flora Tristan. How is one to do justice to them all, without bursting the bounds of literary space? How, on the other hand, can one even begin to comprehend the climate of the socialist movement during this formative period if one reduces it to a set of economic precepts? At the very least an attempt must be made to breathe some life into these dry bones. Let us then for a moment ignore the principal figures and cast a glance at some of the minor stars. Flora Tristan is perhaps the most striking of the lot, but history is not a portrait gallery, and the fascinating details of her short and tragic life must be left to the literary scene-painters. For the most part, this brief section will be devoted to the disciple of Fourier who kept the school going: Victor Considérant.

This is not to slight a remarkable woman who has her place in history as the first socialist to have lived the connection between the emancipation of her sex and the ending of wage-slavery. Flora Célestine Thérèse Tristan (1803–44) was the illegitimate daughter of a Peruvian-Spanish father and a French mother. Notwithstanding her father's wealth and social position (his brother became President of Peru and he himself held high rank in the Spanish army), she grew up penniless and was largely self-taught. Her unhappy marriage to the painter André Chazal, her travels around the world, and her stormy love affairs formed the background to her autobiography, *Pérégrinations d'une paria* (1838), a novel, *Méphis* (1838), and a harrowing description of the life of the London proletariat, *Promenades dans Londres* (1840). Returning to Paris, she discovered the ancient craft unions of the French working class, the *compagnonnages,* then just about to transform themselves into modern labor unions, and it was the poems and pamphlets of the *compagnons* that launched her on the road to her most influential piece of writing, *L'Union ouvrière* (1843), the first preview of the syndicalist Utopia. The notion of getting the workers to contribute to a fund for their own emancipation may have come to her during her stay in England, either from the Chartists or from Daniel O'Connell's Irish Catholic Association. But the "workers' union," as she conceived it, was to be something more: a project for "constituting the working class by means of a compact, solid and indissoluble Union" into a self-governing corporation—an "estate of the realm," to employ British terminology. As such it was destined to have a considerable future. Proposals for feminine emancipation ("to recognize in principle equality of rights between men and women as the sole means of establishing Human Unity") were woven into the general scheme. She was launched upon its propagation among the workingmen of France when death from a typhoid infection overtook her at Bordeaux in 1844 at the early age of forty-one, cutting short a remarkable career punctuated by frequent emotional crises: for she was both beautiful and imperious, and men fell for her like ninepins. As a minor curiosity one may note that Gauguin, the painter, was her grandson.

In our time, feminism as a cause no longer stirs the blood, save in backward countries where woman is still a chattel. Is this the reason why accounts of socialism get written wherein earnest clerical censors of bourgeois morals and "the profit motive" usurp the place that belongs to the disciples of Fourier? In France, where by the 1840's Romanticism and socialism had fused, and where woman's emancipation was perceived as something more than a necessary consequence of modern industry, such a dissociation of reason and sentiment was inconceivable. Like the friendship between Pierre Leroux and George Sand, the story of Flora Tristan forms part of socialist history. But it is not part of the history of socialist theory, save in so far as her project looked forward to the internationalism of the 1860's. Her idea for a workers' union was itself simple. It was that every worker in France (or elsewhere) should subscribe an annual contribution to a fund for the emancipation of labor: not by way of cooperatives, but along lines that subsequently entered into the theory and practice of French and Belgian syndicalism. Put briefly, the project foresaw the establishment, in every sizable urban locality, of a "palace of labor" combining the functions of hospital, home for the aged, elementary school, and center for advanced studies. There were two interlocking notions involved: that of self-emancipation and that of a world-wide workers' international. Both were destined to grow from the seed Flora Tristan had scattered. The title of her book was itself a program. It anticipated a good deal of the mature labor socialism of the next generation, and for all its naïveté it had more immediate relevance than the elaborate schemes for economic planning worked out by writers like Louis Blanc.[9]

Before turning to this tedious subject let us briefly contemplate the dying embers of Fourierism. Here at least there is no boredom to be endured, though the Fourierists never managed to rival the Saint-Simonians when it came to dazzling the public with colorful eccentricities. But it was just this that ensured their temporary success, even winning them the esteem of cautious sympathizers like Victor Hugo (though in his case largely on account of Fourier's cosmogonic speculations, which fitted his own romantic temper). By comparison with Enfantin and Bazard, not to mention

Blanqui, the Fourierists seemed harmless, if a trifle ridiculous, and the decline of Saint-Simonism after the great schism of 1831–32 gave them a chance to make themselves heard. The first of their journals—edited under varying titles by Fourier, Jules Lechevalier, and Victor Considérant from 1832 to 1834—failed to win public attention. But in 1836, when Saint-Simonism had gone into eclipse, Considérant, Just Muiron, and Clarisse Vigoureux founded *La Phalange,* and Fourierism as a movement was well and truly launched. It continued to spread the socialist gospel until the fall of the Orléans Monarchy in 1848, an event that briefly precipitated the principal leader of the school into the political arena.

The first thing to be said about Considérant is that his thinking formed part of the general stream of Romanticism. The connection between socialism and the Romantics, as was remarked above, had established itself on the morrow of the July Revolution, when the classical style was perceived as a potential ally of the newly victorious liberal bourgeoisie. Since the Orléanist liberals were seen as traitors to the democratic cause, their defection, in the eyes of many, discredited rationalism as such. After 1830 democracy and Romanticism thus entered into an uneasy partnership, albeit men like Carrel and Blanqui refused to countenance this abandonment of the Jacobin tradition. There was indeed one aspect of Romanticism that the socialists repudiated: the *l'art pour l'art* (not yet so described) of the aesthetic cult. This too was a feature of that dissociation of thinking and feeling which set in after 1830, when the synthesis of eighteenth-century classicism and traditional republicanism began to come apart: at any rate among artists, if not among republican terrorists, some of whom (as we have seen) continued to cling to the style of 1793.

All this may seem rather tangential, but it is in fact quite central. One cannot understand the Fourierist socialism of the period unless one realizes that the Romantic attitude was at its core. Not, be it noted, the worship of medievalism: this was left to Chateaubriand and other exponents of the Catholic revival. Fourier's disciples, like their Saint-Simonian rivals, were believers in progress: the cult of France's medieval past bored and irritated them. But equally they were repelled by the shallow self-satisfaction of the liberal bourgeoisie, its complacent acceptance of the present as the best of all possible worlds, and its addiction to art forms which exalted the "good sense" of the average philistine. There was indeed an alternative to both philistinism and aestheticism: one could adhere to the heroic style of classical antiquity as the ideal expression of republican sentiment. But to Fourier and Considérant, no less than to the Saint-Simonians, this worship of classicism carried overtones of 1793—of revolutionary rhetoric, marching crowds, the guillotine, and the opening phase of a military adventure culminating in the Napoleonic empire; and it was of the essence of the new socialism that it was anti-militarist and anti-Jacobin. This did not save Considérant from being hurled into the political arena in 1848 (and having to flee for his life when the counterrevolution triumphed), any more than it saved Victor Hugo from exile when Louis Bonaparte sent Parliament home in December 1851 and made himself dictator. But men are rarely able to foresee the consequences of their actions, much less of their ideas. The 1848–51 upheaval was not the sort of thing Considérant had worked for. It went against the grain, and although an opponent like Tocqueville saw him as a leader of the hated *Montagne*—that caricature of the real "Mountain" of 1793–95—Considérant was not really cut out for the role of Tribune of the People. It was a fitting anticlimax to his earlier career that in 1854 he should have emigrated to the United States, there to implant a Fourierist phalanstery in the unfriendly soil of Dallas, Texas.[10]

If one inquires how these general principles came to underpin a democratic and anticlerical doctrine, the answer must be that the synthesis of socialism and Romanticism was precisely the originality of the school. Fourier, unlike Saint-Simon, had made a clean break with religion, and his followers wasted no tears over the lost beauties of Catholicism or the Middle Ages. If they spoke of religion at all, it was in a humanitarian sense; worship of mankind was to become the new faith. Of the existing religions, Christianity was the one they favored least, if only because of its moralism and its hostility to the emancipation of the flesh. Romanticism implied a critique of bourgeois life, hence in his writings Considérant appears as the advocate of a realism that rejects the formal purity of the classics, no less than the philistine worship of what is healthy and "normal." Both are denounced as embellishments of a sordid reality that must be shown up in all its sickness and hideousness. On these grounds *La Phalange* in general and Considérant in particular showed some indulgence for the fashionable cult of the macabre.[11]

The originality of the school and of its chief apostle did not stop there. It extended to politics—specifically the politics of the Left. To the majority of French democrats in the 1840's, anticlericalism was respectable, atheism at least tolerable. Lack of patriotism was not, for no one had been more furiously patriotic than the *grands ancêtres* of 1793, and the republican socialists of the 1840's followed in their wake, to the point of favoring war to recover the left bank of the Rhine for France. Yet *La Phalange* steadily resisted this clamor and, in the teeth of neo-Jacobin war cries in 1840–41, refused to give ground. Considérant's journal indeed has the distinction of having pioneered two quite novel and then highly unpopular attitudes: pacifism and Franco-German reconciliation. Neither was to the taste of republican socialists like Louis Blanc, not to mention ordinary republicans like Victor Hugo or Jules Michelet, the historian. Belief in peaceful progress was to become the special mark of the last Fourierist journal, founded in 1843 under the title *La Démocratie pacifique,* the very title of which was a program. The historian is obliged to note, though, that the pacifism of the school was confined to Europe. Its followers saw no moral objection to the colonization of Algeria (an enterprise begun in the 1830's) since in their eyes it represented a civilizing mission. This enthusiasm for the colonization of distant lands went with a marked hostility to France's principal rival in this field, Great Britain. *La Démocratie pacifique* rarely missed a chance to vent its spleen at the British aristocracy, though it sympathized with the British workers. On balance this attitude perhaps represented no more than a cautious step beyond the familiar universe of the French Left, but the change of tone was important and had lasting consequences.[12]

Considérant's theoretical position was an outcrop of Fourier's, minus the latter's private fantasies and extreme utopianism. Contemporary civilization was to blame for the heightening of class antagonism and the impoverishment of the people. Yet the remedy lay at hand: it was only necessary to turn from preoccupation with politics and war to what really mattered—the social question, i.e., the condition of the poor. "Make revolutions, pass decrees, promulgate constitutions, proclaim any number or kind of republics, nominate whomever you wish as president or consul: you have done nothing for the real freedom of the masses so long as society has not guaranteed to every man, woman and child a minimum necessary for existence." There must equally be a guarantee of "the right to work, that first social right of man, the one which safeguards and carries with it all others. . . . Those individuals and classes who own nothing, have no capital, no instruments of labor . . . are necessarily—whatever the political system they live under—reduced to a state of dependence and helotry, sometimes called slavery, sometimes serfdom, at other times the proletariat." [13]

Such had been the lot of men for ages, but modern civilization, by introducing new tensions, was about to bring matters to a head and give rise to a frightful cataclysm.

> We live in an age when wars, political commotions, senseless and cruel party conflicts, the misery and the atrocious suffering common to mankind in all ages of development have been condensed into a very brief hour and with fearful intensity. Moreover, the sense of social injustice is today more highly developed than it has ever been: pain is more acutely felt, evil speaks louder, and on all sides there is a realization of the urgent need for reform.[14]

This speed-up, in the last analysis, was due to the impact of the new industrial technology which had sharpened class antagonism, while the growth of population aggravated the condition of the poor. On the eve of 1848, Considérant—like many others—saw the hour of doom approaching. In later years Marx was to observe that in those days the socialists (himself included) had mistaken the birth-pangs of modern capitalism for its death-throes. In France, a country perpetually in turmoil for reasons stemming from the great upheaval of 1789–99, illusions of this kind were apt to engender political passions.

Buchez, Pecqueur, Blanc

If 1848 is a watershed, the reason is not only, or even mainly, that it witnessed the publication of the *Communist Manifesto,* for that document was hardly noticed at the time. Nor is the date significant primarily because it marked the collapse of the united front formed by the "bourgeois republicans" and their socialist allies. Other issues were involved as well: the fusion of laborist democracy with socialism, and the first shaky attempt to introduce welfare economics and what was vaguely known as "the organization of labor." These themes are associated with the personality of Louis Blanc, who has some claim to being regarded as the ancestor, or at any rate *an* ancestor, of the particular variety of socialism later brought to prominence in Britain by the Fabians. But Blanc himself had precursors and associates who influenced him and who in some respects possessed a clearer vision of the future. They must be briefly mentioned before we turn to the protagonist.

Philippe-Joseph-Benjamin Buchez (1796–1865) has already caught our passing attention as an adherent of the Saint-Simonist group, which he had joined after passing through the usual school of political conspiracy in the 1820's, the Charbonnerie. Having revolted against the leadership of Enfantin, he reverted to Catholicism, and set out late in 1831 to propagate a species of Christian socialism in his journal, *L'Européen.* He also helped to launch the cooperative movement and in addition composed numerous writings, including a forty-volume edition of contemporary documents, the *Histoire parlementaire de la Révolution française,* of which Thomas Carlyle made extensive use in writing his own work on the subject. In 1840 his followers founded a new journal, *L'Atelier,* which championed the cause of producers' associations. Buchez himself gravitated a short distance toward the orthodox republicans, contributed to their journal, *Le National,* supported Louis Blanc, and in 1848 was briefly elected president of the Constituent Assembly, a position for which he showed no aptitude and which won him no glory. Thereafter he returned to the task of reconciling religion and social progress. His last work, the

Traité politique de science sociale, appeared in 1866, shortly after his death.

Buchez belongs to the mainstream of socialism in as much as he may be conjectured to have influenced Louis Blanc, who was likewise attracted to the notion of marrying the democratic cause with the socialist idea; and the English Christian socialists, notably J. M. Ludlow and F. D. Maurice, like himself believers in cooperative producers' associations. For the rest he was an important precursor of the Christian democratic movement in twentieth-century France, a movement associated with some Dominican theologians and with influential laymen such as Charles Péguy. Buchez is their ancestor in that he tried to reclaim Jacobinism for Christianity or—what comes to the same—to show that the spirit of 1793 was not necessarily hostile to religion. His principal thesis in this regard was that the nefarious influence of Voltaire had been partly offset by the beneficial heritage of Rousseau. If Voltairean liberalism stood for the individual, Rousseauist democracy had an egalitarian bent. Buchez was not alone in having perceived this, but his liking for Robespierre enabled him to bridge the gap between Catholic faith and loyalty to democracy. He could point to the fact that Robespierre detested not merely Voltaire, but atheism in general. As a foundation for a renovated Catholic doctrine, all this perhaps amounted to no more than a statement to the effect that democracy and religion were compatible. But general affirmations of this kind were important in the France of his day, when most Catholics looked upon democracy and socialism with horror. If it took the Church more than a century to make its peace with French democracy, Buchez (like the better known Lamennais) can claim to have been among the pioneers of this belated acceptance of the inevitable.[15]

Constantin Pecqueur (1801–87) is usually mentioned in connection with a line of thought stemming from Sismondi's critique of *laissez-faire* economics. He was primarily an economist, and for his time and place an astonishingly good one. It is this that makes him important, rather than his Saint-Simonian origins, which were not remarkable; or his advocacy of a reformed Christianity, which he shared with Leroux; or his collaboration with

Louis Blanc, from whom, however, he differed in being a more consistent advocate of state socialism. Since this issue was directly connected with his professional work as an economist, it requires some elaboration.

Pecqueur differed from Sismondi in taking a hopeful view of the future which the industrial revolution had opened before mankind. He was, indeed, one of the early propagandists of industrialism. His critique of bourgeois society consequently lacked the doom-filled note so prevalent among the Fourierists and the adherents of Proudhon. As an economist he was distinctly forward-looking and optimistic. What was wrong with capitalism (i.e., private ownership of the means of production) was simply that it did not make the best possible use of the new technology. Science and machinery had combined to open up a new world to all mankind, for not only was industrial productivity vastly superior to pre-industrial manufacture: the new technology was also the means of imposing a new way of life based on great urban agglomerations. The machines were inherently "associantes, socialisantes, agglomérantes," hence destined to alter the face of the earth. What had induced Sismondi's pessimism was the inadequacy of the present social organization, which placed these means of production in the uncontrolled possession of private owners. Well then, the solution lay in vesting their ownership in the community: concretely, the state. To avoid a Saint-Simonian technocracy (Pecqueur had broken with the Saint-Simonists because he disapproved of their elitism), there must be public control of those placed in charge of the economy. But not workers' control! Pecqueur was no syndicalist, but a thoroughgoing state socialist, though he wanted the state to be a democracy. The economy was to be operated by public administrators, and the workers were to be state employees.

The whole scheme was quite realistic, if somewhat premature. The fact that in 1848 Pecqueur (like Blanc, who presided over the abortive experiment in welfare economics) was unable to put his ideas into practice proves nothing. He was a century ahead of his time, a circumstance for which it would be foolish to blame him. When France in 1945–47 adopted a semi-planned economy, it bore a marked resemblance to the scheme outlined by Pecqueur a century earlier. Of course, the change-over did not come about as a result of ethical claims to justice, as he had hoped; rather it was prompted by the collapse of the market economy and the social order resting upon it. In this respect Marx and Proudhon were to prove better prophets than Pecqueur, whose Christian moralism inclined him to believe that major structural changes could be effected by appeals to social solidarity.

Pecqueur's originality as a theorist rests on his understanding of the consequences inherent in the industrial revolution. In his writings he developed a rudimentary sociology of class and a general theory of historical development which formed a link between Saint-Simonism and Marxism. He likewise formulated a labor theory of value based on the notion of labor-time, but meant to apply only to a socialist order, not to the existing capitalist one. This approach was abandoned by Ricardo's British followers who held that capitalist economics was a function of value determination by labor. In consequence of this intellectual revolution, which he lived to see but did not comprehend, Pecqueur's originality (and his influence on Marx) have tended to receive little attention. Among the French socialists of that generation, his contribution to theoretical economics, and to the understanding of the new society, was outstanding. Less influential in the short run than Louis Blanc, whose synthesis of socialism and democracy he helped to underpin, he is of greater interest as an economist.[16]

The name of the protagonist has now occurred so often that some attention must at last be devoted to his views. This is not an easy matter, for Louis Blanc (1811–82) was an extremely prolific writer, the author of historical works such as the *Histoire de dix ans* (1841–44), *Histoire de la Révolution française* (1847–62), and a *Histoire de la Révolution de 1848* (1870), the last two composed during his exile in England, where he took refuge after the failure of the 1848 revolution. Blanc's prolonged stay in England confirmed his original disposition toward democratic reformism, and on his return to France in 1870 he refused to support the insurrection of the Paris Commune, entered the National Assembly as an independent Socialist, and in his last years drew close to the body of left-wing Republicans headed by Clemenceau: the nucleus of the great Radical party which was to govern France almost continuously from 1900 to 1940. In this and in other ways Louis Blanc prefigured the subsequent rise of a reformist movement hostile to Blanquism and Marxism alike. As a curiosity it may be noted that (unlike Blanqui and Proudhon) he retained his faith in Christian ethics. He was, however, a genuine socialist, not a simple-minded meliorist. He had no use at all for capitalism, believed in state regulation of the economy, and for good measure advocated self-government in the workshops. He also favored a species of collective farming.

Blanc's most important work, *L'Organisation du travail,* appeared in 1839, i.e., at a time when Saint-Simonism and Fourierism had both run out of breath. It thus came at precisely the right moment and immediately established him as the exponent of a brand of socialism that was no longer wild-eyed and utopian, but sober and based on the study of economics. Blanc indeed has some claim to being called a "scientific" socialist, in as much as he tried to relate socialism to economics. Pecqueur's first book came out at the same time, and the two men, not accidentally, became political allies in 1848, when Blanc appointed Pecqueur to the commission set up by the Provisional Government to make a study of the "organization of labor." If during the 1830's socialism had been identified with Fourier and the Saint-Simonians, in the 1840's it came to mean Louis Blanc (or alternatively Proudhon, who promptly set up as Blanc's principal opponent and rival). In addition, there was the "utopian" communism of Cabet and the "republican" communism of Blanqui, both descended from Babeuf. This inheritance supplies a clue to the treatment of "socialism" in the *Communist Manifesto* of 1848. Writing at the close of 1847, Marx had before his eyes the division between "socialists," i.e., in the main followers of either Proudhon or Louis Blanc, and "communists," who were prepared to seize power by violence and hold it by dictatorship. His sympathies then lay with the latter, as may be seen from the contemptuous reference to Proudhon in the section on "conservative or bourgeois socialism" in the *Manifesto.* But part of the argument of this section was also aimed at Blanc, in common with the political alignments of the period which pitted revolutionary communists against reformist socialists. This was not to be Marx's mature standpoint, but here we are only concerned with the party divisions on the eve of 1848. Years were to pass before Marx and Engels dropped the communist label and consented to having their cause described as "socialist."[17]

Louis Blanc has gone down in political history as the organizer of the so-called National Workshops set up after the February revolution of 1848 to provide work for the mass of unemployed in Paris. Their brutal dissolution then provoking the June rising of the proletariat against the bourgeois Republic, Blanc found himself in the grotesque position of figuring as the alleged inspirer of a popular insurrection which he had bent all his efforts to forestall. Moreover, the National Workshops—a form of outdoor relief for the unemployed—were thenceforth associated in the public mind with his elaborate plans for the "organization of labor": meaning recognition of the "right to work" and the effective creation of full employment. Like Pecqueur he was ahead of his time, i.e., of what was then possible. This earned him the disdain of Marx, who argued that socialism could not be legislated into existence by a few doctrinaires, but had to await the coming of a politically conscious labor movement. More surprisingly, the debacle of 1848 provoked the ferocious rage of the bourgeoisie, whom Blanc was trying to save from the consequences of their own stupidity. For although socialism was impractical in the France of 1848, unemployment relief was not. Neither were public works—as Louis Bonaparte was soon to show. But then the future Napoleon III had once been a Saint-Simonian, and for all his insipidity was miles ahead of bourgeois statesmen like Thiers and Guizot when it came to sizing up the realities of social strife. Louis Blanc's failure in 1848, and the bloodbath of the "June days," when the Army was called in to save the Republic from the proletariat, led directly to the political collapse of liberalism and the installation of a military dictatorship to which Blanc (unlike Proudhon) refused to accommodate himself.[18]

As a theorist of democratic socialism, Louis Blanc stands and falls with the scheme outlined in his *Organisation du travail*. There he trod the razor's edge between the full-fledged state socialism of the Saint-Simonians and the *laissez-fairism* of the liberals. Unlike the former, he did not want the state to own and operate industry, arguing that such an arrangement would lead to the establishment of a new social hierarchy, with administrators running the show and the workers getting the short end of the stick. Unlike the latter he did not believe that private industry could be left to its own devices. What then was the proper solution? It lay in the establishment of autonomous *ateliers nationaux,* with capital advanced by the government through a central bank, but with the workers electing the directors themselves (after a brief trial period with state appointees) and thereafter keeping control through periodic re-election. The workshops were to obtain official charters from the government and group themselves, or be grouped, into industrial corporations, but were thereafter to be autonomous and self-governing. Their operating funds were to be initially subscribed in the form of loans bearing a fixed rate of interest, but there was to be no profit on invested capital. Pay was to be equalized, though only gradually. For the countryside there were to be rural *ateliers* combining collective farming with centers of light industry. He also favored collectives (not merely cooperative workshops) for the towns, with shared housing and social services. This side of his doctrine was clearly influenced by Fourier. In general Blanc may be termed an associationist. For the immediate future he foresaw more modest measures, notably the achievement of full employment through public recognition of the "right to work." The entire process was to be initiated by a democratically elected government. Blanc would have nothing to do with either communism or dictatorship: his appeal was to the solidarity of all right-thinking people. He was a consistent social democrat—the only sort of revolution whose legitimacy he conceded was one to establish democracy. Once that was done, all the rest would follow. His political attitudes, both in 1848 and in 1871, were consistent with this basic orientation, from which he never diverged and which sustained him throughout a lifetime of disappointments.

From an economic viewpoint the key issue was the relationship of the *ateliers* (supposing them to be established) to the sector of privately owned industry, for Blanc did not favor wholesale nationalization. He wanted his cooperative workshops to compete with private industry, believing that productivity in worker-managed plants would be higher than in the private sector, and that the producers' cooperatives would gradually drive the capitalists out of business. This was the vulnerable point of his scheme, especially since he also insisted that the workers should elect the administrators, that no profits should be made on capital (though loans might be repaid with interest), and that salaries should gradually be equalized. Contemporary socialists are still struggling with the difficulties inherent in such an arrangement, especially in those countries where they are in power and faced with the conflicting pressures of economic rationality and social equality. Blanc was indeed realistic enough to allow for subsidies to uneconomic enterprises and for deductions from the wages fund to permit capital development. In all these respects he anticipated some of the practical problems of a socialized economy—no mean achievement for a theorist writing in 1840. What made him popular with the French workers, of course, was not his socialist blueprint, but the doctrine of the "right to work." This was put to the test in 1848, and the result was civil war. But Blanc proved right in thinking that democracy and socialism would survive, and his legacy was preserved by the democratic labor movement of the 1880's.

5. Proudhon and the Origins of Anarchism

The argument of the preceding chapter concerned itself with the various socialist schools of the 1840's, ranging from the neo-Jacobinism of Blanqui to the reformist socialism of Blanc. Most of the writers in question continued to exercise some influence after 1848, and indeed Blanquism came to a climax in the Paris Commune of 1871, which was run jointly by Blanqui's followers and those of Proudhon. There is thus a certain arbitrariness in allotting Proudhon a section all to himself. On the face of it, it would seem more consistent to bracket him with the "socialism of the 1840's," a decade that witnessed the appearance of his first and most important writings. But consistency, like everything else, can be overdone. Proudhon stands out not so much on account of his personal originality (he was scarcely more colorful than Blanqui or more influential than Blanc), but because the socialist framework is too narrow to hold him. Indeed, it has been questioned whether he was a socialist at all save in the most general sense. In some respects he clearly harks back to Rousseau; in others he looks forward to the reformist socialism of the 1880's, but also to the anarcho-syndicalism of the 1890's.[1]

First, then, a few biographical data—but we shall see that in Proudhon's case it is impossible to distinguish his "life" from his "work." Pierre-Joseph Proudhon was born in Besançon (Fourier's home town) in January 1809 and died in Paris exactly fifty-six years later, in January 1865. Both his parents were of working-class stock, his father a cooper and domestic brewer, his mother a peasant woman by origin. The boy grew up in poverty, was apprenticed to a printer, worked for years as a press-corrector, taught himself grammar and the ancient languages while working at his trade, and amassed a considerable store of miscellaneous information (notably in theology) from the writings he was called upon to correct. Having attracted the attention of the Academy of Besançon, he obtained a scholarship in 1838, moved to Paris, undertook a regular course of studies, and in 1840 published his celebrated tract *What is Property?*, whose well-known thesis ("Property is theft") made him famous, or rather notorious, overnight and incidentally cost him his Academy grant. From 1842 onward the author of *Qu'est-ce que la propriété?* (to cite the original text correctly) had come to the attention of Marx, who in October of that year referred to him in the liberal journal of which he was then editor, the *Rheinische Zeitung*. A sequel to the 1840 work known as the *Deuxième Mémoire* took the form of an open letter to the economist Adolphe Blanqui, while a third publication, the *Avertissement aux propriétaires*, was cast in the form of an open letter to Considérant and took issue with his doctrines. Acquitted by a court of charges of spreading subversive and inflammatory ideas, Proudhon now divided his time between a commercial employment in Lyon and literary activities in Paris. His most important publication during this period was the *Système des Contradictions économiques*, more generally known under its English title as *The Philosophy of Poverty*—a two-volume treatise on economics which had the misfortune of provoking Marx's famous rejoinder *The Poverty of Philosophy*. The two men had met in Paris in 1844 and corresponded briefly in 1845–46, but they did not take to each other, although Marx had been complimentary about Proudhon in *The Holy Family*, where he introduced him to his German readers as the outstanding representative of French working-class socialism. Some time in 1847 Proudhon once again moved to Paris and launched a journal, *Le Peuple* (subsequently called *Le Représentant du Peuple*). The upheaval of 1848 thus found him installed in the capital, and his prominence as a writer undoubtedly helped to get him elected (on June 8, 1848, a fortnight before the great insurrection) to the National Assembly, where he naturally took his seat on the extreme left.[2]

Proudhon's subsequent political and literary career is so closely intertwined with the fortunes of the labor movement under the

Second Empire (1852–70) that only the briefest summary can be given. Although skeptical of all purely political uprisings and hostile to the Jacobin "communism" of Cabet and Blanqui, he sided with the June insurgents, at any rate rhetorically. On July 31, 1848, he provoked a furious scene in the National Assembly with a speech proclaiming the class struggle and announcing the advent of a proletarian revolution that would sweep bourgeois legality aside. An account of this incident is to be found in his *Confessions d'un révolutionnaire,* where he also affirmed his belief that the peaceful emancipation of labor was impossible: it was no use relying upon the good intentions of middle-class reformers. Only the proletariat itself, "par-delà toute légalité . . . opérant par lui-même, sans intermédiaires," could bring about the social revolution. These formulations were close to those of the *Communist Manifesto* (a document Proudhon never took the trouble to read). Marx too had in 1848 asserted that the working class must emancipate itself and could do so only through revolution. Proudhon's defense of the June insurgents furnished one of the few occasions when the two men saw eye to eye, and Marx went out of his way to praise his stand on that issue when in 1865 he penned his generally critical estimate of Proudhon's legacy. He was understandably less complimentary about Proudhon's equivocal attitude toward Louis Bonaparte, an aberration the historians have found it hard to explain. Gurvitch does his best, but is obliged to note that Proudhon's private abuse of the future Napoleon III contrasted strangely with the ambiguous line he adopted in his pamphlet on the *coup d'état* of December 2, 1851, when Louis Bonaparte made himself dictator. This was written in prison, where Proudhon had been sitting since June 1849, and was followed by a personal letter to Louis Bonaparte protesting against the official ban on the work. As a result the ban was lifted. (Proudhon had already been released in June 1852.) The episode does not make happy reading. Proudhon had a poor opinion of Napoleon III (and an even poorer one of the Saint-Simonian financiers who surrounded him). On the other hand, he maintained friendly relations with Jérôme Bonaparte, the Emperor's cousin and the accredited chief of the Bonapartist left wing—a group of malcontents who would have liked to see the imperial regime adopt an anticlerical and socially progressive policy. The least one can say is that these maneuvers do not easily rhyme with Proudhon's pose of total independence and abstention from politics. His convictions fluctuated altogether a good deal during these years. In his *Idée générale de la révolution* (1851) he looked forward to a reconciliation between the proletariat and the middle class "to overthrow capitalism," while in his *Philosophie du progrès* (1853, another of his prison writings), he reverted to his earlier standpoint, appealing to the "revolutionary energy of the working masses" as the means of ending the "industrial feudalism" he saw growing up around him. It is difficult to avoid the conclusion that he was groping about in a rather muddled fashion. He was, however, consistent in retaining his old animosity toward the Saint-Simonians, who duly came to prominence under Napoleon III and in whom he perceived the pacemakers of "industrial feudalism."[3]

As a writer, Proudhon suffered from the handicap of being self-taught, not to mention his ignorance of foreign languages and a certain provincialism which led him to neglect or denigrate non-French ideas. With the touchiness of the autodidact he combined a quarrelsome temper and a vituperative style—far more virulent than that of Marx, who sounds positively restrained by comparison. A born polemicist, Proudhon spattered all his writings with personal abuse of his opponents or of people he disliked: notably Cabet, whom he pursued with tedious persistence, and Louis Blanc, that "professed enemy of liberty."[4] Even Rousseau did not escape his venom: he was "the Genevese charlatan."[5] It is difficult to name a single author, alive or dead, of whom Proudhon ever found anything good to say. His other crotchets included antisemitism, Anglophobia, tolerance for slavery (he publicly sided with the South during the American civil war), dislike of Germans, Italians, Poles—indeed all non-French nationalities—and a firmly patriarchal view of family life. For good measure he extolled war (in *La Guerre et la paix,* a boring tract of 800 pages) as a necessary, albeit barbarous, means of promoting "justice." After this it comes as no surprise that he believed in inherent inequalities among the races or that he regarded women as inferior beings, fit only to provide a tranquil domestic repose for their husbands. In all these respects Proudhon simply reflected the milieu from which he had sprung. His mental crudities were commonplace and not peculiar to him. The remarkable thing is rather that he retained them after having shed the religious and political superstitions usually associated with such sentiments. He thus presents the curious case of a semi-civilized autodidact who is always being pulled back by the rural barbarism of his origins. Half peasant, half townsman, he was the embodiment of the average French workingman of his day. He spoke his language, translated his feelings, reflected both his coarse prejudices and his vague intimations of a better future. Not surprisingly, his writings obtained a ready echo. An entire generation was to pass before the movement he helped to found outgrew his personal limitations, while retaining what was valuable and original in the message he had proclaimed.[6]

The message has often been described, generally by sympathetic biographers who have cast Proudhon in the role of a consistent libertarian, or of a new Rousseau struggling to uphold the autonomy of the peasant-craftsman in an increasingly machine-ridden universe. This is indeed an important aspect of Proudhonism, accounting both for its short-run success and its long-range failure as a political movement. However, in justice to Proudhon one needs to remember that he was more than a latter-day agrarian populist. He is after all the father of anarcho-syndicalism, a doctrine that outgrew its originator and became an important influence upon the labor movements of France, Belgium, Italy, Spain, and Latin America. There is a parallel here between Marx and Proudhon. Both men reacted to the catastrophe of 1848 by revising their doctrines in important respects, making them applicable to the new world of democracy, industrial capitalism, and autonomous labor unions. Marx abandoned communism (without saying so in public) and transformed himself into the theorist of democratic socialism. Proudhon dropped agrarian populism and invented what was later called syndicalism.

As noted before, there was nothing very original about the social doctrine put forward in *Qu'est-ce que la propriété?* The well-known reply he gave, "La propriété c'est le vol," for all· its evident absurdity (or because of it), had a suitably Rousseauist ring and thus helped to establish Proudhon in the tradition of Morelly and the Natural Law school.

Later, after the publication of the *Système des contradictions économiques,* another catch-phrase fastened itself to him: "Dieu, c'est le mal" ("God is evil," or rather, "God is the principle of Evil").[7] Lastly, in *Du Principe fédératif* and elsewhere, he developed the full implications of his doctrine that the political authority (the state) must be abolished. For the more simple-minded of his followers and for the general public, these notions represented what was essential in Proudhon's teaching. Taken together they formed the sediment of that popular anarcho-syndicalism which began to spread in his life-time and became an increasingly powerful influence after his death.

Now there can be no doubt that as a social thinker Proudhon stands in the succession of Rousseau (though he himself thought otherwise). Equally one may agree that he belongs to that group of nineteenth-century thinkers (Carlyle, Ruskin, and Tolstoy being the best-known representatives) for whom modern civilization stands condemned because it has divorced politics and economics from ethics.[8] The moral pathos of Proudhon's writings is directed not simply against the fact of exploitation, but against the presumption of the economists, and the *laissez-faire* liberals in general, that in teaching a bloodless doctrine made up of abstractions (Carlyle's "dismal science") they were giving an adequate account of reality. Against them he insisted that "justice" must be made to prevail, not as a mere ethical postulate to be invoked on suitable occasions, but as the regulatory code of everyday life. Justice to Proudhon is no abstraction, but a descriptive term applicable to a state of affairs where men deal equally and fairly with each other, i.e., where true morality reigns. Any departure from this norm is by definition evil and destructive of human happiness.

Now all this might serve well enough as a critique of modern society, but it is not easy to perceive how it could become the foundation of an economic doctrine. Before turning to this question, which was to involve Proudhon in his celebrated quarrel with

Marx, let us see what "justice" signifies when placed in the context of Proudhon's general view of history and society. The starting-point, as with Rousseau, is the distinction between natural and un-natural forms of social life, or (as he occasionally puts it) between a state of affairs governed by mutual "reciprocity" and a condition distinguished by an absence of reciprocal relations. Reciprocity is "the principle of social reality, the formula of justice." It is a pre-supposition of life itself, and its neglect necessarily leads to chaos. In the social order there is a "natural" economy based on work and equal sharing. It is realized by mutual exchange among the associated producers, resulting in a balance that perpetuates itself, unless it is disturbed by the intrusion of hostile forces: notably the state or some form of monopoly. The ideal social order is one in which individual producers freely exchange their products in ac-cordance with the principle that labor creates value. Production then is for use, not for profit, and only surpluses are exchanged, nor is any toll levied by middlemen. This mutual reciprocity is the concrete manifestation of the cosmic principle of justice. So far we are on familiar ground, and it is plain enough why Proudhon felt able on occasion to say that socialism was simply the application of Christian principles. He was in fact describing the kind of social order to which the doctrine of the "just price" was applicable: a society composed of independent artisans and peasants, exchang-ing surplus commodities on the basis of labor-created value rela-tions. If this state of affairs was "natural," then it followed that capitalism was unnatural.

Proudhon's critique of bourgeois property relations was gov-erned by these assumptions. It has often been noted that he was inconsistent in his treatment of this topic. In *Qu'est-ce que la propriété?* he started off by reviving Brissot's absurd phrase "Prop-erty is theft." As Marx was not slow to point out (in his obituary notice on Proudhon, which the latter's followers much resented be-cause it cast doubt on their master's capacity for logical thinking), the notion of "theft" presupposes the existence of property, so that one cannot wax indignant about it unless one regards property as intrinsically valuable. Proudhon's confusion on this point stemmed from the general muddle into which he had got himself as early as

1840 by attempting to appear simultaneously as a socialist and as a defender of personal property. A careful reading of his voluminous writings makes it clear that he was not really opposed to individual ownership as such, but to what, in his *Premier Mémoire* of 1840, he called the *droit d'aubaine:* the right which property gives to its owner to levy toll on others. The advantage thus obtained may take the form of profit on capital, rent on land, or interest on loan—in any case it represents an infringement of the principle of justice, since it enables the owner to exact a revenue from the nonowner. It is this *droit d'aubaine* which makes possible the *droit de vol,* or right to theft. Proudhon thus seeks to purify private ownership by freeing it from those accretions that are "hostile to sociability." This may be a worthy aim, but it has nothing to do with what is commonly known as socialism, although it can be argued that even in a socialist order there is a subordinate problem of preventing individuals from misusing their private possessions (which, however, do not include capital and thus do not give them any real power over others).

Whatever one may think of the argument, it is retained in the posthumously published *Théorie de la propriété,* where Proudhon makes a fresh attempt to expound his thesis. He now explains that by "property" he really means the sum total of the abuses inherent in the institution of private ownership. When infused with the principle of justice, property is no longer damnable but praiseworthy, notably as a counterpoise to the threatening power of the state. The latter can be balanced only by endowing individuals with possessions which are theirs by right, i.e., private ownership. Such ownership is a liberating influence and a guarantee of individual independence.[9] If Proudhon had said all this in 1840, it is unlikely that he would have become the terror of the French bourgeoisie, but then it is equally unlikely that he would have attracted much notice. It is somehow typical of him that he should have been indignant when reminded that Brissot had already described property as theft before 1789. Brissot, he asserted, did not know what he was saying![10] On the other hand, he (Proudhon) had made a world-shaking discovery. "Not in a thousand years is utterance given twice to a saying such as this."[11] Proudhon's writings are full of such childish boasts, a circumstance which makes their perusal a very wearisome task indeed. In fairness it should be noted that he is also the inventor of the term "scientific socialism" and that he shared Marx's distaste for collectivist blueprints worked out in detail.

Up to this point it may appear that Proudhon is merely echoing Rousseau and Morelly, and indeed he has in common with them that he normally thinks of property as consisting in land. However, he is also concerned with the exploitation of labor in its modern sense: the exaction of profit by the industrial capitalist through withholding from the laborer part of the value created in industry. How does this fit into a doctrine of private ownership as the source of (*a*) personal independence and (*b*) those abuses which have turned it into an instrument of power over others? First of all, Proudhon denies that mere occupancy can establish an absolute right to ownership as against latecomers or later generations. Next, he asserts (against Locke) that property cannot be constituted by mixing one's labor with a plot of land, or some other gift of nature, since those in possession quite plainly have never labored (the reference here is not to peasant proprietors, but to the bourgeoisie). Bourgeois property then is an usurpation, at any rate in so far as it is absolute, i.e., in so far as it implies a denial that other people have a right to it. There is a balance between individual and social claims to the same plot of land, or the same piece of urban property, and while it is right that individual owners should be secure in their possession of as much as is needed by them and their heirs for their actual work, it is wrong that they should have power to compel others to work for them. In this somewhat roundabout fashion Proudhon arrives at a doctrine of exploitation. The latter is present wherever the laborer is not remunerated in accordance with the value of his product. But what is the measure of value? Proudhon seems to waver between a labor theory of value and the notion that the "value" of a product is equal to what it is "worth" to other producers. Plainly these two concepts can be made to rhyme only under fairly simple conditions, where the producers employ roughly similar tools, and indeed Proudhon most often gives the impression of referring to a

society of small craftsmen, though elsewhere he does deal with
the situation in the industrial workshop.[12]

In view of the conditions created by industrial capitalism, the
solution of the social problem could not be found uniquely in
measures for safeguarding the family farm or the independent
craftsman: that much Proudhon was willing to concede. His principal attempt to grapple with the problem was made in the *Système
des contradictions économiques* and in his later writings. Here we
are mainly concerned with the 1846 work, which provoked Marx's
rejoinder and the ensuing dispute between the followers of the two
men. Since it runs to almost 1,000 pages, all we can do is indicate the general line of thought and the principal issue dividing
the Proudhonist from the Marxist critique of capitalism.

Unlike the *Théorie de la propriété,* which may be described as a
sociological tract dealing with the institution of private ownership,
the *Système* is intended as a treatise on economics. Its inordinate
length is due to the fact that Proudhon comes forward as a critic
of the liberal economists (including the British, in so far as they
were available to him in translation). At the same time he sets
out his objections to the socialism of Louis Blanc and the communism of Cabet. Both systems are denounced as dictatorial, subversive of personal freedom and private life, and destructive of the
family. The proper aim of the legislator should be the widest
possible distribution of private possessions (though not of property in the bourgeois sense), so as to make a healthy family life
possible. Liberalism and communism are equally damnable:

> The community [of goods] is nothing but the exaltation of the State,
> the glorification of the police. . . . Communism reproduces . . .
> all the contradictions of liberal political economy. . . . Mankind,
> like a drunk, hesitates and flounders between two abysses, property
> on the one hand, community [of goods] and Statism on the other:
> the question is how [humanity] can traverse this mountain pass
> where the head is seized by vertigo and the feet refuse their service.
> . . . Capital and power—the subordinate organs of society—are
> the gods which socialism adores. If capital and power did not
> exist, [socialism] would invent them. Owing to this preoccupa-
> tion with power and capital, socialism has completely misunderstood
> the meaning of its own protestations.[13]

The partisans of centralist collectivism are the victims of a strange illusion: "fanatics of power," they expect the instauration of a new social order through the intrusion of the government. But the new corporate power of property would be worse than the old. "Property cannot become social by being made common. One does not cure rabies by biting everyone."[14] The collectivists, by relying on the state, make nonsense of their own professed aims.

The more strictly economic parts of Proudhon's argument are set out at wearisome length in Volume I of the *Système des contradictions économiques*. As the title indicates, his aim was to demonstrate the self-contradictory nature of the prevailing mode of economic organization. It was this approach that attracted Marx's special scorn, since by his standards Proudhon was not only a poor economist, but an even worse philosopher. Attempts have been made to show that he was not in fact quite so naïve as Marx supposed, but these apologies relate chiefly to his later writings. So far as the 1846 work is concerned, even his stoutest defenders are obliged to concede that his handling of the dialectical method was amateurish. The more technical passages, on the other hand, suffer from Proudhon's unfamiliarity with those British economists whose writings had not been translated. Marx, who in 1846 already possessed a thorough grasp of contemporary British literature, had an easy time demonstrating Proudhon's lack of control over his material. Proudhon does indeed make a sad muddle of concepts such as scarcity, supply and demand, and so forth. However, the real weight of Marx's criticism falls upon his attempt to demonstrate that one can arrive at egalitarian conclusions by taking Ricardo's economic theory at its face value.[15]

Proudhon starts from the observation that use value and exchange value conflict with each other, since the more there is of some useful commodity, the less it will fetch in the market. He regards this as a contradiction and wonders how it has come about. His explanation is that use value is constituted by the producer, exchange value by the consumer, who estimates the scarcity of the product. Marx objects with reason that Proudhon has overlooked the real conditions of exchange: supply and demand bring production and consumption together because the producer has to sell and the consumer has to buy. They are not free agents, but partners whose respective positions are determined by the existence of a market economy. Producer and consumer are held together by their mutual involvement in the exchange mechanism, which is a social process, not a matter of their personal whims. "The conflict does not take place between utility and estimation; it takes place between the marketable value demanded by the supplier and the marketable value supplied by the demander."[16]

Proudhon next proceeds to what he calls "constituted value," a formula which he regards as an important theoretical discovery of his. In his usual manner he takes the opportunity to patronize earlier writers:

> The synthetic idea of value had been vaguely perceived by Adam Smith. . . . But with Adam Smith this idea of value was entirely intuitive. Now, society does not change its habits merely on the strength of intuitions: its decisions are only made on the authority of facts. The antinomy had to be stated more palpably and more clearly. . . . It is incredible that for the last forty years so many men of sense should have fumed and fretted at such a simple idea. . . . Values are compared without there being any point of comparison. . . . This, rather than embrace the revolutionary theory of equality, is what the economists of the nineteenth century are resolved to uphold against all comers. What will posterity say about it?[17]

The "revolutionary theory of equality," whose discovery Proudhon attributes to himself, is this: since (as Ricardo had argued) labor is the source of value, and the measure of labor is time, the "constituted value" of a product is the value "constituted" by the labor-time incorporated in it. Hence it is only necessary to lay it down, once and for all, that goods shall be exchanged in proportion to their embodied labor-time. This will do away with the distortion introduced by supply and demand and will satisfy the demand for justice. Marx replies that Ricardo's formulation describes the actual condition of things in bourgeois society. Equal labor values are in fact exchanged, but the outcome is not a society of equals, but rather the perpetuation of inequality. The reason is that labor is paid for under conditions where it is a commodity among others.

Proudhon confuses the *value* of labor with the *quantity* of labor embodied in a commodity. The cost of production determines the exchange value, or price, of a commodity. The value of labor, on the other hand, is the price which labor commands, its wages. This price is settled in the labor market, by competition, and thus tends toward a minimum. The laborer gets in wages what it costs to maintain him, that is, the amount of labor embodied in his means of subsistence.[18] Proudhon's solution is utopian:

> Ricardo takes his starting-point from present-day society to demonstrate to us how it constitutes value. M. Proudhon takes constituted value as his starting-point to construct a new social world. . . . The determination of value by labor-time is for Ricardo the law of exchange value; for M. Proudhon it is the synthesis of use value and exchange value. Ricardo's theory of values is the scientific interpretation of actual economic life; M. Proudhon's theory of values is the utopian interpretation of Ricardo's theory.[19]

What Proudhon is looking for in this part of his work is an invariant standard of value which will enable a future hypothetical society to fix a "just price" on the basis of labor-time. He holds that if the value of all things can be "constituted" (i.e., if a price can be fixed for everything), there will be an end to unearned income and the exploitation of the laborer by the capitalist. Marx's comment on this is that, given the existing system of capitalist production, exploitation is a necessary consequence. If one wants to end it, one must do away with private property in the means of production. Proudhon's solution is inoperative under capitalism and unnecessary under socialism. "In a future society in which class antagonism will have ceased, in which there will no longer be any classes, use will no longer be determined by the *minimum* time of production; but [rather] the time of production devoted to an article will be determined by the degree of its utility."[20]

Marx is not the only critic to have remarked on Proudhon's misuse of the dialectic, notably in his handling of the notion of contradiction or antagonism. Proudhon sees contradiction everywhere, particularly in the categories of political economy, but unlike Marx he does not treat contradiction as the motor of development. For him, every social phenomenon (machinery, division of labor, etc.) has two sides: good and bad, positive and negative. The division of labor, for example, "is the mode in which the equality of conditions and intelligences is realized," but on the other hand, it degrades the laborer. In this way he arrives at the "antagonistic effects of the principle of division," namely wealth and degradation. The synthesis is found by Proudhon to lie in the invention of machinery. This again has its "antagonistic effects," which in turn are harmonized by competition, and so on through all the successive stages. To this Marx objects: firstly, these distinctions are merely conceptual, not related to real historical epochs; secondly, Proudhon has overlooked the function of what Hegel had termed "negativity"—he sees only antinomies but gets no meaning out of them, because he will not admit that what he calls the "bad" side is the one that keeps the process going. In trying to neutralize the second term of the contradiction, he does away with the real movement of history. In the real world, the "positive" and the "negative" element interact, whereas in Proudhon's mental universe they merely confront each other. Marx is enough of a Hegelian to hold that history is propelled forward by its "negative" side, e.g., that capitalist exploitation is the price of economic progress. Proudhon will have none of this. He wants to do away with the contradiction, not realizing that the true historical synthesis lies beyond the conflicting forces which have their logical counterpart in his "contradictions."[21]

Proudhon's later writings, notably his posthumous *De la capacité politique des classes ouvrières* (1865), which became important for the French labor movement of the 1860's, do not concern us. On the other hand, note must be taken of the fact that in 1848 he proposed what he called his *système mutuelliste*. "Mutualism" was the middle term between economic liberalism and state-controlled socialism or communism. Its principle was simple enough: there should be a means of enabling the producers to obtain monetary credit without having to pay interest, the taking of interest being a particularly noxious form of the *droit d'aubaine*. As he put it in his *Organisation du crédit,* what was needed was not the organization of labor (as Louis Blanc had supposed), but something more urgent: "What we need, what I call for in the name of the workers, is reciprocity, equity in exchange, the organization of credit." Gratuitous credit is the solution of the social problem. A system of unlimited bank credit will ensure economic justice without the intervention of Louis Blanc's *ateliers nationaux* or any other form of state interference. Indeed, the government should keep out of the economy altogether. "The task of the State is merely to pronounce on the justice of economic relationships, not to determine the manifestations of freedom." What was needed was quite simply an exchange mechanism based on the principle that the producers be remunerated in proportion to their labors. This done, they would be able to enter into "free contracts" with each other, leaving the government at liberty to attend to other matters (if indeed there was need for a government at all).[22]

Gratuitous and unlimited credit is the foundation of "mutualism," for once the producers are freed from the tyranny of the banks and of interest payment, the only brake upon production is their own capacity to supply each other's needs. Full employment will thus be assured. Moreover, commodities under this system will exchange in accordance with their real values, thus securing social justice as well. The producers (who are also described as the workers) require credit, which they will obtain from a central bank established for this purpose; but in a sense they will provide their own credit by rendering each other mutual support, i.e., by exchanging their goods and accepting token money (the gold standard having been abolished) as a symbol of their mutual interdependence. This is the *système mutuelliste* to which Proudhon looked for the gradual emergence of a new and better order. It is not, in the usual sense, a socialist system, since it has no room for central planning, and it is certainly not communist. What is it then? Perhaps it is best described as Proudhon's private version of socialism.[23]

The disappearance of the state is not envisaged by Proudhon as the final term of a process set in motion by the introduction of "mutualism." On the contrary, it is presupposed. The social revolution consists precisely in the dissolution of the state and the inauguration of a social order held together by "free contract." In

1848 Proudhon regarded the socialism of Louis Blanc as the principal obstacle to the adoption of his own principles. The revolution must be spontaneous, it must come from below, and it must set itself the aim of dispensing with the state, an institution counterrevolutionary by its very nature. This was the message of Proudhon on the eve of 1848 and during the stormy events of that year. In all fairness it has to be recognized that the "mutualist" project was neither more nor less impractical than Louis Blanc's schemes for legislating full employment into existence, and that Proudhon did not share Blanc's illusions about getting such legislation passed by a government and an assembly dominated by bourgeois Republicans without a single constructive idea in their heads. Proudhon's credit bank would at least have been popular with a large section of the electorate, whereas Blanc's National Workshops— had they come into existence—would have made the operation of the market economy impossible under the conditions then prevailing. Proudhon was also quite realistic in forecasting the election of Louis Bonaparte to the Presidency of the Republic in December of 1848. In this respect his contempt for the Republicans served him well. Whether their behavior entitled him to flirt with the Bonapartists and to call on Louis Napoleon in 1852 to fulfill his mission by introducing Proudhon's schemes for mutual credit is another matter.

Having thus completed our review of the socialist tradition in France, we must make the Channel crossing into England before turning to the concluding part of our story: the Marxian synthesis.

PART TWO

Critics of the
Industrial Revolution

And did those feet in ancient time
Walk upon England's mountains green?
And was the holy Lamb of God
On England's pleasant pastures seen?

And did the Countenance Divine
Shine forth upon our clouded hills?
And was Jerusalem builded here
Among these dark Satanic mills?

WILLIAM BLAKE

6. *The Heritage*

It is a commonplace that Britain was first with the industrial revolution, just as France was first with a large-scale experiment in political democracy. It is equally a commonplace that North America during this period was uniquely successful in establishing a functioning liberal-democratic political system while at the same time undergoing an economic transformation stimulated by the British example. When these circumstances are taken together, they make up a complex picture which Marx later on was to describe as the "bourgeois revolution," an example of the kind of shorthand that traditionally has been the despair of people brought up in the empiricist tradition. What justification was there (they might ask) for subsuming these widely separated and quite distinct phenomena under a common heading? There had indeed been a connection between the American and the French upheavals, even though the more conservative American and the more radical French theorists were apt to stress the differences rather than the similarities. But what did either or both have to do with the economic transformation in Britain? Was it more than a coincidence that all these developments got under way during the last quarter of the eighteenth century? And if there was a common factor, why did it pass unnoticed at the time?

A possible reply to this last question might be that a community of destiny was in fact perceived by radicals whose sympathies were successively engaged with the American struggle for independence, the defense of the French Republic, and the popular protest movements in England and Ireland. Thomas Paine is the obvious example that comes to mind, and one might add the leaders of the Irish rebellion in 1798 who notoriously counted on French help. But all this does not quite go to the roots of the matter. It is indeed plain that there was a democratic upsurge around 1800 on both

101

sides of the Atlantic and that its leaders were conscious of having certain broad principles in common. But it is equally plain that the social origins of this movement were basically agrarian and that its aims were at variance with the actual outcome of the economic transformation then under way. Moreover, in so far as it was urban, the movement was largely sustained by independent artisans whose position was being undermined by the growth of industrial capitalism. And indeed where it gained power, as in France, the democratic party (taking that term in its widest sense) proved a hindrance rather than a help to the economic core of the industrial revolution: the accumulation of capital. It was Britain, not France, that took the lead in transforming the ancient mode of production—Britain, the stronghold of oligarchic government and the leader in the struggle against Jacobinism. It was as though the two most important countries of Western Europe were acting different roles in the same play. From the historian's viewpoint the "play" could be described as the emergence of a new type of civilization whose economic base was being laid in Britain, while its political and ideological structure was being worked out in France (and rather less dramatically in the United States).

This is the first point to be made in examining the origins of British socialism. It needs to be stressed lest it be forgotten that socialism presupposes the existence of capitalism. Not every anti-capitalist movement is necessarily socialist. It may represent a conservative reaction, or an attempt to stabilize an order of things antedating the industrial revolution. So far as Britain is concerned, socialist thinking properly so called made its appearance in the 1820's, when an urban factory proletariat had begun to form. What had earlier passed for social criticism bore the familiar imprint of tradition: agrarian, clerical, or philanthropic. The solutions proposed would, if adopted, have conserved the ancient order of things. Not surprisingly, the nascent class of industrial entrepreneurs was not to be found on the side of such reformers. This is enough to explain why the democratic movement of the 1790's, which had formed under the impulsion of events in France, obtained so little middle-class support. A Jacobin republic of craftsmen and peasants held no attraction for pioneers of technical change who also happened to be pacemakers of capitalism. For that matter, it would have held no great attraction for socialists either, but socialism was not then an issue. What doomed the democratic movement before 1830 was lack of support from the manufacturing middle class and its theorists. A "bourgeois revolution" was not possible without them, and, as events were soon to show, it was not possible (at any rate in Britain) with them.

This is the background to the intellectual movement which laid the foundation of the English radical tradition. The term "radical" has traditionally been employed by historians of this period to designate groups or parties which sympathized with the ultimate aims of the American and French revolutions. Plainly this does not include the Whigs or those utilitarian thinkers who merely stood for cheap and honest government. Yet Bentham is conventionally described as a "philosophical radical." On the other hand, the term has been stretched to accommodate Tory democrats like William Cobbett, who loathed republican France but were hostile to the ruling oligarchy and its merchant allies. So defined, radicalism becomes synonymous with democracy in the literal sense of popular rule. But who were "the people" in radical parlance? Not the urban factory proletariat, for this stratum was only just beginning to form. Artisans and small farmers? That would have been Paine's understanding of the term, but Paine's republicanism —albeit moderate by French standards—was too extreme for most English democrats, while his deism was uncongenial to Cobbett. Paine's writings influenced men who later became Chartists, while the hard core of the manufacturing middle class found its creed in Bentham's utilitarianism and in the new science of economics. Radicalism in *this* sense was a class ideology—that of the industrial bourgeoisie, although its exponents would have been surprised to hear it said. Were they not uniquely concerned with the good of society, and did the public interest not demand that society be remodelled in the image of the industrial entrepreneur?[1]

Radicalism, then, was both less and more than a democratic movement. Less because its effective leadership lay with the Benthamite "philosophic radicals"; more because in its Painite form it raised issues transcending the popular horizon, then still bounded by the struggle for a broader parliamentary franchise. In the second part of his *Rights of Man* (1792), Paine had sketched the outline of the modern welfare state: a graduated income tax to pay for general education of all children; old-age pensions ("not as a matter of grace and favor, but of right"); public housing; and help for the needy. William Godwin's *Political Justice* (1793) questioned the need for centralized government, and Mary Wollstonecraft's *Rights of Women* (1792) inaugurated a century-long struggle on yet another sector of the front. These writings of the 1790's established a tradition on which the socialists of the next generation were to draw, but their authors were "bourgeois" democrats. Of Paine it has been said by a modern historian of the labor movement that his proposals "were in no special sense aimed at the working people, as distinct from farmers, tradesmen, and professional men. His was a doctrine suited to agitation among 'members unlimited'; but he did not challenge the property-rights of the rich nor the doctrines of *laissez faire.*" His targets were the monarchy, the aristocracy, and the clergy. The social reforms he advocated could have been adopted by the middle class of his day, though in fact they were not. There is no sense in treating *The Rights of Man* as a socialist pamphlet. It is no more socialist than the *Wealth of Nations,* nor could it have been. A socialist doctrine could not be formulated until industrial capitalism had unveiled its secret, and even then the bulk of the British labor movement remained wedded for many years to the nonsocialist radicalism of an earlier day.[2]

If Bentham was a pioneer of "free enterprise," and if Paine was neutral on the issue, Cobbett represented a species of agrarian populism quite compatible with loyalty to the British Monarchy and the Anglican Church. Further to the left, some of the English "Jacobins" of the 1790's carried democracy to the borders of utopian socialism, but the people whose cause they took up were artisans, not factory workers. Neither John Thelwall nor Thomas Spence can properly be termed socialists. Their concern was with "the poor" or with dispossessed farm laborers. The Spenceans perhaps came closest to outlining something that Babeuf might have recognized as familiar. But Thomas Spence (1750–1814), a cranky schoolmaster with an absorbing interest in promoting a phonetic alphabet, struck no terror in the hearts of the ruling class (though he was duly put on trial in 1801 for treasonable activities). Britain was not a suitable field for Babouvism. Anti-Jacobin sentiment, widespread among the people, reinforced a conservatism which had its roots in the rapidly growing wealth of middle class and farmers alike. The obverse of the coin was the misery of the pauperized artisans and the gloom of Blake's "Satanic mills." But no popular movement crystallized around these issues. Their evocation in literature passed almost unnoticed and at a later day served only to remind people of the horrors an earlier generation had endured.[3]

That the condition of the laboring poor was appalling, no one denied, least of all those economists who took the lead in explaining the meaning of the industrial revolution to the middle-class public. A good many writers asserted that living standards were deteriorating, and even the more optimistic held out no hope of rapid improvement. Down to the 1840's, the Malthusian theory, which maintained that the growth of population must always outrun the means of subsistence, served to explain why pauperization appeared to be spreading. After that date, the visible betterment in living conditions (in part a consequence of cheaper food imports) was held to have disproved these pessimistic forecasts. Either way the middle class preserved a good conscience. During the earlier period, proposals for welfare legislation were countered by appeals to laws of nature which supposedly rendered poverty and misery inevitable. Thereafter it was affirmed that such legislation was unnecessary, since real wages showed a tendency to rise— as indeed they did from about 1850 onward. By then the prolonged and dreadful birth pangs of the industrial revolution were over, and pauperism was no longer an important issue. Moreover, it was no longer a case of "the poor" facing "the rich," but of the new factory proletariat facing the employers. Unless this is grasped, the difference between old-style radicalism and authentic socialism must remain obscure.

The political line-up had altered too. The French Revolution had given birth to the democratic movement; the industrial revolution brought forth the labor movement. The two might and did intermingle, notably in the Chartist agitation of the 1830's and 1840's which sought political remedies for economic problems. But socialism was something new, whereas democracy was very ancient indeed, at any rate as an aspiration. The Chartist movement itself was agrarian-populist rather than socialist in orientation. Many of its leaders still thought in terms of reviving pre-capitalist, if not pre-industrial, forms of economic life. Others conceived the issue in strictly corporate terms: labor as the main producer of wealth was entitled to bargain for fairer shares. Even when working-class interests were counterposed to those of the "masters," the emphasis was on the division of the product, rather than on the elimination of private ownership. A rudimentary form of working-class consciousness, Chartism must not be confused with socialism, even though some of its leaders had been influenced by the new doctrines. What makes the movement important is its working-class character and the spur it gave to new methods of combat, such as the strike, which took the place of machine-wrecking or of the traditional hunger riot. Intellectually it remained for the most part confined within the limitations of Painite radicalism, the watered-down British version of Jacobinism. Had it succeeded, Chartism would have turned Britain into a democracy (and correspondingly hindered the capitalization of wealth, since middle-class savings would have been reduced by taxation). It would not, and could not, have introduced anything worth being described as socialism.[4]

None of this detracts from the general truth of the statement that the most advanced radicals of the 1790's had already anticipated some of the issues subsequently made familiar in socialist literature. For the theme of pauperism this is obvious, and in confronting it writers like Paine passed beyond the confines of respectable middle-class radicalism à la Bentham, with its stress on self-help. Here is Paine in 1797 on the need for an inheritance tax:

> Personal property is the *effect of Society;* and it is as impossible for an individual to acquire personal property without the aid of Society, as it is for him to make land originally. Separate an individual from Society, and give him an island or a continent to possess, and

he cannot acquire personal property. He cannot become rich. . . . All accumulation, therefore, of personal property, beyond what a man's own hands produce, is derived to him from living in Society; and he owes, on every principle of justice, of gratitude, and of civilisation, a part of that accumulation back again to society from whence the whole came.[5]

This states the case well enough, a generation before Owen and his followers applied it to the new world of industrial capitalism. It is of course no more than an explication of what is inherent in traditional Natural Law doctrine, faintly preserved in Locke and thereafter reaffirmed by Rousseau. But then socialism is ultimately rooted in the self-evident fact that man of necessity depends upon his fellow-men for the satisfaction of his needs, from the simplest and most basic to the most refined and complex. But for this perception of a universal truth independent of changing circumstances, the first socialists could not have presented their doctrine as a necessary corrective to the then prevailing liberal-individualist creed.

Spence and Paine were agrarian reformers, though Paine was also a theorist of republican democracy. Even Owen, the father of British socialism, is in some ways a transitional figure linking the reform movements of the pre-Waterloo period with the socialist theorizing of the 1820's and 1830's. By then, anti-capitalist notions were put forward by writers who had gone to school with the economists, absorbed Ricardo's doctrines, and later turned them against their originator. What was it, then, that linked the socialism of the 1830's to the radicalism of the 1790's? Primarily, it would seem, a residual faith in the ancient doctrine of Natural Law: the doctrine that there are human rights antecedent to, and in some sense more fundamental than, the positive enactments made by law-givers. Stoical and medieval ethics alike asserted that every man has a claim to certain rights and freedoms simply because he is a man. In the strict sense there was no Biblical foundation for this kind of universalism, but primitive Judeo-Christian ethics were compatible with it, in so far as they tacitly assumed that the community had a responsibility for the welfare of its members. In the later development of institutionalized Christianity, all these notions fused into Natural Law ethics. The fusion was made possible, so far as material circumstances were concerned, by the fact that medieval society provided a place for everyone whom it recognized as a member. Its social structure did not prevent poverty and inequality, but it excluded unemployment of the early capitalist type: partly because the economy was still primitive, in part because it was supposed to be the duty of the authorities to provide work or relief for everyone who counted as a member of the (Christian) community. If these arrangements broke down, religion could be invoked to warrant a crude egalitarianism, based on the notion of an equitable share-out. This had been the faith of seventeenth-century Levellers and Diggers, who otherwise differed—the former defending private property, the latter projecting a primitive form of agrarian communism. Although preached by the extreme left wing of the Puritan movement, these doctrines were never effectively put to the test, and intellectually they were displaced by Locke's far more influential formulations. Yet Locke retained the concept of a state of nature, albeit not a pre-social one. The citizens of his ideal commonwealth own property, whose possession is defined as a natural right; but the title to property is secured by labor, which is the source of value. Almost a century later, this seemingly innocent proposition recurs in Adam Smith, to describe a state of affairs in which the producer is still the owner of his tools. In the eighteenth century this kind of talk sounded harmless enough, at any rate down to the French Revolution. To the leaders of American democracy, indeed, even Paine's rather more radical formulation of the creed appeared inoffensive.[6]

It is tempting to conclude that the socialists started from principles laid down by Locke and by the more radical democrats among his followers. Yet we have seen that the term "radical" is ambiguous. It covers Bentham as well as Paine, and Bentham had no use for Natural Law, nor did he care for the egalitarian conclusions derived from it by writers hostile to private property. Bentham's "greatest happiness" principle could be turned in any direction, and it was to become part of the Owenite armory; but its author was resolutely hostile to communism and convinced that private ownership furnished the only possible foundation of civilized life. If property was incompatible with equality, then equality must be sacrificed; and if the utilitarian principle could not be demonstrated on Natural Law grounds, this was an additional reason for dispensing with *ius naturale* altogether. For the respectable middle-class radicals of the 1820's and 1830's, Bentham supplanted Locke, much as in France the new post-revolutionary liberalism after 1815 abandoned Rousseau: his doctrine (it was said) had been discredited by Robespierre. The appeal now was to experience, or to empirical psychology, rather than to philosophical abstractions. Yet Bentham's rather simple-minded pleasure-pain calculus was to become the intellectual premise of Robert Owen: the object of men's exertions being the attainment of felicity, social institutions must be so designed as to remove the causes of misery. For experience had shown that institutions were infinitely malleable. They could be designed and improved at will; hence it was the duty of governments so to model them as to promote that happiness which Robert Owen too regarded as the ultimate aim of men's strivings on this earth.

7. The New Commonwealth

General Principles

It is customary to describe as "utopian" the earliest representatives of British socialism: at once a doctrine and a movement constituting a parallel to Fourierism and Saint-Simonism across the Channel. There is much to be said for this view, provided one retains a firm hold upon the distinction between utopianism in general and the particular form it took among the writers retrospectively classed as early socialists. Unless it is borne in mind that socialists had no monopoly of perfectionism, some confusion must arise in contemplating other specimens of the genre, such as William Godwin's *Enquiry Concerning Political Justice,* already mentioned among the literary monuments of the enthusiasm uncorked by the stirring events in Paris. Godwin is usually classed among the philosophical fathers of anarchism, and with good reason. His principal concern, after all, was to disabuse his contemporaries of the erroneous notion that government was at all times a necessity. His trust was in the good will and common sense of the individual, and this is just why socialists have been reluctant to claim him. But that he was a true eighteenth-century rationalist, hence a true utopian, there can be no doubt. He took the view, as others of that school have done before and after him, that it was possible to imagine—and therefore to construct—a harmonious order adjusted to the unchanging needs of human nature. Such a society (of which the imaginary model might be found either in a past Golden Age or in a future Utopia) would be stable and permanent because uniquely designed to make men happy. Having attained this condition, they would clearly not desire to alter it. History therefore would come to an end, for history was simply the record of men's unavailing attempts to attain perfect felicity.

110

It is important to stress this point, for the spell of utopianism is understood only when one penetrates to its core: the belief in a possible state of harmony (or equilibrium) to be attained by designing a perfectly stable social order. The idea itself has a long and venerable history, going back all the way to Plato, albeit his proposed solution was designed to perpetuate a system of class (or caste) distinctions based on the acceptance of slavery and social inequality. In principle this does not matter, for the utopian message as such is rooted in the notion of history as a falling away from (or a preparation for) a just and stable order in a state of equilibrium. It is the philosopher's task to describe the arrangements necessary to bring the actual social order into conformity with this ideal. Utopian thinking antedates the concept of history as a real and irreversible process of change, a discovery commonly associated with Vico, Montesquieu, and Hegel. In this sense, writers like Godwin and Owen fall under the same description, for Owen too believed himself to be in possession of an ideal scheme conformable to the true needs of men and capable of being instituted by the simple exercise of reason. If in what follows we take no further account of Godwin and his progeny, the reason is that we are concerned with utopian socialism, not with its anarchist twin. So far as the philosophical origins are concerned, however, their common source is unmistakable.

The same cannot evidently be said of what has sometimes been described as the "Germano-Coleridgean" school, a line of thought nurtured by German metaphysics and destined to introduce into England the notion of history as an "organic" process. What is organic must evolve—indeed, this is the whole point of the organic-mechanical contrast elaborated by the founders of the Romantic school. Of these, Samuel Taylor Coleridge was the most influential so far as England is concerned, but his guiding ideas (as he was the first to admit) were derived from the Germans, principally F. W. J. Schelling and A. W. Schlegel. German Romantic philosophy will be examined later on, in connection with the pre-Marxians. Here it is sufficient to say that the organismic creed, as transmitted to the English Romantics by Coleridge, had much in common with the doctrines already put forward in 1790 by

Burke in his critique of the French Revolution. It was essentially a conservative approach stressing the slow growth of historical institutions (a point already made, in a different context, by Montesquieu). In what sense, then, was it favorable to socialism? Principally in that it cast doubt upon the rationalist doctrines about human nature underlying much of contemporary liberal writing. These doctrines were held, by conservatives and socialists alike, to be erroneous in that they imposed a rigid intellectual framework upon the living tissue of real, concrete, human relations: the family, the nation, the "organic" community of the village and the workshop. In due course, the "mechanical" rigor of rationalist philosophy came to be associated with the destructive effects let loose, by way of the new industrial technology, in the life of the "organic" community or the nation. This is the sense in which the organismic creed was understood by writers like Coleridge who had imbibed the new Romantic philosophy. But the point is worth making that these writers were conservatives, even if they came forward as Christian social reformers. They thus linked up with an older tradition, ultimately going back to the medievalists and to Thomas More, for the idea of an "organic" community was commonly joined to the notion of reverting to a social order based upon individual craftsmanship. Once again, empirical history was to be bypassed or brought to a stop.[1]

If there is a sense in which these writers prepared the ground for socialism (as distinct from social romanticism), it must be looked for in the emphasis they laid upon the concrete needs of real historical communities. Indirectly, too, the organismic model was of value to the emerging socialist movement in that it suggested the possibility of altering social relationships—including property relationships—as against the doctrinaire affirmations of the reigning orthodoxy, which tended to equate what was "normal" with what was advantageous to the new mode of production. Presumably this was what John Stuart Mill had in mind when, many years later, he praised the Germano-Coleridgean school for introducing the historical approach:

> They were the first who inquired, with any comprehensiveness and depth, into the inductive laws of the existence and growth of human

society. . . . They thus produced not a piece of party advocacy, but a philosophy of society, in the only form which is yet possible, that of a philosophy of history, The brilliant light which has been thrown upon history during the last half century, has proceeded almost wholly from this school.

Coming from Mill—neither a Romantic nor a socialist, for all his cautious criticism of the prevailing economic order—this was high praise. Not much needs to be said about Thomas Carlyle's rather similar utterances, for in his case the anti-individualist line of thought issued in a philosophy of history unacceptable to the emerging socialist movement. Owen's followers, like those of Fourier, never renounced the heritage of the Enlightenment nor the fundamental optimism of the French materialists from whom they were descended. They were in this sense within the democratic mainstream, however much they might differentiate themselves from the liberal heirs of eighteenth-century rationalism and individualism.[2]

Robert Owen

In what has been said so far about the utopians, some of the information relevant to Robert Owen and his school has already been anticipated. Let us now retrace our steps, so as to obtain a more adequate picture of what the first generation of socialists in Britain actually stood for.

It is natural to start with the Owenites, for Robert Owen's *New View of Society* (1813–15) in its way is as much a foundation-stone of the socialist creed as the work of Charles Fourier. Like his French counterpart, Owen derived a critique of society from an ethical doctrine ultimately rooted in a religious humanitarianism. The book's original title as published in 1815—*Essays on the Principle of the Formation of the Human Character*—plainly states what was at all times central to its author's view of the world: namely, that the social problem is a moral one, in the sense that it depends upon those in authority what sort of world they intend to make for other people to live in. In words often cited by his followers:

Any general character, from the best to the worst, from the most ignorant to the most enlightened, may be given to any community, even to the world at large, by the application of the proper means; which means are to a great extent at the command and under the control, or easily made so, of those who possess the government of nations.[3]

So far there is nothing very new here. Reliance is still placed upon the benevolence of those in control. It was Owen's disappointment with the existing governments that drove him into unorthodox channels and eventually turned him into an advocate of labor's emancipation. The story of his long life—he was born in 1771, a year before Fourier, and died in 1858—is the record of a spiritual pilgrimage from the naïve faith of an enlightened and philanthropic businessman to the cheerful stoicism of an elderly sage presiding over a group of trade unionists. Simply by enduring until well into the second half of the nineteenth century, he bridged the gap between the world of William Blake and that of Karl Marx. He also survived a string of disappointments that would have broken the spirit of anyone less confident in the effectiveness of his principles.[4]

These principles had their foundation in Owen's optimistic view of human nature as infinitely plastic, hence capable of indefinite improvement. He seems to have held this conviction already at the time when, as a youthful factory manager in Manchester in the 1790's, he entered the cotton-spinning business. But his first great field of experimentation was the New Lanark textile establishment in Scotland, where from the age of thirty he combined the duties of owner-manager with the task of rationalist educator of his numerous labor force. The story is tediously familiar. Its interest lies in the fact that it shows Owen at the start of his career in the role of enlightened autocrat which he never really abandoned. The son of a Welsh ironmonger, with an education that began and terminated at the village school, Owen was one of the "new men" who transformed Britain in the age of the industrial revolution. That, unlike most of his fellow employers, he was an instinctive humanist doubtless accounts for his gradual conversion to a form of socialism. In other respects he represented the industrial middle class of his age, not least in his boundless optimism, his faith in science, and his conviction that machinery, from being a curse, could be turned into a blessing for mankind.[5]

It is arguable that this characterization does not do justice to the second phase of Owen's career, which coincided with the great upsurge of trade unionism in the early 1830's. It is indeed remarkable that Owen should at the age of sixty have become the guiding spirit of an autonomous labor movement (not to be confused with the Chartist campaign which got under way in the late 1830's and immediately assumed a political character). The early trade unions had taken advantage from the repeal in 1824–25 of the Combination Acts passed in 1799 and 1800 at the height of the anti-Jacobin panic. The effect of this was to legalize the already existing bodies of organized workingmen, so that on his return to Britain in 1829 from the United States, Owen found himself unexpectedly in contact with labor organizers who used his ideas to promote both trade unionism and cooperatives. The movement spread rapidly, notably after the passage of the parliamentary Reform Act of 1832 which enfranchised the middle class (but not the workers), thereby encouraging the idea of a "General Union" of the working class to provide a "parliament of labor." The second and definitely socialist phase of Owenism belongs to this period. In 1833 Owen put before the Cooperative Congress a plan for a "Grand National Moral Union of the Productive Classes," whereby the new social order was to be introduced at one blow, by a concerted (though peaceful) refusal to continue working under the capitalist system. In practice this became something very different, namely the Grand National Consolidated Trades Union of 1834: an unsuccessful attempt to assemble the entire working class under socialist leadership. Owen incorporated a demand for the eight-hour working day in the program of his "Society for National Regeneration," but the Grand National Union was to have more ambitious aims. As visualized by Owen, it would unite the whole working class in a single organization and then, on a given day and in response to a proclamation from headquarters, declare a general strike and take over all the means of production: an interesting anticipation of both syndicalism and what was later called "guild socialism," for the Grand National Union was to transform itself simultaneously into a country-wide cooperative society, so as to provide the actual economic framework for the new socialist order.

Needless to say, nothing came of all this. During the early months of 1834 hundreds of thousands of workers briefly flocked to Owen's Grand National Trades Union, but the only concrete political action they ever undertook was an entirely peaceful procession through the streets of London in the spring of that year, to protest against the savage sentences inflicted by the Whig administration of Lord Melbourne upon six Dorsetshire laborers, the famous Tolpuddle Martyrs. These men—all of them peaceable Methodists, and two of them local preachers—had committed the crime of trying to organize the farm laborers in their district. The local landlords and farmers, with memories of the agrarian riots of 1830–31 fresh in their minds, promptly panicked, and the six organizers were brought to trial. Found guilty on a charge of administering illegal oaths, they were sentenced to seven years' transportation to Australia. The sentence aroused indignation among trade unionists and middle-class liberals (then known as "radicals") alike, but it was wholly effective so far as the government's purpose was concerned. At the first whiff of legal repression—hardly worth mentioning by the standards of contemporary France, where simultaneously the first workers' revolts and republican risings had broken out in Lyon and Paris—the entire movement collapsed. Nothing more was heard of the eight-hour day, not to mention the seizure of power by the working class. The Grand National Union dissolved within a few months, to be succeeded by the Chartist movement, which was a failure too, but at least had an attainable aim: the broadening of the parliamentary franchise.

But the history of the British labor movement lies outside our subject. Here it must be sufficient to note that Owenism after 1834 was associated with the cooperatives rather than with trade unionism. Owen himself remained active in other fields as well, notably in a Home Colonization Society, while some of the younger socialists (now proudly bearing this new label) organized the Rational Society, a forerunner of later humanist movements, not all of them socialist. Meanwhile what of Owenism as a doctrine? We

have seen that its core was a belief in the need for reshaping the social environment, but this might have been urged without reference
to practical proposals such as factory legislation or the establishment of consumer cooperatives. As for the idea of communitarian land settlements, this had been urged by Owen from 1817
on as a means of unemployment relief. These issues must not
be confused, nor must it be supposed that because at one stage
in the early 1830's Owen was drawn into trade-union organization,
he approved of class conflict. His basic approach never altered:
there were certain remedies for the social ills of the age, chief
among them the establishment of Villages of Cooperation to serve
as a model of the new social order. These settlements formed part
of an early project for combating unemployment, and they remained central to Owen's vision of the future. In this respect they
resembled Fourier's phalansteries, albeit Owen (no great reader,
and moreover intent upon asserting his originality) insisted that he
had not derived his ideas from Fourier.

The original scheme was simplicity itself. Pauperism and unemployment being among the major preoccupations of the Poor
Law administrators in the 1820's, Owen in his *Report to the
County of Lanark* (1821) proposed a form of unemployment
relief which was also a project for what a century later would have
been called collective farming. Instead of being maintained in idleness, the unemployed were to be settled on the land and made to
grow their own food. Later versions of the plan allowed for industrial production as well, but at first the emphasis was on farming,
specifically on spade cultivation. (Owen disapproved of the plow.)
In addition to raising crops, the settlers would also improve their
physiques and acquire an education. Their bodily and mental
powers would thus be developed and placed in the service of the
community. All these advantages could be secured by establishing
Villages of Unity and Cooperation, each consisting of 500 to 1,500
persons settled on 1,000 to 1,500 acres of land, with blocks of
houses built around large squares. Within the squares, public buildings would be erected so as to divide the squares into quadrangles:
hence the derisive label "Mr. Owen's parallelograms of paupers,"
which attached itself to the project after Cobbett had denounced

it in his usual robust fashion. Parliament and the government did not respond, although Owen was invited to London to lay his scheme before them. What is of interest is his belief that these largely self-subsistent settlements would help to solve a pressing problem of early capitalism by exchanging their surpluses with each other: the market was to be bypassed. It is this feature of the scheme which connects it with Fourier and with the early socialists in general, for Owen had by 1820 come to the conclusion—then fairly widespread—that both industry and farming, in so far as they were conducted on commercial lines, were "on the eve of bankruptcy."

The *Report* proceeds from a rudimentary labor theory of value, along lines later made familiar by the Owenite socialists. Its foundation is the traditional doctrine—as yet unquestioned by the economists—that labor is the source of value, hence ideally its standard of measurement. As Owen puts it: "The natural standard of value is, in principle, human labor, or the combined manual and mental powers of man called into action." To the objection that human labor is unequal, he replies that so is horse-power, which nonetheless has been found suitable as a standard of measurement. The average worth of human labor having been established by investigation, a certain quantity of such labor should form the basis of a unit of value, skilled labor counting for more—though the proportion is left obscure. The standard having been fixed, work would be remunerated by paper certificates stating the number of labor units credited to the individual, and these notes would entitle their owner to draw stores representing an equal number of units from the community warehouse—the whole arrangement to last until the progress of science might make it necessary to undertake a revaluation of labor's productivity. Thus justice would be served and consumption remain in step with production. It is uncertain whether Owen meant the laborer to receive the full value of his product (including the imputed value of machinery and management) or merely a standard wage reckoned upon labor's collective share in the total product; but the second interpretation seems more plausible. Certainly Owen conceived his project as being in the interest of the community as a whole, including its propertied classes. There need be, he argued in 1821, no fear of social revolution. Properly managed, his scheme would literally "let prosperity loose on the country." One catches the familiar accent of the reformer armed with an infallible plan for circumventing the obstacles raised by human folly and perversity. It did not occur to him that the economy might simply be operating in accordance with its built-in principles. As he saw it, all the trouble was due to a simple failure to perceive that labor certificates were a better medium of exchange than gold and silver. For needless to say, the worship of these metals was at the roots of social misery. Owen is the ancestor of a long line of currency cranks. His view of the matter was breathtakingly simple. The Bank Restriction Act of 1797 had made paper money legal tender, but unfortunately this wise measure had been contravened by the restoration (after the Napoleonic wars) of gold to its ancient dignity. There being a shortage of this metal, trade had been cramped and the general disease of the body politic aggravated. Hence the unparalleled depression of manufactures and the consequent fall in real wages. The remedy was a change in the standard of value, which at one blow would install prosperity and introduce social justice. This line of thought later became the starting-point for those of his followers who elaborated schemes for reforming the currency. Owen did not commit himself wholly to monetary reform at the expense of his main theme, which had to do with the maldistribution of property. His writings after 1821 (some of them published in the *New Harmony Gazette* while he was busy with his communitarian project in the United States) indicate that he was drifting toward a form of agrarian communism, with the stress upon complete equality and the virtual disappearance of private property. But this had not been the tenor of his writings while he was still a successful manufacturer appealing to the enlightened self-interest of his fellow businessmen.

Owen always regarded the *Report to the County of Lanark* as one of his best writings. In his autobiography, looking back upon a long life studded with many failures and disappointments, he still maintained that it gave—

a full view of society in its whole extent, including every department of real life necessary for the happiness of our race. It was the first time that the outlines of a science of society were given to the world; . . . and it was after the circulation of this report that the imaginative Fourier imagined his notions for forming a practical community society, mixing old and new principles and practices, which never can continue long to work together.[6]

Cooperation versus Competition

A glance at the issues prominent in the discussion of Owenism must take account of a group of men who may be described indifferently as socialists or laborists, depending on whether one notes their views on society or the more technical aspects of economic doctrine. In principle it makes no difference at this stage whether one calls them Owenites, since it was possible to share Owen's general outlook without adopting his specific proposals for dealing with pauperism or his views on education. Owen's working-class followers in the 1820's and 1830's were among the earliest socialists in England (or Britain) to deal with questions of economic theory. They claim our attention also because, unlike their predecessors, they were concerned with the particular set of problems brought to the fore by the industrial revolution. It is this which makes them significant and indeed enables one to describe them as socialists.[7]

The term "socialism" itself, as noted before, emerged from this formative decade of the 1820's, when Owen's rather vague doctrines received an indispensable theoretical stiffening in the shape of laborist deductions drawn from the theory of value. Before turning to this topic, it may be as well to note that these early socialists were able to make headway as critics of capitalism only after they had acquainted themselves with economic theory in its Ricardian guise. Prior to this, the only choice for radicals lay between some form of utopianism—agrarian or communitarian—and simple defense of labor's immediate interests against the claims of capital. Once they had absorbed Ricardo's explanation of how industrial capitalism worked (together with the rather paradoxical theory of value he had inherited from Adam Smith), it was possible to take a further step: the industrial revolution could now be regarded as potentially beneficial, and in any case irreversible, with the reservation that there was no need why it should profit only the capitalists. Both on theoretical and on practical grounds it might be argued that labor, being the principal creator of the new industrial wealth, should also be its owner. This was what "socialism" meant to those who first employed the term—specifically the editors of the Owenite journal in which this argument made its first appearance in November 1827. The London Co-operative Society founded in 1824 was among other things a debating society, and its journal, the *Co-operative Magazine,* from 1826 to 1830 formed the principal vehicle of what has been called orthodox Owenism. The Society held debates on such topics as "Is there any principle in human nature which presents an insurmountable obstacle to the co-operative system?"—meaning the system of egalitarian communism which Owen was then trying to establish at New Harmony. But along with these philosophical disputations the debaters also gave their attention to more immediate and pressing questions, e.g., "Is the laborer entitled to the whole produce of his labor?" "Why is, in the present state of society, the lot of the producing classes poverty and wretchedness?" Self-educated workingmen who had been induced by Owen's writings to discuss such topics as "Man is not properly the subject of praise or blame, reward and punishment," also let their minds rove over the implications of the labor theory of value, not to mention such down-to-earth questions as "Can the working classes permanently improve their condition by combinations to raise the rate of wages?" Or, to put it differently: while they made the first halting attempts to form trade unions and cooperatives, they also debated the relevance of Owenite philosophy to the new conditions of urban industrial life.

The term "socialist" was born in these disputations and thus from the start implied a critique of the prevailing individualist doctrines which underpinned the conventional wisdom of the middle class. In Owen's terminology "social" signified the opposite of "selfish." Self-love found expression in economic competition, while the "social" sentiment favored cooperation, hence "social-ism" or communalism. For people brought up in the habit of relating every historical mode of production to some inborn or acquired trait of human nature, there followed the plain moral that the existence of a "social" sentiment permitted the reorganization of society along cooperative lines. Those who favored selfish individualism would naturally be on the side of competition, while those who condemned it on moral grounds would, in their attitude to the holding or sharing of property, come to be "Communionists and Socialists."[8]

In strict logic, socialism and cooperation were not the same thing. Owen himself was not the only apostle of practical co-operatism (in the form of stores that sold provisions on a noncommercial basis). Neither was it necessary for Owen's followers to be "socialists" in the sense of holding that the ownership of capital should be lodged with those who had created it. It is true that such conclusions were drawn by George Mudie, a Scottish journalist who in 1821 founded a weekly propaganda organ, *The Economist,* to spread Owen's doctrines among the London printers. (When in the same year the printers formed the Economical and Co-operative Society, they did so with the object of promoting "a village of Unity and Mutual Co-operation, combining agriculture, manufacture, and trade upon the plan projected by Mr. Owen, of New Lanark.") Mudie himself was an agrarian, although he also believed that labor (after nature) was the creator of capital or wealth. For the rest, he proclaimed Owen's doctrine that the choice lay between two different economic systems: one based on strife and competition, the other on harmony and cooperation. In practice, many of these early cooperators gravitated toward communitarian settlements on the land, the best-known experiment in this direction being that associated with the Scottish Owenite. Abram Combe (1785–1827). In later years Owenism gradually merged with the cooperative movement in the form given to it by the Rochdale Pioneers in 1844: self-help through mutually owned stores selling industrial goods. The application of the cooperative principle to the ownership of industry was effected by those among Owen's followers who had absorbed Ricardo. There is no hard-

and-fast line separating the true Owenites from those writers who drew socialist conclusions from Ricardo's doctrines: it was possible to adhere to both groups simultaneously. Nonetheless there is a difference in emphasis, just as Owenism must not be confused with Chartism. Owen's experiments with cooperative producers' societies—intended to sell products at values determined by "labor time"—formed part of a movement which ended harmlessly with cooperative stores trading in goods produced under capitalism, albeit sold at prices designed to cut the usual distributors' margins. Some of this went back to William King's *Brighton Co-operator,* a journal which ceased publication in 1830. Trade unions and cooperatives both owed much to Owenism, but it was not necessary to be a socialist to be active in either of them.

As for Owen's later career, it will be sufficient to note that after the failure of his political schemes he retreated to higher and securer ground. His search for a secular religion which would be the animating spirit of a new form of community life, culminated in the establishment of Harmony Hall, at Queenwood (Hampshire), over which for seven years (1839–46) he presided as Social Father of the Society of Rational Religionists. There he held converse with the spirits of the departed, Shelley and Benjamin Franklin among them, for in his old age he had become a believer in this form of communication with the dead. Not untypically, the experiment was terminated by a quarrel between its working-class adherents (who wanted the settlement run on democratic lines) and Owen's wealthy supporters who had advanced the capital for its founding and installed their own trustees. Also, the middle-class members were not prepared to do manual labor. In the end Queenwood was closed down by the trustees, after a final quarrel over democratic self-management. The enduring monument to Owen's work is to be found in the cooperative movement, but cooperation was never synonymous with socialism.

8. *British Socialist Economics, 1820–40*

The Labor Theory of Value

The doctrine that labor is the sole (or at any rate the main) source of wealth, although not literally as old as the hills, is of respectable antiquity. Mention has already been made of the formulation given to it by Locke, for whom, however, labor was not distinguishable from capital, since both were conjoined in the person of the farmer or manufacturer: in short, the early entrepreneur. It is curious, by the way, that the definitive formulation of the private enterprise ideology owes so little to the British economists who founded what is known as the "classical" school. Neither Smith nor Ricardo discriminated clearly between the monetary and the managerial function. Initiative and risk-taking, as distinct from the provision of investment capital, were somehow taken for granted. It was left to the French economist J. B. Say (better known as the inventor of "Say's Law," i.e., the proposition that production creates its own demand) to bring out the importance of the entrepreneurial function. In Ricardo's writings, which set the tone for the British discussion from 1817 onward, the idle landlord is indeed contrasted with the active man of business, but the latter appears in the role of owner or investor, rather than as the organizer of a new mode of production, a theme celebrated in contemporary French literature. This approach opened a flank to critics who treated the employer of labor as a monopolist levying toll on the "real" producers, the workers. However, this was not quite enough. There also had to be a theory of value (as distinct from an assault on the social function of property-owners), and this too the critics of capitalism discovered (or believed they had discovered) in Ricardo's formulation of the older Smithian or Lockean doctrine.[1]

The seventeenth-century version of Natural Law ethics derived a juridical right to private ownership from the personal toil and care bestowed upon material objects (principally the land and its products) by an individual who was at once an owner-manager and a farmer or artisan. This was the assumption underlying Locke's discussion of the topic in the *Two Treatises of Government,* a work that retained canonical status for the British economists of the classical school, as well as for the authors of the American Constitution. Locke, however, also retained the ancient notion that—in addition to the "value" created by "labour"—there was an "intrinsick value" in objects which sprang from "their usefulness to the life of man." This had been the Aristotelian view, an echo of which may be found in Shakespeare's *Troilus and Cressida,* where Hector explains that "Value dwells not in particular will; It holds his estimate and dignity As well wherein 'tis precious of itself As in the prizer." Hector was an Aristotelian before his time, or perhaps one should say Shakespeare followed the medieval canon law. Sir William Petty (1623–87), half a century later, tried to make room for the new concept of exchange value (as distinct from use value). Thereafter the economists of the mercantilist school, and eventually Smith in his *Wealth of Nations,* established the principle that "labor" was the source of both use value and exchange value. Smith added to the confusion by laying it down that the owners of capital employed in manufacturing, transportation, etc., "are themselves productive labourers." Ricardo, while avoiding these and other Smithian muddles, did not make it clear what precise role the employer of (salaried) labor played in the process of wealth creation. He can hardly have supposed that the capitalist was essentially nonproductive, but this conclusion was drawn by the socialist writers of the 1820's and 1830's.

Before going further, it is as well to guard against a possible misunderstanding: nothing said here is to be taken to imply that the labor theory of value was central to Ricardo's system. Nor need it be inferred that those writers who derived socialist implications from Ricardo understood him better than his more orthodox followers. Least of all is it to be supposed that Ricardo himself (whose death in 1823 removed him from the scene before the debate between liberals and socialists had properly got under way) would have sided with the Owenites. It is true that he had been influenced by Owen to the extent of conceding that there might be a conflict of interest between employers and workers with regard to the introduction of machinery. But this modification of his earlier standpoint occurred in 1819, when his views on all other subjects were already fully formed; and while important, it was not enough to suggest an effective critique of capitalism. Basically, Ricardo's doctrine is one of social harmony where the interests of capital and labor are concerned. Class conflict makes its appearance in his system in a different context altogether: the division of the social product between the owners of the soil and the producers in charge of manufacturing industry.

Confusion on this topic is best avoided by distinguishing what is specific to Ricardo's doctrine from the traditional quasi-philosophical concepts he inherited from his predecessors. These concepts had originally been evolved during the seventeenth and eighteenth centuries in response to the new phenomenon of a market economy. Historically, the notion of "exchange value" served to legitimize the profits accruing to manufacturers and traders, as well as farmers, from the conduct of their business. Exchange value arose from the sale of commodities and thus was not quite respectable in the eyes of clerical medievalists. Hence the economists, from Sir William Petty in the seventeenth century to Ricardo in the nineteenth, took pains to establish that exchange values were created by labor. The labor they had in mind was that of the property-owner: the sort of person whom Marx later called the bourgeois. It never occurred to them that "labor" might one day become a description attached to men deprived of all title to property: the class of industrial proletarians. For this to happen the early socialists had to discover the rift set up by the appearance of two new strata, capitalist employers and salaried workers. This new class division had arisen from the industrial revolution and thus postdated the formulation of a value concept which in effect treated "labor" as an aspect of "capital." Ricardo indeed had already seen the difficulty and tried to meet it by suggesting that capital was stored-up labor. This took care of the traditional notion that wealth was created by "labor." Beyond this he saw no problem other than the practical one of reconciling the competing claims of employers and workers to their respective shares of the total product.[2]

What did the argument about use value and exchange value have to do with the actual remuneration that salaried laborers received in the industrial production process? Ricardo had an answer to that one too; witness the opening passage of Chapter V of the *Principles:*

> Labour, like all other things which are purchased and sold, and which may be increased or diminished in quantity, has its natural and its market price. The natural price of labour is that price which is necessary to enable the labourers, one with another, to subsist and to perpetuate their race, without either increase or diminution.

He goes on to explain that "the natural price of labour" depends on the price of food and other necessities, while "the market price of labour" is "the price which is really paid for it, from the natural operation of the proportion of the supply to the demand." The natural price and the market price might correspond or diverge; in either case, labor was a commodity to be bought and sold. But "labor" had traditionally been defined as the source of wealth and the standard, or measurement, of "value." Here, then, was an entity which appeared in the shape of wage-earners, while at the same time furnishing a standard for measuring the wealth they were busy creating. It was all very baffling, and the socialists made the most of it. They were encouraged by Ricardo's habit of treating capital as stored-up labor. From there it was no great jump to the conclusion that labor was the original factor in production, or even the only one. Ricardo did not actually say this, but his treatment of the subject lent itself to such conclusions. In the words of a modern interpreter of his work, he "does ultimately seem to adhere to the view that the expenditure of physical energy constitutes a unique real cost of production and a fundamental cause of value."[3]

Ricardo's approach thus raised two quite different issues which were frequently confused in the subsequent disputations. There was, on the one hand, the purely theoretical problem of using the concept of labor, or labor-time, as a unit of measurement in reckoning up the "values" created in production. In addition there was the quite separate problem of deciding whether or not labor was being defrauded. When manufacturers hired laborers and then sold the goods they had produced at a net profit, was this profit legitimate or not? That it arose in the process of production seemed plain enough, and equally it was plain that the wages paid to the laborers fell short of the marketable value (price) of their product. As Adam Smith had already observed, employers earned a profit because workmen "stand in need of a master to advance them the materials of their work, and their wages and maintenance till it be compleated." Workmen (i.e., craftsmen) were made to part with a portion of their output, in return for money wages for which they could not wait. Combined with Smith's rather fanciful picture of an early state of society when the laborer received the whole product of his toil, this led to the notion that capitalist profit was a form of monopolist exploitation. Ricardo, and even more so James Mill and McCulloch, felt uncomfortable with this conclusion and tried to avoid it by introducing the notion that profits represent a return upon that stored-up labor which exists in the form of machinery. This explanation failed to satisfy the socialists, for whom there was a distinction (neglected in Ricardian theory) between the capitalist and his capital. They were ready enough to concede that machinery and other fixed equipment might add value to the product, but they saw no reason why this addition should be credited to the capitalist, or indeed why the employer of living labor should ever have been permitted to become an owner of "stored labor" in the first place. They also extended the Ricardian value concept by insisting that labor was not merely the *measure* of value, but its *creator*. In all these respects Ricardo's ambiguities opened the door to a debate in which the socialists came to differentiate themselves from his more orthodox disciples.

The Ricardian Socialists

We are now in a better position to understand the group of writers generally known as the Ricardian socialists: "that small band of economic radicals who between 1820 and 1840 put forth the claim of labor to the whole product of industry."[4] In particular it should be clear that we are dealing with men who have some claim to be regarded as theorists. This is not to say that they speculated in the abstract. On the contrary, it was precisely the fusion of theoretical and moral concerns that made them noteworthy. Politically, they were submerged by the broader Owenite current, not to mention the Chartist movement, which climaxed (and failed) in 1848. Intellectually, they figure in socialist history as pre-Marxians, for it was Marx who made effective use of Ricardo's doctrine for the critical interpretation of capitalism. But precursors have their place in history, and the Ricardian socialists can claim to have pioneered into virgin territory. On some points they anticipated Marx; and it is arguable that he might not have reached his goal had they not blazed a trail for him.

Piercy Ravenstone's name is seldom encountered in standard histories of socialism.[5] His pamphlet *Doubts on the Subjects of Population and Political Economy* (1821) was, however, read by some of the Owenites. It presents the socialist case with the help of arguments drawn from the labor theory of value. In addition to expounding the theme that labor is the source (not merely the measure) of all wealth, and capital merely appropriated labor, Ravenstone also attacked Malthus' population theory, which conservatives had been using for two decades in support of the thesis that nothing could be done about pauperism. Ravenstone was followed by the anonymous pamphleteer whose tract *The Source and Remedy of the National Difficulties* (1821) made use of Patrick Colquhoun's *Treatise on the Wealth of the British Empire* (1814), with its challenging statement that "more than one fifth part of the whole community are unproductive labourers, and . . . these labourers receive from the aggregate labour of the productive classes about one third of the new property created annually."[6] Colquhoun's statistics furnished material for John Gray (1799–

1883), of whom little is known save that he was of Scottish origin, grew up in London, and around 1820 became a follower of Owen. His *Lecture on Human Happiness* (1825) offers one of the earliest syntheses of Owenite and laborite (the two must not be confused) reasoning. In a later work, *The Social System* (1831), Gray came forward as a currency reformer, a theme further developed in his *Lectures on Money* (1848). However, it is his early tract which concerns us, since it was here that he gave eloquent expression to what was to become the standard socialist indictment of unearned wealth. Was he a Ricardian? It is perhaps safer to call him a Smithian, since he operated with a rather simple-minded version of the labor theory, in which labor is equated with manual toil in field, factory, and mine. All other occupations are unproductive, although some of them may be useful. The useful as well as the useless live on the wealth produced by wage-labor in fields and factories. This is a fairly unsophisticated standpoint, and one can see why some authors would rather not have Gray included among the Ricardian socialists. However, in a general sense he belongs to the group, though it may be surmised that Ricardo's more technical arguments were above his head.[7]

Gray's *Lecture on Human Happiness* starts off from the Owenite (or Rousseauist) proposition that man's nature, if not interfered with by evil influences, conduces to harmony and happiness. The principle that satisfies man's natural desire to live in peace with his fellows is barter, i.e., the giving and taking of equal quantities of labor. Properly applied this would lead to a condition of equality, whereas under the existing system the workers are robbed of four-fifths of their produce, which is then distributed among the non-workers. At this point Gray invokes Colquhoun's statistics, which demonstrate that "the rich man who, in point of fact, pays nothing, receives everything, while the poor man who, in point of fact, pays everything, receives nothing. We put it to the candour of every honest man whether such a state of society as this ought to be preserved!"[8] If the non-producers should argue that they live upon their own property, Gray rejoins that property not acquired by labor is held unjustly. Moreover, the present inequitable distribution of wealth conduces to further evils, for the competition among laborers presses down the rate of wages, while competition among employers lowers the rate of profits. Were competition replaced by cooperation (as proposed by Owen) the whole of society would benefit. As matters stand, production is limited by effective demand, whereas it ought to be limited only by the satisfaction of material wants. The result is that the inhabitants of Britain are "in possession of powers by which they can create wealth without any known limits, and yet one-half of them are in a state of actual poverty."[9] The argument, though rather confused, points to lack of purchasing power as the cause of insufficient production, and in his later writings Gray quite consistently comes forward as a monetary reformer, while socialism drops out of sight. If inadequate purchasing power is at the root of the trouble, then the remedy may be found within the terms of private ownership and the market. In this sense Gray can be called a forerunner of the under-consumptionists. However, in 1825 he was still an Owenite and as such a socialist, at least in intention. As an economic theorist he does not rank high, but his pamphlet had some influence on later and abler writers.

With William Thompson (1775–1833) we enter the field of economic theorizing properly so described. A wealthy landowner in County Cork, he was already a firm believer in Bentham's utilitarian principle before turning to Owen's doctrine as a remedy for society's ills. His major work, published in 1824 under the title *An Inquiry into the Principles of the Distribution of Wealth Most Conducive to Human Happiness,* runs to 600 closely printed pages, which by the standards of the age was not extraordinary. As a stylist, too, Thompson is very much the cultivated gentleman of leisure. There is more than a touch of the eighteenth century about him. He had, however, absorbed economic theorizing and in some manner fleshed out his utilitarian ethics with a rudimentary doctrine of exploitation. He may thus be described as a socialist Benthamite—an odd case, but after all no odder than Owen himself.

In the *Inquiry,* Thompson, while critical of capitalism, is still uncertain about the alternative. The full socialist implications of Owenism, notably the critique of private ownership as a matter of principle, make their appearance in his second work, usually cited as *Labour Rewarded* (1827), though the actual title is a good deal ampler. The earlier work, however, already operates with the notion that labor is the only source of value. From this it would appear to follow that the laborers ought to receive the full product, but Thompson is willing to let the capitalist have a share, on the grounds that the producer must pay for the use of tools when so unfortunate as not to own them himself. There is perhaps a hint here that Thompson thought of the craftsman rather than the factory worker. In general his argument implies that the laborer is the real producer, the capitalist merely the owner of means of production put at the producer's disposal. Ideally, the craftsman or laborer, being the creator of value, ought to retain his product free from all deductions in the shape of rent or profit. But since we do not live in an ideal world, the capital-owner may be allowed a limited return on his investment. There will then be a deduction for depreciation of capital, plus compensation to the owner, so as to enable him to live "in equal comfort with the more actively employed productive laborers." This of course assumes that the laborer is the real producer, whereas Bentham, like Ricardo and James Mill thereafter, had treated capital as creative, labor as its more or less willing tool. In siding with labor against capital, Thompson adopts what would later be called a class standpoint, but his reasoning, at least in intention, proceeds from theoretical considerations. The source of all profit is "the value added to the raw material by the labour, guided by skill, expended upon it. . . . The additional value proceeds from labour alone." The laborers need buildings, machinery, and raw materials, and must pay for their use. But how much? Certainly the capitalist ought not to appropriate the entire surplus. In opting, as he does, for "almost perfect equality," Thompson appears to follow ethical rather than strictly economic considerations, which might have pointed in a different direction. In his later writings he gets around the difficulty by abandoning the whole notion of competing claims under an assumed system of private ownership. His standpoint is now frankly Owenite: the workers, through their cooperatives, are to become joint owners of the entire apparatus of production. This is the thesis of *Labour Rewarded,* a work written in reply to Thomas Hodgskin's *Labour Defended* (1825). Thompson's position in socialist history is secured by his belated, but unswerving, adherence to Owen's cooperative doctrine, as against the individualism of writers like Hodgskin who still clung to the dream of a society of free and independent producers. In 1830 he published *Practical Directions for the Establishment of Communities.* It has been conjectured that, in addition to amplifying the Owenite system, he influenced Owen by clarifying in his mind the operation of capitalism, of which for his time he had a remarkably good grasp. He also anticipated Marx by introducing the term "surplus value," although in the Marxian system this has a different connotation.[10]

Thompson, then, was an Owenite socialist, although perhaps not much of a Ricardian in the technical sense. Thomas Hodgskin (1783–1869), after a variegated career as a naval officer and strenuous voyager in post-Napoleonic Europe (he did most of his travels on foot and on his return to England in 1820 published a two-volume account of his wanderings, interlarded with libertarian musings), became a self-taught economist in the Ricardian manner. In 1825 he published the pamphlet which gives him his place in socialist history, *Labour Defended Against the Claims of Capital.* Meantime he had become involved in the establishment of the London Mechanics' Institution, a college for workingmen where he taught a course subsequently condensed into a book under the misleading title *Popular Political Economy* (1827). This was followed by his *Natural and Artificial Right of Property Contrasted* (1832), where the labor theory of value was set out in a form that made it relevant to the nascent trade-union movement— a movement in which he participated until 1833, when his public career came to an end, just as the working class was beginning to assemble under the banner he had helped to unfurl.[11]

Hodgskin is interesting for two reasons: he was resolutely indifferent to both Bentham and Owen; and he was a critic of capitalism who did not want to abolish private property. Rather he contended, in the Lockean manner, that ownership was sanctified by personal labor. The general tendency of his thought was toward a society of free and independent producers. On these grounds he has sometimes been described as an anarchist. Certainly the Owenites thought him misguided on the issue of private ownership, and Thompson chided him for adhering to a belief in competition and the market. In this respect Hodgskin in 1825 seems to have anticipated his subsequent conversion to liberalism. At any rate he ended his career as an editorial writer on *The Economist:* not the short-lived Owenite weekly started by George Mudie, but the famous financial journal founded by James Wilson in 1843 and for many years edited by Walter Bagehot as the organ of *laissez-faire* liberalism. The Mechanics' Institution, after being recaptured by the orthodox Benthamite radicals headed by Francis Place and George Birkbeck, survived to become a constituent part of London University. In short, the early attempt to divorce socialism from radicalism ended in failure so far as Hodgskin was concerned. Yet he has retained a small niche among the English pre-Marxians, and for this his pamphlet of 1825 is clearly responsible.

Labour Defended is not a blueprint for a socialist alternative to capitalism. It is an exposition of the doctrine of class struggle, couched in terms that Hodgskin had borrowed from Ricardo. Its starting-point is the Ricardian theory of value, plus an analysis of the actual conflict between masters and men, capital and labor, let loose by the formal abrogation of the Combination Laws in 1824–25 and the workers' attempt to form trade unions. As a writer Hodgskin sides with their efforts, in which he took part, but he also presents a theoretical argument. Labor being the source and measure of value, the laborer has a prior right to the whole product of industry. Yet the existing system keeps the wages of labor down to a subsistence level, while all the fruits of productivity accrue to the landlord and the capitalist, both useless to society, which only requires a market for goods turned out by different kinds of producers. Hodgskin favors private ownership and free competition. His objection is to the capitalist monopoly of the means of production. Capital (as Ricardo has shown) is simply stored-up labor, a part of the product of industry set aside from current consumption. This does not entitle the capitalist to appropriate everything over and above the subsistence wage paid to the worker, who for Hodgskin is the real producer.

It is the overwhelming nature of the demands of capital, sanctioned by the laws of society, sanctioned by the customs of men, enforced by the legislature, and warmly defended by political economists, which keep, which ever have kept, and which ever will keep, as long as they are allowed and acquiesced in, the labourer in poverty and misery.[12]

From these premises Hodgskin draws a conclusion that may be described as laborist rather than socialist: the conflict between capital and labor is destined to continue until labor shall possess and enjoy the whole of its produce, while idleness shall no longer be rewarded by wealth and power. The vagueness of this doctrine was suited to a time when it was still possible to envisage a society of independent producers held together by free competition. Yet Hodgskin was familiar with the emerging factory system which made nonsense of such notions. In fact the Owenites had already passed beyond him by developing the principle of association. It is not altogether clear why Hodgskin retired from labor politics at the very moment when Owen's more radical followers moved towards Chartism. The subsequent political reaction made Owenism synonymous with cooperation, a subject in which Hodgskin took no interest.

The 1830's witnessed the rise of the Chartist movement, led by working-class organizers whose thinking had been radicalized by Owen's doctrines and by the writings of the "Ricardian socialists," so far as they understood them. This accounts for the growing irritation with which advocates of laborism (in the sense of adherence to the doctrine of labor as the only source of value) were viewed by orthodox Benthamites like Francis Place and James Mill, who were committed to democracy but also to private property, and who sensed in this agitation a threat to the projected alliance of the middle class and the workers. Writing to Lord Brougham in 1833, James Mill refers to the "mad nonsense of our friend Hodgkin [sic] about the rights of the labourer to the whole produce of the country. . . . These opinions, if they were to spread, would be the subversion of civilised society; worse than the overwhelming deluge of Huns and Tartars."[13] In actual fact this was the moment when early English socialism went into eclipse. Thompson was dead, Gray was about to become a "monetary reformer," i.e., a currency crank, and Hodgskin had just started on the road which was to turn him into a liberal journalist and lecturer for the free-trade movement. The last, and in some ways most effective, shot in the socialist campaign of the 1830's was fired by an American resident in England but not destined to stay there for long: John Francis Bray.[14]

Bray's book, usually cited as *Labour's Wrongs and Labour's Remedy* (1839), has been described as "a synthesis of Owenism and anti-Ricardian economics"—a characterization which assumes that Ricardo's doctrine, properly understood, does not lend itself to the conclusions which writers like Bray extracted from it. At any rate it is plain that Bray was an exponent of the labor theory of value—but then so were some pre-Ricardians, e.g., Charles Hall. Perhaps it is best not to argue over whether or not Bray understood Ricardo. Basically he was an Owenite who had read Hodgskin and the other anti-capitalist writers of the period and combined their views in what was for its time an effective statement of working-class socialism: labor is the source of wealth, and the laborer has a right to the full value of his product, justice demanding that products should exchange in accordance with their imputed labor costs. Under capitalism this natural right is filched from the worker, who is paid a subsistence wage, while the nonproducer appropriates the product of unpaid labor. The nature of the remedy follows from that of the disease: capitalism being founded on unequal exchange (of unpaid labor against wages), the workers must seek to establish an equal exchange of their labor—i.e., an exchange of equal quantities of labor. This, however, is only possible in a society based on common ownership, as envisaged by Owen, although as an interim measure Bray outlines a system of joint-stock companies enrolling as many people as would volunteer to pool their savings. These are to be used to establish commonly owned enterprises, which would issue their own money in the form of labor-notes. There would be a national bank to finance the operations of these enterprises—in effect, producers' cooperatives to furnish goods outside the capitalist market system. Transport and services would be municipalized or run by elected boards. The whole project had affinities with

Louis Blanc's contemporaneous schemes in France. It was never put to the test, but as a sketch of a functioning socialist system it has some claim to originality. Marx thought well of Bray's work, although he criticized the utopian side of his proposals.[15]

Bray's subsequent career in the United States—as a banking reformer, advocate of farmer-labor cooperation, and vice-president of the American Labor Reform League—in some ways ran parallel to the evolution of those Chartists who, after the failure of their hopes in the 1840's, turned toward trade-unionism or the cooperative movement. The socialism of the 1840's had been immature; not only intellectually—for none of the pre-Marxians were really able to handle theoretical economics—but in that it had run considerably ahead of the political opportunities open to them. America at least was a democracy, and France briefly looked like becoming one in 1848, although it took another quarter-century before the Republic was finally established (and then in a purely bourgeois form). In Britain the collapse of Chartism in 1848 ushered in a period during which the labor movement first became altogether non-political and then entered into an alliance with middle-class liberalism in order to secure at least a broadening of the franchise. The year 1848 is in this sense a watershed for Britain as well as for France, since it marks the temporary eclipse of the socialist movement. When the British branch revived, it had outgrown its utopian origins, although a certain underlying continuity can be traced from the more radical Benthamites to their Fabian successors. At any rate the "greatest happiness" principle was not challenged. Whether it supplies an adequate basis for a socialist system of ethics is a question that need not concern us here. It was effective as a link between the liberal-radical reformism of the mid-Victorian era and the revived socialism of the following generation. The founding of the First International (1864) falls midway between the collapse of Chartism (1848) and the birth of the new Marxian or Fabian socialism in the 1880's. The International Working Men's Association (to give it its official name) was from the start backed by a considerable section of the British trade unions, and one may suppose that Owenite reminiscences had something to do with the willingness of their leaders to cooperate with foreigners. But the Chartist inheritance appears to have been more effective, and the Chartist movement, while radical-democratic enough, was not socialist. Nor did Ricardian socialism survive the great free-trade boom of the 1850's and the consequent spread of liberal *laissez-faire* doctrines among the unionized upper stratum of the British working class. Its leaders retained the conviction that labor was entitled to a more egalitarian kind of share-out, but for about a generation they did not challenge "the system." It seemed to work, and this pragmatic argument retained its effectiveness until the 1880's, when a new generation began to cast a questioning look at the operation of British capitalism.

Critical Summary

The origins of a movement, whether in philosophy, in the arts or in politics, frequently supply a pointer to its eventual outcome. In the case of British socialism one may confidently assert that its subsequent evolution was already inherent in its relatively peaceful and reformist beginnings. While French socialism and communism, having grown up on revolutionary soil, passed through the bloody turmoil of 1848 and 1871 before settling down to a more tranquil form of existence, the British labor movement reflected the relatively conformist pattern of middle-class liberalism during the Victorian era. Neither the middle class nor the workers seriously challenged the ruling oligarchy; the political system continued to operate within the confines of parliamentary government; and the revived and revitalized socialism of the 1880's, including its Marxist component, was at bottom just as reformist as its ancestor.

There is, however, a different aspect of the matter if one considers the intellectual formulation of the socialist creed. It is, after all, quite possible for a new phenomenon to manifest its true originality at the outset. In the arts this has ever been the rule. In the words of an eminent literary critic:

Here is a very odd thing. In literature the best in each kind comes first, comes suddenly and never comes again. This is a disturbing, uncomfortable, unacceptable idea to people who take their doctrine of evolution over-simply. But I think it must be admitted to be true. Of the very greatest things in each sort of literature, the masterpiece is unprecedented, unique, never challenged or approached henceforth.[16]

If this is true generally, one may inquire how it applies to our present theme. The answer would appear to be that the rule holds good for the British socialist movement, albeit with an important qualification: the unique intellectual creation did make its appearance at a fairly early stage, but its author—although resident in London and working within the tradition of British economics—was technically a foreigner. The greatest of the Ricardian socialists was Karl Marx. The true monument to the spiritual travail of that generation is *Das Kapital*.

Although not particularly shocking, this circumstance does raise a problem. Why, one may fairly ask, did it take a German-born thinker to stand British economics on its head? One possible answer might be that the early socialists simply happened not to possess the required theoretical capacity, but this hardly explains why they found no true successors. Ricardian socialism in its original form did not survive the onslaught of its critics, just as Chartism and Owenism did not survive the collapse of 1848. It was abandoned because Ricardo's doctrine had meanwhile come under critical scrutiny from a new generation of liberal economists, who quite specifically rejected the labor theory of value in the form Ricardo had given to it. In order to salvage its content, Marx was obliged to reformulate it. By that time, however, another Ricardian —John Stuart Mill—had begun to waver in his attachment to liberal economics. When after 1848 he moved toward a cautious acceptance of welfare economics and "consumer socialism," he laid the basis for the Fabianism of the future. Mill was all the more influential because he did not really challenge utilitarianism, although he had reservations about it. Altogether he built a bridge across which intellectuals and union leaders could at a later stage cross from liberalism to a kind of socialism. In doing so they saved themselves the trouble of having to read Marx (the first

English translation of whose major work did not see the light before 1887). All told, the empiricist tradition won out. Narrow and unsatisfactory though it was, it had the advantage of being familiar. It also imposed no great intellectual strain—an important consideration. As an economist, Mill was thoroughly eclectic, a circumstance which did him no harm with his readers. Thus, e.g., while he went on affirming his devotion to Ricardo's work, he also adopted the "abstinence" theory of profits in his own *Principles of Political Economy* (1848). That is to say, he committed himself to the proposition (first urged by Ricardo's critics in the 1830's, and then taken up and popularized by Nassau Senior) that the employer's "abstinence" (from what?) could be treated as a factor of production, along with the involuntary "saving" imposed upon the working class by the existing distribution of property. At the same time he retained the labor-cost approach, although he was careful to avoid the pessimism of Ricardo and Malthus about the level of real wages. Lastly, he advocated steep inheritance taxes as a social equalizer, and peasant proprietorship as a solution of the Irish land problem. All this made a splendid stew from which socialists and non-socialists alike could fish whatever they chose.[17]

There was, moreover, the direct impact of events in France upon public opinion in England. In the first edition of the *Principles,* Mill had professed sympathy with the egalitarian aims of the socialists (whom he clearly distinguished from the communists) but questioned whether any kind of socialist system could be made to work. By 1852 the upheaval in France and the concurrent growth of "Christian socialism" in England had made so deep an impression on him that in the third edition of his book he eliminated most of the theoretical objections to socialism, save for "the unprepared state of mankind in general and the labouring classes in particular" (as he phrased it in his *Autobiography*). What attracted him in the socialist doctrines of his time, which he discussed in his correspondence with Comte and others, was the notion of a "stationary state," originally suggested by Ricardo as a purely conceptual limit to the accumulation of capital, but treated by Mill as possible and desirable. Mill's stationary state is not socialism, but it is compatible with the notion of a social equilibrium such that all reasonable demands will have been satisfied and further technological progress will be regarded as unnecessary and undesirable. The first edition of the *Principles* already contained an adverse comment upon "the ideal of life held out by those who think that the normal state of human beings is that of struggling to get on." What of the United States which possessed "the six points of Chartism, and . . . no poverty?" Were the Americans to be envied for having made a fresh start? "All that these advantages seem to have yet done for them . . . is that the life of the whole of one sex is devoted to dollar-hunting, and of the other to breeding dollar-hunters." The theme was to become rather tiresomely familiar. Its interest for us lies in the fact that it should have been voiced in 1848 by the official philosopher of liberalism. But of course it was the Christian socialists who made the most of it, and a generation later it was taken up by the Fabians before being given its final and classical formulation by R. H. Tawney.

All of which is merely to say that the renascent British labor movement of the 1880's had at its disposal an indigenous tradition of liberal-laborism shading off into reformist socialism by way of J. S. Mill and his Fabian descendants. By that time, of course, the industrial revolution as such was no longer an issue; socialist critics, save for eccentrics like William Morris, who were perhaps closer to the anarchist tradition than they knew, now focused on capitalist property relations. Marxists and Fabians alike accepted industry and science, though not private property in the means of production. But there was a lengthy interval lasting from about 1850 to 1880, when socialism had little relevance in Britain. To understand why and how it became a living force on the Continent, we have to cross the North Sea and make a landing on the coast of Germany.

PART THREE

German Socialism

9. The Precursors

Romanticism and Reaction: 1800–1830

Something has already been said (and a great deal more ought to have been said) about the tension between the utilitarian doctrine subtending classical British economics and the philosophy associated with the Romantic movement. Insofar as the "Germano-Coleridgean" school in Britain around 1800 bore the imprint of German idealist metaphysics, one can speak of a fusion of cultures. For the period immediately antedating the July Revolution of 1830 and the subsequent British political and social agitation, it would be difficult to maintain that there was something like genuine cross-fertilization, although it is a fact that the leading German philosophers of the age were familiar with economic theory in the form given to it by Smith and Malthus. So far as theoretical economics went, even the most learned Germans in those days were in the position of pupils sitting at the feet of the British. In philosophy the relationship was less one-sided, but we have already seen that Coleridge and Carlyle condemned themselves to the role of prophets crying in the wilderness. Whatever the profundity of their social vision when compared to the productions of the Benthamite school, they had not mastered the new intellectual discipline and were thus reduced to deploring the inroads of the "dismal science."

The Germans faced a different problem. In philosophy they could hold their own, if only because the organismic conception of history was substantially their achievement. But in order to proceed from there to a critique of classical economics they would have needed a clearer view of the British situation than they actually possessed. As Germans they also had to get rid of mental cobwebs associated with the nationalist reaction against the French Revolu-

145

tion and Napoleon. This became easier after 1830, when German liberalism at long last picked up some steam under the impact of British and French developments. But it was precisely during the three decades between 1800 and 1830 that classical German metaphysics took shape in the great systems of Fichte, Schelling, and Hegel. The period is of crucial importance, since it witnessed the birth of those philosophical concepts which were to revolutionize the understanding of history, once Marx had fused them with French political theory and British economics. But it is idle to pretend that the German philosophers of this generation had anything original to say about matters economic: their interest lay elsewhere, and if they took note of the new science, they did so primarily because it served them as an example of the kind of theorizing they were determined to reject.

In saying this one must distinguish between Kant and the post-Kantians, the latter being then virtually unknown abroad, while they were beginning to exercise a growing influence among their own countrymen. Kant had an audience, if not a following, among British philosophers and theologians. Herder, Jacobi, Fichte, Schelling, and Hegel did not, even though Carlyle had read Jacobi. Among the utilitarians, James Mill earnestly grappled with Kant, and the moral philosophers then influential at Edinburgh thought well of him (which considering the Scottish origin of much of Kant's thought is hardly surprising). But Kant was pre-Romantic—indeed he represented just that side of the Enlightenment which the Romantics found intolerable: a rigorous separation of reasoning from the emotions, and a bleak refusal to engage in the kind of imaginative thinking proper to the understanding of life in its concreteness. Even the greatest and most influential of his pupils, Fichte, in the end found it impossible to adhere to the rigid Kantian orthodoxy. As for the Romantics properly so called—that is to say, the group of writers and critics who invented and then popularized the organic-mechanical dichotomy—they had a philosophical champion in Schelling, in addition to the consolation they would naturally derive from the writings of J. G. Herder, a pre-Romantic like Goethe and, like the latter, an instinctive opponent of Cartesian and Newtonian "atomism." The

British situation was different, for while the organismic view of history and society had its defenders (it was, after all, the foundation of Burke's critique of the French Revolution), there was no radical revolt against the Enlightenment as such. For the same reason, the abstract notions underlying the "dismal science" of economics did not provoke quite the virulent hostility they encountered in Germany.[1]

In general one must guard against supposing that Romanticism meant the same thing on both sides of the Channel. When the first generation of German Romantics appeared on the scene around 1800, they were confronted with the overwhelming authority of Kant and the prestige of Fichte, then a dogmatic rationalist. They needed a philosophical spokesman and found one in the person of Schelling, who supplied them with a metaphysical system. (In England it was possible to be a Romantic in politics without for that reason abandoning the empiricist tradition in philosophy. Coleridge was the exception, and he had no followers.) Inversely, when the next generation of German writers, having by then become politically liberal, discovered Byron, they adopted his principles but not his neoclassical style. The outstanding German Byronist around 1830 was Heinrich Heine, through whom the Byronic mood reached the youthful Karl Marx, as well as thousands of others who became (or remained) liberals rather than socialists. Since this theme is crucial to an understanding of both German socialism and German nationalism (subsequently destined to form an alliance which proved fatal to a great many people), some attention must be given to the topic before we enter upon our main theme.

In itself the Romantic movement was compatible with a variety of political creeds. In Central Europe, for political reasons, it eventually became associated with an anti-Western and anti-liberal outlook, but down to 1848, when the liberal-democratic movement failed to produce the long-desired national integration of Germany, this outcome was in doubt. Yet it is fairly obvious that German Romanticism was from the start affected by an undercurrent of hostility to the Enlightenment as such. The long-term consequence of this fateful orientation was to give the German

Weltanschauung a bias toward irrationalism: not merely in the arts (where it did no harm and may even have acted as a stimulant), but in politics and economics as well. Romanticism stood for a general attitude to the world—one hostile to uniformity, rationality, and abstraction. But in Germany there was also something more definite: a passionate rejection of the kind of reasoning which the Benthamites and their Ricardian allies were beginning to work out. It was not that the Germans—or even the Romantics among them—disliked empirical generalizations as such. What repelled them was the generalizing procedure employed by the British economists and the utilitarian philosophers to the end of demonstrating that, if individuals behaved reasonably, the final result was certain to benefit the community. To this the Germans of Goethe's and Hegel's generation replied that the whole was more than the sum of its parts, and that in order to determine what was beneficial for individuals, one had first of all to make up one's mind concerning the ultimate truth about history and society, as well as man and nature.

It could be argued that not all Germans who mattered held such views. Some influential statesmen and civil servants clearly did not. Adam Smith had his followers within the Prussian bureaucracy around 1810 (typically they were men who adhered to Kant's philosophy), and free-trading principles were surreptitiously introduced in Prussia from this time onward, under the aegis of enlightened administrators whose military colleagues at the same time were busy reforming the Prussian army. But in regard to economics this movement took place in a stealthy fashion and never became popular. Certainly it evoked no emotional response from the students who during these stirring years flocked to hear Fichte's patriotic lectures. We shall return to Fichte, a greatly underrated thinker who among others had a considerable influence upon the youthful Marx. For the moment let us consider briefly what it was that lay at the heart of the Romantic reaction against Kantian rationalism and individualism.

The subject can be approached by asking what it was that Kant got out of Rousseau (whom of course he had read); and the answer must be that he somehow missed the point Rousseau had made about society. Rousseau was concerned to describe the sort of community in which men could live harmoniously with each other, and this led him to envision certain kinds of social relationships (cooperative rather than competitive) as being more desirable than others. Now Kant too aimed at social harmony, but —reasoning along individualist lines—he thought it sufficient to lay down certain general rules of conduct whose observance would promote the common good. These rules were negative rather than positive: they specified what sort of behavior one ought to avoid. For the rest, they left the individual free to do as he liked, on the understanding that he would not misuse his freedom to encroach upon others. The moral world was thus ideally constituted as a realm of free and autonomous personalities, all obeying the dictates of their conscience and rejecting any external authority. It was an impressive construction rigorously deduced from first principles. There was only one thing lacking: it did not specify any particular ends to be pursued, or actions to be undertaken. To put the matter in different terms, it did not tell people what they ought to do, except that they ought to behave morally. It was this formalism which the Romantics found intolerable, and they could point to the fact that Kant's own disciples had trouble adhering to the rigid system of their master. This is where Fichte proved important: not because around 1810 he became one of the prophets of German nationalism after having shed his earlier sympathies for republican France, but because his philosophy meshed closely with his public role. Fichte was far and away the most important follower Kant ever had. He was also—and this is crucial—the author of a socio-political doctrine which was anti-liberal and authoritarian. *Der geschlossene Handelsstaat,* the tract on economics he published in 1800, outlined an anticipation of later autarchic and corporatist systems. It did not matter that Fichte was not, in the technical sense, an economist at all. What mattered was that the greatest of Kant's followers had broken away from liberalism. By comparison with this shattering reversal of roles, all the rest was trivial.[2]

J. G. Fichte (1762–1814) is so great a figure in the history of philosophy that it is tempting to describe his political attitudes as accidental, in the sense that—while doubtless important to him as the man he was, living in the Napoleonic age and reacting to its stresses—they may have been quite unrelated to his work as a philosopher. Unfortunately this will not do. Fichte's metaphysical nationalism was not just something he adopted because as a German patriot he felt impelled to resist the Napoleonic empire. It represented a coherent doctrine whose principles he had begun to develop years before he transformed himself from an ardent "Jacobin" and cosmopolitan democrat into the prophet of a national uprising. Moreover, it is arguable that his emphasis upon the *nation* (as distinct from the state) possessed permanent value and constituted something like a theoretical discovery. It can also be held that he became important to later generations of Germans (Marx among them) because, unlike Kant, he understood that a community is more than the sum of its individual members. This had both positive and negative implications. In principle it was quite compatible with the universalism of the Enlightenment, but in the populist and nationalist interpretation it received in Germany from the Napoleonic era onward, the doctrine had distinctly reactionary implications.

The point has already been made that the political theory of Romanticism, in so far as there was one, went back to Herder, in whose prerevolutionary philosophy the idea of mankind's essential unity still conserved an important place. What his successors did was to divorce the notion of an "organic community" from the humanism and cosmopolitanism of the eighteenth century. In doing so they became the precursors of German nationalism, while at the same time they laid the ground for the conservative critique of modern society as "soulless" and "atomistic." This is where the organic-mechanical contrast becomes politically relevant. Where does Fichte stand in this line of succession? As a Kantian he was out of sympathy with the irrationalism of the true Romantics, who eventually found their spokesman in Schelling. As a nationalist— indeed the founder of German nationalism, at any rate so far as Prussia and the Protestant North were concerned—he took over the Herderian concept of a *Volk*-state, with its racial overtones, although the emphasis in those days tended to be on language and culture rather than on "blood and soil." At the same time he moved away from Kant's liberal individualism toward the idea of a community (the nation) which was more than the sum of its parts. His *Naturrecht* of 1796 (written at a time when he was still an ardent democrat and Rousseauist) already employs the (Kantian) distinction between the group as *totum* and as *compositum* so as to arrive at conclusions foreign to Kant, for whom the social whole is ideally made up of autonomous individuals. Fichte's early writings—composed at the peak of his short-lived Jacobin enthusiasm—already suggest the vision of a process whose final aim is not the emergence of the autonomous personality, but rather the concretization of the human species into a number of distinct national collectivities. In this respect as in others, Fichte is a link between Kant and Hegel. What needs to be borne in mind, though, is that his subsequent conversion to nationalism also made it possible for the Romantics to treat him as an ally. He and they held in common a notion already implicit in Herder's philosophy of history: the belief that every ethnic community (*Volk*) is a uniquely determined sub-division of the human race whose spirit is embodied in its language. This spiritual essence constitutes the "organic" foundation of nationhood and of the state.

So far, there is nothing here to which Rousseau and his French followers could not have subscribed, but the German nationalists of the early nineteenth century added something else: the various folk communities were on principle not merely different from each other but impenetrable to each other. They might dwell peacefully side by side, but their spiritual essences were not communicable. Furthermore, the true repository of the national spirit, or folk culture, was the peasantry, plus those sections of the population that were closest to it: the small-town burghers and artisans. The aristocracy on the one hand, the "rabble" on the other, were not genuine members of the community. This belief too could be given a democratic coloration, as indeed was the case during the French Revolution, but the German Romantics chose to turn it into a doctrine hostile to the universalism of the Enlightenment. It was Hegel's refusal to accept these notions, rather than his political conservatism, that angered them. To Hegel—in this respect an individualist—the state mattered more than the folk. On these grounds the demagogic nationalists of 1820 denounced him— quite rightly, from their viewpoint. He was a conservative; they were racists, even though some of them still masqueraded as populist democrats.[3]

Mention of Hegel introduces a topic whose relevance to any discussion of socialism needs no emphasis, and this quite irrespective of how one evaluates his general philosophy. It is enough that part of his intellectual inheritance survived in Marx's thought (and even more in what is conventionally known as Marxism). The trouble is that one cannot in this context do justice to Hegel the philosopher, nor is it possible to present even the briefest outline of his system. It must be enough to indicate in what respect his thinking became relevant for Marx and his followers. After what has been said about the Romantics and Fichte, the main point can be stated, however inadequately, by saying that Hegel synthesized the Enlightenment and the Romantic upheaval. How and why he did this does not concern us. It is sufficient to say that he worked out a philosophy of history which embodied the "organicism" of the Romantic school, without for this reason abandoning the classical rationalist vision of a universal history of mankind—a movement whose logic could be discerned by the philosopher, albeit only in retrospect. The vision in Hegel's case was a contemplative one. Unlike Fichte (and unlike Marx, who on this issue reverted to Fichte), Hegel felt no urge to "transform the world." Indeed, he regarded such an enterprise as inherently absurd, at any rate for a philosopher. His standpoint was one of pure contemplation, and his perspective upon history makes sense only for someone who adheres to a theoretical mode of approach. The moment one abandons it, one also ceases to be a Hegelian.

This, by the way, accounts for the fact that no one actively involved in the shaping of history has ever been able to make consistent use of the Hegelian categories, although it is easy enough, after the event, to invoke Hegel by way of clarifying what actually happened (as distinct from what the participants imagined themselves to be doing). This is not a matter of choice or of individual temperament. Hegel's mode of thought becomes meaningless if it is employed for any purpose other than that of contemplation. It is a platitude that for Marxism to come into being, Marx had to abandon the Hegelian posture. But the same holds good for other writers—no matter what their political orientation—who made the transition from speculative thinking to practical involvement. Even as theorists (supposing them to have been such) they could not remain orthodox Hegelians but had to become something else if they wanted their thinking to make contact with some sort of practice. This applies impartially to conservatives and radicals alike. It is no less true of Kierkegaard than of Marx. It holds good for Prussian Conservatives, Russian Communists, Italian Fascists, or anyone else who has ever tried to operate with Hegelian notions (and a great many people have). It also holds for the folk enthusiasts of Hegel's own generation and for the nationalists who succeeded them. They too had to abandon his system—although they might conserve isolated fragments of it—if they intended to become politically effective. On pure Hegelian principles it was not possible to *do anything,* although one might *comprehend everything.* This was precisely what made Hegel acceptable to the Prussian government (and to the Lutheran theologians) so long as there was no radical movement in Church and state to disturb them. When such a movement arose, from about 1840 onward, Hegel (who in 1831 had left the scene) was retrospectively viewed as a subversive thinker, and the aged Schelling was imported from Munich to grapple with the "dragon seed" of Hegelianism. For by then the Hegelian school had split up into conservatives, liberals, and radicals, and the latter—the "Young Hegelians"—were reverting to the radicalism of Hegel's own student years. Only—this is the point—in order to do so they had to abandon their master's system.

None of this is to deny that certain elements of Hegel's thought were immensely influential already in his own lifetime. These aspects of his system were not what made him the greatest speculative thinker of his age, but they did have some connection with his general philosophy, and they enabled his immediate followers to exercise something like an intellectual dictatorship during the decade following his death. This is particularly true of Hegel's philosophy of religion which for a while managed to satisfy Lutherans, pantheists, and rationalists alike. It also applies to his philosophy of history, which was Hellenic and "tragic" rather than Christian, and thus eluded the debate then raging between the rationalist heirs of the Enlightenment and the Romantics. By the 1840's the latter had made themselves ridiculous with their yearning for a golden age which they generally located in the medieval past (when by a fortunate coincidence the German Empire was the greatest power in Europe). All this is important for the intellectual history of Germany and Europe in the later nineteenth century, but it is not pertinent to our theme and must therefore be left aside. We can only note here that Hegel was the successor of Kant and Fichte, but also of Herder and the Romantics, and that his system represented a grandiose synthesis of these conflicting strands. In as much as he made use of the organic-mechanical contrast he can be said to have underpinned the basic intuition of the Romantics. In so far as he rejected the reactionary ideology of the Restoration era, he remained in the central tradition of German idealism, as expounded before him by Kant and Fichte. His secret has already been noted: he was able to transcend all the conflicting parties of his day because he had fixed himself once and for all in an attitude of pure contemplation. In this respect he differed profoundly from most of his contemporaries, for both the followers of Kant and the Romantics in their different ways strove to unite life and thought, theory and practice, fact and value, what is desirable and what merely happens to exist. Hegel did not. For him there was no such problem, and it was precisely for this reason that he proved able to found a school, but not a religious or political party.[4]

And yet there clearly was something in Hegel's thought that made it possible for the radicals of the 1840's to bridge the gap between theory and practice. How else can one account for the phenomenon of a thinker such as Ludwig Feuerbach, who began his career as a fairly orthodox Hegelian in the 1830's and became the inspirer of Marx and Engels a few years later? Even a writer like Bruno Bauer—Marx's first teacher and for some years his friend—who disdained any share in political involvement, counted as a radical and indeed regarded his criticism of Lutheran theology and the Prussian state as a truly revolutionary act. Yet Bauer and his friends remained left-wing Hegelians. That is to say, they rejected their master's political conservatism, while retaining what they considered the essential aspect of his thinking—the dialectical method. Contrary to a popular legend, this had little to do with the celebrated triad thesis-antithesis-synthesis, a Fichtean invention rarely employed by Hegel. What was it, then, that enabled these writers, and those whom they influenced, to transmute Hegel's speculative philosophy into an instrument of revolution?

Paradoxical though it may sound, it was precisely Hegel's all-embracing rationalism which made possible the world-transforming activism of his radical followers. They could do nothing with Kant, for the Kantian disjunction between physics and ethics led to the conclusion that moral and political decisions could not be reached theoretically: what *ought* to be cannot be deduced from what is. Hegel did away with this distinction, and thereby opened the road to revolution. Not that he had the slightest intention of doing anything of the sort: he was an instinctive conservative long before he had become the official apologist of the Prussian state. But his grandiose metaphysical construction had implications of the most world-shaking kind, once its meaning had been grasped. For what was it that he affirmed? Simply that the Kantian *ought* was unnecessary, because the "noumenal" realm, the realm of absolute knowledge, was accessible to Reason after all!

For Kant, "practical" philosophy had been a matter of the individual conscience. Its true ground could not be met anywhere in actual experience and hence took on the character of an "ideal," of something that *ought* to be but *is* not. Hegel demolished this barrier, along with the Kantian thing-in-itself and the cautious agnosticism that flowed from it. Not that Kant lacked self-confidence: his ethics (by implication at least) did away with the idea of a supersensible deity. But the notion that *there is absolutely nothing beyond the reach of human thought* belongs to Hegel. Once this faith had sunk in, it did not take his bolder followers long to conclude that *the material world can be* (and therefore must be) *transformed,* so as to turn it into a creation of the human spirit (itself consubstantial with the divinity).

But how could the link between Reason and Revolution be forged by men who thought of themselves as interpreters of the Master? No group of theorists ever detonated a greater explosion than the Hegelians, yet none was less aware of the practical consequences of what they were doing. Hegel's mature system rivaled Aristotle's in its attempt to interpret the universe as a *mundus intelligibilis,* satisfying both to the minds and to the hearts of men. What he demanded of his readers was an ascent to a standpoint from which it became evident that reality was exactly as it ought to be—namely, rational. The real world having thus been transfigured into an Absolute, how could theory turn into practice? The answer is that the urge to make the real truly rational could be read into the system because Hegel had affirmed that world history represented the gradual emergence and the eventual breakthrough of Reason. As if this were not enough, the first decisive step away from contemplation toward revolution was taken by a conservative aristocrat, who for good measure was a Catholic mystic: the Polish nobleman and Hegelian philosopher August von Cieszkowski.[5]

Were this a history of nineteenth-century Europe, as distinct from an account of socialist origins, more would have to be said about the spiritual crisis into which Germany was plunged once Kant and his successors had extruded the last shadowy remnants of the older medieval world picture. It would then be necessary to explain in some detail that Hegel and his pupils were wrestling with a set of problems which were ultimately "existential," to employ the fashionable term. And lastly one would have to indicate how and why Hegel's grandiose attempt to recover a pre-Kantian sense of the objectivity and universality of truth was vitiated by the hidden subjectivism of the idealist approach. Regretfully, these fascinating topics must be set aside. But something further needs to be said before we come to Marx—namely, that as a Hegelian of the Left in the early 1840's he confronted the same problem which had already baffled Feuerbach and the other radicals: What was to be done about the world if Hegel's system had brought traditional philosophy to a close? Specifically, how could one (and should one) proceed from theoretical contemplation to political practice? On Hegelian principles, even as reinter-

preted by Cieszkowski, Bauer, or Hess, there was no very con-
vincing answer to such questions, which is why Marx in the end
broke with Bauer and the Left Hegelians generally. Yet he never
quite came to terms with an ambiguity in his thinking which had
probably been implanted by the early influence of Hegel's great
predecessor Fichte. The eleventh of the *Theses on Feuerbach*
(1845) simply does not make sense on any interpretation other
than the "idealist" one that "the world" must be "changed" because it is not as it ought to be: which was just what Hegel had
stigmatized as nonsense.

From Democracy to Socialism: 1830–48

So far as Germany and the remainder of Central Europe are
concerned, the three decades from 1800 to 1830 represent a fairly
uniform reaction to the French Revolution: taking the term "reaction" both in its narrower political and in its broader ideological
sense, for the emergence of conservative Romanticism (mainly in
Catholic Austria and Bavaria) and militant nationalism (chiefly in
Prussia and the Protestant north) were alike reaction-formations
provoked by the Revolution and Napoleon. After 1830 the picture
changed, in as much as liberalism now made its appearance as a
political force—at first in some of the south German states and
later in Prussia—and eventually entered into an uneasy alliance
with nationalism, both movements having for their aim the unification of Germany and the modernization of its internal political life.
The whole phenomenon was restricted to the middle class or, to
be precise, its educated section, led by university lecturers and
students. Both the aristocracy and the peasant masses were indifferent to nationalism (at any rate down to 1848) and hostile to
liberalism, in so far as they were at all aware of it. Notwithstanding
some democratic efforts in the south, liberalism on the whole made
no attempt to clothe itself in popular forms. So far from concealing
its middle-class character, it gloried in it. One may say that the
Central European *Bürgertum* (the French term *bourgeoisie* does
not quite convey the deliberately archaizing sonority of its German analogue) was conscious of itself as a *Stand* (estate) be-

fore it acquired the economic significance of a class in the modern sense. Germany was still economically backward compared to Britain and Western Europe. The industrial revolution did not really touch the country until about 1830, and thereafter the social tensions resulting from the growth of pauperism in the towns impinged upon the consciousness of a politically inert and philistine middle class which was literally "in the middle": wedged in between the landowning nobility and the laboring classes of town and country. This awareness of belonging to a social stratum bereft of political power, but possessing some influence upon the absolutist governments and the ruling bureaucracy, rendered the German *Bürgertum* peculiarly susceptible to legal and constitutional arguments, while barring the way to the kind of social vision that had opened up before its West European counterparts. Even after the July Revolution in Paris had enthroned a constitutional monarchy and a government solidly based upon the liberal bourgeoisie, the German middle class did not really envisage anything so alarming as the notion of actually having to govern. All it desired was an extension of its influence and some concessions to liberalism in the realm of the written and spoken word. In brief, it tended to behave not like a politically conscious class, but like a pressure-group.

On the other hand, the change in the intellectual climate after 1830, with the increasing inroads of Anglo-French liberalism, made it difficult for the Romantic school to conserve its intellectual hegemony. Romanticism—notably in its Roman Catholic and aristocratic aspect—had underpinned the politics of the Restoration era from 1815 to 1830. Its dissolution left the authoritarian regimes in Central Europe ideologically naked, although in Lutheran Prussia the more conservative Hegelians for a while did what they could to provide a substitute by extolling the state as such. When the Hegelian school began to disintegrate in the 1840's, the crisis of the official ideology coincided with the growing impact of economic change upon the absolutist regime and its social base: the class of great landowners. The upshot was the revolution of 1848, which failed to introduce parliamentary democracy but gave the *Bürgertum* some additional leverage. It also ushered in the reign of what in later years came to be described by German writers as *Scheinkonstitutionalismus* or pseudo-constitutionalism: a form of rule ostensibly modeled on British parliamentarianism, although the constitutional façade barely concealed the reality of military and bureaucratic power. During the seven decades from 1848 to the collapse of 1918, Germany and Austria were to be distinguished or disgraced (according to one's point of view) by this peculiar form of government, which combined the effective supremacy of the military and the bureaucracy with the gradual implantation of the *Rechtsstaat,* or rule of law. The middle class on the whole accepted this state of affairs and made no serious attempt to introduce parliamentary democracy on the Western model, although the franchise was gradually extended to include most of the adult male population.

The struggle for democracy thus became the affair of groups and parties lower down in the social scale, ranging from dissatisfied bourgeois radicals to socialists and communists; and from the lower middle class of the towns, by way of the peasantry, to the new industrial proletariat. Not surprisingly, those who stood for democracy imagined themselves to be carrying a banner already displayed during the French Revolution. This ignored the fact that in France the political struggle had laid bare the existence of class interests which could not be harmonized by the simple expedient of broadening the franchise. Moreover, when manhood suffrage was finally introduced in France after the February Revolution of 1848, its immediate practical outcome was the election of Louis Napoleon to the presidency of the Republic. Democracy, that is to say, proved incompatible with bourgeois liberalism. In Germany and Austria, where the Old Regime survived until 1918, this sort of problem did not arise. Nor, for different reasons, did it arise in Britain and Belgium, where from 1830 to the 1880's liberal rule (based on a restricted franchise) when hand in hand quite comfortably with the social pre-eminence of a mixed aristocratic-patrician stratum based on what the French called the *grande bourgeoisie.* But then Britain and Belgium were the two most industrialized countries of Europe, and neither had a serious agrarian problem. Germany and Austria (not to mention Russia, where serfdom lasted until 1861) had to face not only industrial tensions, but also peasant unrest, at times mounting to the point of insurrection. In Central and Eastern Europe, therefore, "the revolution" signified the threat of actual violence and the overthrow of the state: the sort of thing that the governments and their more or less lettered supporters were in the habit of describing as "Jacobinism." To put it briefly, in Germany and Eastern Europe, society down to 1918 remained pre-bourgeois, while the state remained autocratic. Hence democracy could be had only by violence, and its triumph was tantamount to republicanism—even "red republicanism," i.e., with inroads being made upon private property. Liberalism in these areas was quite simply the class ideology of a propertied minority and perceived as such by all concerned. The German liberals themselves made no secret of the matter. In their terminology, *Bildung und Besitz* (education and property) were necessary qualifications for the exercise of the vote.[6]

In the light of this unbroken record of political passivity and accommodation to the established authorities in Church and state, it may seem paradoxical that this very same German *Bildungsbürgertum* gave birth to a culture—and notably to a philosophy —which in important respects transcended not only the authoritarian regime, but contemporary bourgeois civilization itself. The paradox is lessened if one bears in mind that the great age of classical German literature, art, and philosophy, from about 1760 to 1830, ran parallel to the "bourgeois revolution" in France, England, and North America. The Germans accomplished in thought what others achieved in practice. Moreover, their relatively sheltered position, and their attachment to forms of life which elsewhere had begun to crumble under the impact of industrialism, afforded their intellectuals a unique insight into problems destined to become acute at a later day. Spectators rather than actors in the historical drama, they possessed a vantage-point which for a generation or so enabled some of them to take a critical view of what was going on around them. This applies not only to the Romantics, who set themselves more or less consciously in opposition to the entire trend leading toward specialization and "mechanism," but also to Hegel. It is true that Hegel—having by 1820 digested Smith and Ricardo—made a very deliberate attempt to come to terms with the new reality of "civil society": an entity clearly distinguishable from a more ancient political concept, the state. Yet for all his awareness that the situation had changed, Hegel in the end adhered to the pre-liberal tradition of thought which viewed the state as the realm of moral principles, whereas society by contrast appeared as a subordinate arena torn by strife and given over to "subjective," egoistic appetites and passions. This authoritarian doctrine, for all its Hobbesian undertones of pessimism, still carried a dim echo of the message the youthful Hegel had once extracted from his reading of Rousseau and the Greek and Latin classics: the ideal of a political community of equals. Hegel never recaptured his early faith in the possibility of realizing such a community, but his utterances held implications unflattering to middle-class liberalism. He had at any rate perceived the Rousseauist dilemma inherent in the distinction between the *citoyen* and the *bourgeois*. For practical purposes citizenship had come to be identified with ownership of private property, which was why the more realistic Jacobins (and their Jacksonian counterparts in the United States around 1830) could envisage a democratic commonwealth only as a society of independent property-owners. When this vision dissolved under the impact of industrial capitalism, the democrats had a choice: they could accommodate themselves to the logic of a market economy, i.e., turn into liberals (albeit liberals who believed in universal suffrage and equality before the law). Alternatively, they could repudiate private property and the market in the name of social equality, in which case they had left bourgeois society behind (at any rate in thought) and become socialists or communists of some sort.

In the philistine Germany of 1830–48, then undergoing the first faint stirrings of the industrial revolution, this was not yet an urgent practical problem. The key issue was still the attainment of democracy, or rather the merging of the nascent democratic movement with the mounting nationalist current in and around the universities. Romanticism and nationalism had fused in the so-called "war of liberation" against Napoleon, which in its turn had prepared the way for the Restoration era of 1815–30. The task of the liberals, as they saw it, was to de-fuse the two: in other words, to make the French Revolution respectable, while retaining the patriotic image. In Italy, then undergoing similar stresses, this mental renovation was successfully accomplished by the generation which held the stage from 1830 to 1848, so that in 1848 the leadership in the national struggle against Austria-Hungary could be seized by democratic republicans. But then all Italian patriots knew in their hearts that the liberation of their country from the Habsburg yoke was impossible without French aid (it was in fact set in train in 1859–60 by an alliance between Piedmont and France, then both governed on authoritarian lines). Italian nationalism, whether Jacobin or Bonapartist, was at any rate pro-French, whereas in Germany the liberal opposition had to make its way in a country profoundly marked by the anti-French and anti-Jacobin orientation inherited from the war of 1813–15. Except for the small Jewish community, which owed its (very recent and rather incomplete) emancipation to the after-effects of the French Revolution, the bulk of the provincial middle class was hostile both to France and to democracy. Still, from 1830 to 1848 a liberal current—in some instances even a democratic and "Jacobin" one—made itself felt among an elite of the younger generation, the poet Georg Büchner being the outstanding representative of its radical vanguard. Büchner, an authentic genius and an instinctive Jacobin (as one may see from his magnificent drama *Danton's Death*) rang a bell whose sound continued to reverberate long after his untimely death in 1837. At a different level—that of Byronic liberalism and individualism—the note of rebellion was struck by writers like Heine and Lenau, not to mention a number of lesser figures. In the academic world, liberalism of the English rather than the French variety became the dominant faith among the historians then prominent in Germany (with the exception of L. von Ranke, who throughout his life remained a faithful exponent of Prussian conservatism and authoritarian state-worship). Lastly, there was the disintegration of Hegel's school and the emergence of a liberal trend among former Hegelians, typified by the eminent publicist Arnold Ruge, for a few years an emigrant in Paris and an associate of Marx. From about 1840 onward the movement also possessed a philosophical figurehead of some eminence—Ludwig Feuer-bach.[7]

Here were the makings of a successful liberal-democratic alliance which might have pushed the "bourgeois revolution" through to a conclusion in 1848. Why did it fail? The principal obstacles have already been mentioned: economic backwardness, the national problem, dislike of Jacobinism and of France in general. A further point that needs emphasis is the way in which the unsolved problem of national unification reinforced the traditional reverence for the state. Historically, the rule of absolutism in Western Europe had become superfluous with the establishment of national unity and the provision of a legal framework for the operation of the market economy. In England, this stage had been reached by the seventeenth century, in France by the eighteenth. From this point on "civil society" is seen as an entity distinct from "the state," which latter tends increasingly to be viewed by the commercial and manufacturing middle class as a useless encumbrance. This is particularly true if the state is authoritarian and its government autocratic. In a situation of this kind, the emerging middle class and its more or less liberal spokesmen will begin to find reasons for subjecting the government to the control of an elected legislature. The critique of absolutism may or may not draw upon *ius naturale,* according to circumstances and the individual taste of the philosopher, but in any case it counterposes the will of "the people" to the authority of the government. ("The people" of course does not include "the mob," i.e., all those who own no property at all).

Natural Law systems are quite capable of underpinning a critique of this sort, but a doctrine of the social-contract type will do equally well. The peculiarity of German liberalism lies in the fact that it employed all its ingenuity for the purpose of divorcing the demand for the *Rechtsstaat* (rule of law) from the cause of democracy, and that it did so consistently and from the start. The reason was quite simply that Germany lacked a national state: what it had was the medieval Empire. When this collapsed during the Napoleonic era, the emerging liberal movement fastened upon the centralizing and modernizing Prussian state as the next best thing to a genuinely constitutional regime; and when the Prussian autocracy in its turn broke down in 1848, the liberals contented themselves with a shadow-parliament elected on an undemocratic franchise. Not only was there no republican bourgeoisie in Germany: there was not even a democratic bourgeoisie, although there were plenty of democrats among the lower middle class and its spokesmen. The liberals sought a compromise with the existing regime because they needed the state—any state. Their spokesmen, with few exceptions, did not pass beyond the demand for enlightened rule by a bureaucracy carefully trained to observe its own rules and regulations. This, more or less, was what the "rule of law" had signified to Kant at the close of the eighteenth century, when he postulated a legal framework such that the government would be bound by general laws of its own manufacture. But who would see to it that the state did not transgress its own rules? Presumably the law courts. When the liberals of the following generation came to reflect upon British and French experience, they realized that this was not quite enough: there also had to be an uncensored press and an elected legislature to supervise the executive. But—and this is the point—the legislature did not have to be democratically based. On the whole, it had better not be. In these circumstances there could be no appeal to Natural Law and the Rights of Man. German liberalism from the start was undemocratic and remained so to the end.[8]

At first sight all this may seem to be only very vaguely connected with our subject, but then it is not possible to draw a sharp dividing line between democrats and socialists in the Germany of that period. A youthful "Jacobin of the Left" like Büchner, who had to flee after circulating revolutionary pamphlets among the peasants of his native Hesse, could be regarded as either. The slogan he took up—"war to the palace, peace to the cottage"— was in the tradition of 1793. Yet it entered the Social Democratic consciousness when a labor leader like August Bebel repeated it (under the impact of the Paris Commune) in 1871. One must always bear in mind that the Germany which experienced the abortive uprising of 1848 was still overwhelmingly an agrarian country. "Red republicans" like Wilhelm Liebknecht or Wilhelm Wolff (in later years close associates of Marx in his London exile) on the eve of 1848 looked forward to a popular insurrection that would carry their party to power. These men were radical democrats, not elitist conspirators. It is true that the embryonic Communist League, then operating secretly within the orbit of a loose "popular front" of democratic movements, had a more sophisticated understanding of society than the ordinary run of democrats. But down to 1848, and for a few years thereafter, "communism" still signified radical egalitarianism. Communists and democrats worked together, not against one another. Had the 1848 revolution succeeded, Büchner would retrospectively have appeared as one of its literary heralds. The same applies to better-known figures such as Ludwig Börne and Heinrich Heine—emancipated Jewish intellectuals who had exiled themselves to Paris after the July Revolution of 1830, thereby furnishing a model for political and philosophical radicals of the next generation, Marx and Engels among them. Yet Börne, although a democratic republican, was no socialist; while Heine, who sympathized with Saint-Simonism and in 1844 belonged to Marx's personal circle, remained at heart a Romantic and politically a moderate liberal. The truth is that between 1830 and 1848 it was uncertain where democracy ended and socialism began. Nor was it possible to deny that the Romantics, for all their medievalism, had in some respects made a contribution to the radical cause. Retrospectively it could even be argued years later that their critique of liberal individualism, however reactionary in intent, permitted valuable insights into the historical process. This indeed was to become the judgment of Marx. By then of course a great deal of water had flowed beneath a great many bridges, and political passions had cooled. Romanticism was no longer the enemy, and one could begin to fuse the "organic" sense of historical continuity with the radical urge to "change the world."[9]

To invoke this key phrase is to lay bare one source of the revolutionary ardor which in the 1840's took hold of those German exiles in Paris who had grouped themselves into secret fraternities, from which in due course the Communist League was to emerge. It can never be sufficiently stressed that this source was the French Revolution—specifically its radical culmination in 1793–94, with the aftereffects it produced upon the nascent workers' movement. The filiation from radical republicanism, via Babouvism and Blanquism, to the Parisian upheaval of 1848 has been traced in the first part of this study. Here it simply remains to be added that the notion of a revolutionary change in the material structure of society could arise among Germans in the 1830's and 1840's only because the French example was constantly before their eyes. In their own manner the conservatives saw this quite clearly, which is why a distinguished observer like Tocqueville in the 1850's became increasingly gloomy about the outlook for the sort of hierarchically stratified society in which, as an aristocrat (albeit a liberal one), he believed. Thus in 1852 he told a correspondent that the French Revolution ("We may now venture to call it the European revolution") had arisen from a profound social change; while in the unfinished second volume of his *Ancien Régime* he dwelt upon what he called the "permanent results" of the Revolution. The radical distemper, he thought, had become chronic because of its "doctrinal character," which in turn arose from "the democratic character" and "the essentially ideological character of this revolution." In Tocqueville's use of the term, "ideology" stood for the doctrines of the group of writers known as the *idéologues* who had prepared the great upheaval, whereas Marx would subsequently assign a rather more philosophical meaning to the term. Setting this difference aside, both men concurred in regarding the French Revolution as the precursor of the socialist movement, and so far as France and Germany were concerned, they were of course quite right.[10]

From Populism to Utopian Communism: Weitling

In relation to the embryonic German workers' movement of the 1830's and 1840's, the decisive step from conspiratorial republicanism to utopian communism is associated with the group of exiles who in 1836 came together in a secret society self-styled the League of the Just (Bund der Gerechten): itself an offshoot from an earlier organization, the League of Outlaws (Bund der Geächteten), which after 1834 published a paper, *Der Geächtete,* and maintained contact with German emigrés and working-class fraternities in Switzerland. Unlike its parent organization, which had remained within the tradition of the Carbonari-inspired brotherhood of outlaws, the League of the Just, whose headquarters were in Paris, set itself definite political aims: Article II of its statutes proclaimed the need for a democratic revolution in Germany and at the same time called upon the working classes in all countries to become conscious of their common aims. The League maintained friendly links with the Société des Saisons, then headed by Blanqui and Barbès, took part in the Blanquist uprising of May 1839, and in consequence suffered police persecution, some of its leaders being obliged to emigrate to Britain. They included the printer Karl Schapper, who had worked with Georg Büchner in Hesse (and with Mazzini in Savoy) and subsequently became a leading figure in the Communist League when that body took shape in 1846–47, after the reconstruction of its parent society. The Workers' Educational Association founded by Schapper in London took for its motto the slogan "All men are brothers," around which the League of the Just reconstituted itself after its earlier failure. Most of the members of these various organizations were artisans or, rather, traveling journeymen steeped in a tradition similar to that of the French *compagnonnages* which then were just about to undergo a similar transformation. Like other secret brotherhoods of the period, the German fraternities had a hierarchical structure and elaborate rites of initiation inherited (or copied) from the Freemasons. These ancient paraphernalia were dropped when the League of the Just became the League of Communists. In the 1840's there was nothing unusual about secrecy or Masonic rites. What is noteworthy is that Marx and Engels should have been able to persuade the German workers to dispense with these time-honored rituals.[11]

But before this could be done, an ideological issue had to be fought out—an issue associated with the name of Weitling. This is frequently represented as a personal quarrel between Marx and Weitling, whereas in reality it involved crucial questions of doctrine and organization. The defeat of Weitling was the defeat of utopian communism, in the form it had assumed among the German artisans of the period. Elements of this tradition nonetheless lingered on into the 1850's, giving rise to further dissensions, which in the end resulted in the dissolution of the Communist League itself. This latter event not accidentally coincided with the adoption by Marx, in 1852–53, of a theoretical position incompatible with Blanquism, whereas during the preceding phase the League of Communists had functioned within an international movement of which the Blanquists formed a part. This, however, is by the way. The topic that concerns us here is the League of the Just and Weitling's role within it.

Wilhelm Weitling (1808–71) was born in Magdeburg, the illegitimate son of a French officer and a German seamstress. Apprenticed as a tailor, he led the usual life of an itinerant artisan, meanwhile nourishing his mind with the writings of Fourier and Lamennais. In Vienna and Paris between 1834 and 1837 he made contact with the League of Outlaws and the League of the Just, and in 1838 he published the first of his many tracts, *Mankind as it is and as it should be.* Obliged to leave France after the Blanquist rising of May 12, 1839, he made his way to Switzerland, where his *Guarantees of Harmony and Freedom* appeared in 1842, soon to be translated into various European languages and to make him famous. A third publication, the *Gospel of a Poor Sinner,* which proclaimed Jesus the precursor of communism, led to prosecution for blasphemy and brief imprisonment in Zurich, followed by expulsion across the German border. From there he made his way to London, where Schapper's Arbeiterbildungsverein received him with open arms. At a meeting arranged in his honor on September 22, 1844, he was described as a "martyr to the communist cause" by French and British, as well as German, speakers. The gathering appears to have been a factor in the subsequent formation, in March 1846, of a body known as the Society of Fraternal Democrats. This was a forerunner of the International Working Men's Association of 1864, in the sense that, although it had no foreign branches, the Society (which had been founded by Harney and other Chartists) was organized on the basis of affiliated national groups from various European countries, each with its own representatives on the standing committee. Young Italy (Mazzini's organization) did not participate, communism being anathema to its founder. On the other hand, the Democratic Association in Brussels, which by 1846 included Marx among its members, entered into correspondence with the London society. In the meantime Weitling had quarrelled with Schapper and his friends who did not accept his utopian religious communism. This was the background to a more dramatic personal clash between Marx and Weitling in Brussels, on March 30, 1846, at a meeting of the nascent League of Communists. Weitling, with his religious utopianism and his demand for an immediate rising in Germany, on this celebrated occasion found himself in a minority of one. His subsequent career was anticlimactic. He played no important part in the German drama of 1848–49, withdrew gradually from politics, and emigrated to New York, where he died on January 25, 1871.[12]

Weitling is important for our theme as a representative of a kind of primitive quasi-religious communism which inevitably marked the first emergence of a workers' movement in a country such as Germany. It was quite in accordance with the outlook of the wandering journeymen of his time that in 1843, while settled in Switzerland and preaching Christian communism (as well as the immediate communization of women), he should have concocted a fantastic scheme for invading Germany at the head of forty thousand outlaws who were to bring the ruling classes to their knees by means of armed violence (of the sort celebrated in 1782 by the youthful Schiller in his play *The Robbers,* an enthusiastic glorification of brigandage whose spirit was still echoed in the title assumed in 1834 by the League of Outlaws). Weitling is thus a transitional figure, and this quite apart from the fact that around 1844 he was perhaps a trifle mad. He represented the spirit of the old millenarian fraternities, from which working-class communists like Karl Schapper, Heinrich Bauer, and Joseph Moll were beginning to emancipate themselves—even before they had encountered Marx—under the influence of the Chartists and the British milieu in general. By 1846–47 these men were ready for the transformation of the conspiratorial League of the Just into the League of Communists. This latter was no longer a "brotherhood," with secret rites and self-appointed leaders, but a democratic organization which dispensed with ritual and elected all its officers. Marx, who detested secret brotherhoods, had stipulated this as a condition of his own adherence and that of his associates. By the same token, Weitling, in fact if not in form, was bound to be excluded.

Yet the same man was the author of a work in which Feuerbach and Marx found much to praise: the *Guarantees of Harmony and Freedom*. The contradiction is more apparent than real. Weitling, having spent a few years in Paris, had assimilated the Babouvist tradition and transmitted it to the nascent German proletariat in a language which made a profound appeal to men brought up in the spirit of Evangelical Christianity. The triadic scheme—a golden age, then private property, lastly the communism of the future—which he expounded in that eloquent pamphlet, gave his readers what they needed: an historical perspective couched not in Hegelian, but in Biblical language. His indictment of money as the source of all evil was simple-minded enough, but he did not stop there: he embedded his denunciation in a vision of the historical process, a vision he had seen in Paris. He thus became a link between the inheritors of the French Revolution and the immature German workers' movement of his day: a movement still struggling to free itself from the dead weight of medievalism. In this respect at least Weitling resembled another autodidact of genius, Joseph Dietzgen (1828–88), who lived to become a follower of Marx. But Dietzgen really belongs to the history of philosophy, among the disciples of Feuerbach, and in any case his chief work, a critique of Kant, was published in 1869. By then its author was already a Social Democrat in the full sense of the term, whereas Weitling had come on the scene at a moment when the primitive egalitarianism he represented was still popular, but already beginning to fade out. It is noteworthy that his gospel was repudiated by the Workers' Educational Association in London (in June 1845) before either he or they had made the acquaintance of Marx. The speech he delivered on that occasion was typical of the man, and at least one phrase from it is worth quoting: "In my opinion, everyone is ripe for communism, even the criminals.

Criminals are a product of the present order of society, and under communism they would cease to be criminals. Humanity is of necessity always ripe for revolution, or it never will be." The audience listened respectfully and then sided with Schapper, who replied that the people were not yet ready for the sort of utopia Weitling had in mind.[13]

From Reform to Revolution: Rodbertus and Hess

Any consideration of the revolutionary movement that erupted in March 1848 must of necessity deal with disparate tendencies brought together in the act of revolt itself. What is known in German historical literature as the *Vormärz*—literally "pre-March" —can be viewed under a double aspect: as the moment when the absolutist regime began to disintegrate, or alternatively as the time when the first stirrings of the industrial revolution made themselves felt. Depending upon how one looks at it, the crisis of 1848 appears as the final convulsion of the old order or as the painful birth of modern society. If the former, one will tend to stress the revolt against Church and state associated with the Young Hegelians (to be precise, the Left Hegelians)—Ruge, Heine, Hess, Stirner, Bauer, Feuerbach, and Marx, plus two important non-Germans: Bakunin and Cieszkowski. If one is concerned with the emerging socialist critique of capitalism rather than with the approaching political storm, one will place the emphasis upon writers who were instrumental in bringing Ricardo or Proudhon to the attention of the German public. So far as Marx is concerned, there is no problem, since both streams met in his person. To some slight degree this also applies to another radical Hegelian: Moses Hess. In general, though, one must choose between two distinct topics, for it was quite possible to be a revolutionary democrat without being a socialist. Equally, one could be a socialist without sharing either the general philosophy of the Left Hegelians or the particular revolutionary program of Marx and his associates. Indeed the majority of German socialists—then and later—were "reformists," while some of the more radical democrats around 1848 were either indifferent to socialism or opposed to it on libertarian grounds. Feuerbach, to take a notable example, was a democrat without being a socialist, except in a sense so vague as to be virtually meaningless. (He did proclaim himself a Social Democrat shortly before his death in 1872, but this is hardly relevant.) On the other hand, an economist such as Rodbertus combined a species of purely meliorist socialism with a conservative outlook which made him the ancestor of the Prussian *Kathedersozialisten* of the Bismarck era: men like Adolf Wagner (1835–1917) and Gustav Schmoller (1838–1917) who stood high in the estimation of the ruling elements in German society. Finally, there is Lassalle, a one-time associate of Marx who by the time of his sudden death in 1864 had moved fairly close to the political standpoint of Rodbertus. How is one to accommodate all these diverse personalities under a general label?

A possible answer to this question might take the form of saying that all these conflicting tendencies were aspects of the general crisis of German society. But although true enough, this does not help us with our immediate problem. What mattered most in those days was the coming democratic upheaval, but our chosen topic is the socialist movement, and however feebly it may have been represented in the relatively backward Germany of those days, its theorists must be considered on their merits before we come to Marx. We therefore begin with a brief analysis of German socialism on the eve of 1848, reserving until later the question what it was that distinguished Marx from either the "true socialists" or the Left Hegelians. Fortunately Moses Hess can be considered under both headings, and the same applies to the less known (and certainly less important) Karl Grün. In passing, mention must also be made of Lorenz von Stein, a conservative Hegelian who introduced his contemporaries to the socialist and communist movements in France. Stein's work may have been a factor in drawing Marx's attention in 1842 to the socialist implications of the French Revolution. He also merits attention as a precursor of what was later called sociology. Yet Stein was no socialist. His standpoint corresponded to that of the mature Comte who had abandoned Saint-Simonism. If a summary is permissible, Stein's doctrine amounted to saying that every society is necessarily a class society, and that the relationship of domination and subjection must be accepted as unalterable.[14]

With Karl Marlo (pseudonym of Karl Georg Winkelblech, 1810–65) we are on different and safer ground, but his *Untersuchungen über die Organisation der Arbeit* (1849–50), for all their gloom about the condition of the working class, are not really socialist, albeit favorable to the nationalization of large-scale industry (and corporative organization of the remainder). Perhaps Marlo can be described as an early advocate of state planning. He certainly had little use for the market economy, or for free competition among entrepreneurs, which he thought would always tend to depress labor's real wages to the lowest possible level. On the other hand, it did not occur to him to suggest that the working class could transform the system, nor did he approve of communism. Moreover, he came on the scene at a time when Germany's belated industrial development had just begun to get under way. This circumstance places him among the pre-socialists, i.e., the group of thinkers who still found it possible to argue that the complete development of a capitalist economy could be avoided—at any rate in Germany, if not in England where the system was already in full operation. To some degree this also holds for a more influential writer who somehow bridged the gap between the pre-socialism of the 1840's and the conservative "social reform movement" of the 1870's: Rodbertus.

Johann Karl Rodbertus-Jagetzow (1805–1875) has already been mentioned as a precursor of the Bismarckian era and its bureaucratic essays in social insurance and conservative welfare legislation generally: a German analogue to the Disraelian Toryism of the 1870's. The fact that his first writings appeared around 1840 makes it possible to group him among the early socialists. His subsequent activities (including a brief career as Prussian Minister of Education in 1848) place him among the conservatives; while to his later German followers in the 1880's he was important chiefly as a witness to the truth that one could be simultaneously a conservative monarchist and a socialist: in other words, even if one happened to dislike capitalism and liberalism, one did not have to follow Lassalle, let alone Marx. All this became important in the Bismarck era, when the cult of Rodbertus fitted in with the official attempt to discredit the growing Social Democratic movement; and it explains why Engels, in his 1885 preface to the German edition of Marx's polemic against Proudhon, thought it necessary to dispute Rodbertus' claim to have anticipated Marx's critique of capitalism. But it has little to do with Rodbertus' standing as an economist. This topic can be summarized by describing him as a Ricardian who in the 1840's introduced his readers to some of the theoretical problems then agitating the British. Contrary to the fixed opinion of his later devotees, this circumstance does not make him a precursor of Marx. The latter for his part took no notice of Rodbertus, for the sound reason that by the time he became acquainted with his writings he had already gone to the source and did not stand in need of an interpreter.[15]

What, then, is the core of Rodbertus' theorizing? First, there was a "social problem" to be solved. The problem had two aspects: pauperism and commercial crises. Both were viewed from a Ricardian standpoint, as was natural with a theorist of his age. What gave Rodbertus some claim to be regarded as a socialist was his demand that the state intervene to counteract the operation of the market economy. Rodbertus is the ancestor of a certain kind of theorizing which proceeds from a critical analysis of the market economy to the indictment of *laissez-faire*. Left to itself (so the argument runs) the free play of economic forces will always depress wages to a subsistence level and at the same time promote cyclical crises. This vicious circle can only be broken by the state —ideally by a socially enlightened monarchy, which incidentally will also strive to aid agriculture by arranging for cheaper credit facilities. (Rodbertus was a substantial landowner.) For the state is a living organism and politics the noblest of all arts. Indeed, the soul of the state is divine, a proposition in support of which Rodbertus cites the words of Ulysses in *Troilus and Cressida:*

> There is a mystery—with whom relation
> Durst never meddle—in the soul of state;
> Which hath an operation more divine
> Than breath or pen can give expressure to.

These sentiments (not to mention the author's loyal attachment to the monarchy and the fatherland) presumably account for the fact that in the 1880's Rodbertus' literary legacy was edited, published, and defended by the Prussian conservative Adolf Wagner, notwithstanding the latter's rejection of most of Rodbertus' theoretical postulates.

The "hungry forties," when Rodbertus composed his major writings, were a time when pessimism about the operation of the market economy could make some appeal to the facts. In his case this took the form of asserting that with the workers' share in the social dividend steadily diminishing, labor could not buy back a sufficient amount of its own product. Rodbertus based this gloomy forecast upon a literal interpretation of the labor theory of value: the market price of commodities reflected the cost of the manual labor incorporated in them. In addition to giving the worker a moral right to "the whole product of labor," this proposition also led to certain theoretical conclusions about the operation of an economy in which wages were typically held down to a subsistence level. For if social wealth increased while wages were constantly depressed, it followed that the aggregate income of wage-earners must represent a steadily diminishing proportion of the gross national product. Aside from being manifestly unfair, this arrangement was also nefarious for society as a whole, since it resulted in periodic crises of overproduction. In this fashion Rodbertus arrived at a doctrine which has always been popular with the more simple-minded critics of capitalism: crises are due to lack of purchasing power, which latter in turn is due to the unfair distribution of the social product. There is (to employ the Lassallean phraseology of the 1860's) an "iron law" of wages. The "law" is rooted in the operation of the market economy, and the cure for the resulting evils is to be found in state intervention. The trouble with Rodbertus, as with the pre-Marxians generally, was that he had adopted a naïve and untenable form of under-consumptionism. No space can be given here to his other writings, which included some historical studies. We simply note that on the eve of 1848 it was possible for a conservative Prussian landowner to put forward a socialist doctrine of economics derived from the labor theory of value. In this respect Rodbertus rather than Marx is the ancestor of Lassalle's peculiar brand of state socialism—this quite apart from the fact that Lassalle and Rodbertus were for a while personal and political allies.

Lorenz von Stein, Rodbertus, and (notwithstanding his earlier relationship with Marx and the fact that he came to prominence only in the 1860's) Lassalle represent one particular reaction to the impact of capitalism upon German society. One can say that in all three cases the socialist element was derived from specifically Prussian considerations leading back in the last resort to the ideology of German idealism, as formulated by Fichte and his adherents. The cleavage between state and society was treated by these writers as an implicit threat to the collective existence of the German nation: the state must, in its own interest, reform society by imposing upon it the moral and political principles worked out by the reformers. The obverse of this attitude was to be found among those radicals who consciously placed themselves in the tradition of the French Revolution. For obvious geographical reasons such men were more likely to be found in the Rhineland than east of the Elbe. To the Rhenish radicals the annexation of their province by Prussia in 1815 represented a retrograde step. If— like Heine, Hess, and Marx—they were of Jewish ancestry, the reactionary character of the Prussian government manifested itself in the most palpable manner through its emphasis upon the link between the terms "Christian" and "German." The emancipation of the Jews from civil disabilities—officially proclaimed in France since 1791—had been introduced into the western regions of Germany by the armies of the French Revolution and Napoleon. The official restoration of legal distinctions between Christians and Jews was an aspect of the Prussian regime after 1815 (and the proximate reason why Marx's father felt obliged, in the interest of his family, to assume the Protestant faith). In this context it is immaterial that Heine reacted to this situation by treating all forms of religion with ironic indifference, while Hess eventually returned to Judaism, and Marx adopted the radical atheism of the French materialists. This first generation of emancipated Jewish intellectuals had to make a choice. They felt themselves to be

Western Europeans living in a country which had not entirely accepted the values of the Enlightenment: indeed the more conservative Romantics made a point of requiring conversion to the Christian faith as evidence of spiritual regeneration. If one happened to be an atheist—and the Left Hegelians had broken with their master precisely on this issue—this sort of thing simply added insult to the injury already experienced by young men who had come up against the conventional Judeóphobia of German society. At a deeper level their attitudes were shaped by the spiritual crisis of a generation which had experienced the conservative reflux in the aftermath of the French Revolution. The question they had to face, as youthful radicals brought up on the philosophy of the Enlightenment, was whether the Prussian state, with its "Christian German" ideology and its autocratic form of government, was worth preserving. The negation they opposed to it did not by itself turn them into socialists. It simply meant that (unlike their elders, who were content to hope for gradual progress toward constitutional liberalism) they identified themselves with the cause of radical democracy as represented by the French Revolution.

In this of course they were not alone, as Marx discovered when, as a student in 1837, he encountered the Berlin Hegelians. But the Jewish descent of these Rhenish radicals did make it somewhat easier for them to see the Prussian monarchy as an anachronism. This is all that needs to be said here on a familiar and not very fascinating topic. It is immaterial for our purpose that Hess in later years became a precursor of Zionism or that Marx in 1844 involved himself in the then current controversy over Jewish emancipation with an essay (aimed at his former teacher and friend Bruno Bauer) containing some remarkably doctrinaire and quite unfounded utterances on the subject of Judaism. In strict logic his atheism did not oblige him to vent his spleen on the topic in the way he did, and it is perhaps noteworthy that in later years he contented himself with the then customary remarks about Jewish financiers. The theme is commonly discussed without reference to the fact that in 1844 Marx was polemicizing against Bauer, who had argued that the emancipation of the Jews (i.e., the removal of legal disabilities) was possible only on condition that

Christians and Jews alike abandoned their religion. All concerned had adopted Hegel's and Feuerbach's characterization of Judaism as a religion of practical egoism. Thus Hess (writing in 1843–45) described the Jewish God as an insatiable Moloch who in his subsequent Christian incarnation even demanded the sacrifice of his only son! This did not prevent Hess from reverting to Judaism in his later years, just as it did not prevent Marx from losing all interest in the subject (or his daughter Eleanor from stressing her Jewish parentage). The entire topic is solely comprehensible within the context of German-Jewish life in the nineteenth century and has only a remote connection with our theme. Suffice it to say that Marx's and Hess' utterances about Jewish egoism and materialism in 1843–45, whatever one may think of them, were part of an internal controversy within the radical intelligentsia. It is perhaps significant that whereas Marx's youthful indiscretions are frequently cited as evidence of an insoluble spiritual dilemma, the even more repellent picture then drawn by Hess of the ancestral faith has been forgiven him by Jewish spokesmen—possibly because in his later years he became a pioneer of Zionism, indeed one of the most important philosophers of the movement.

As democrats, all these writers stood on a foundation already worked out by the French writers who had become their guides to the problems of the modern world. When Hess in 1841 encountered Marx, then aged twenty-three and about to enter upon a brief and stormy career in radical journalism, his reaction was characteristic: "Try to imagine Rousseau, Voltaire, Holbach, Lessing, Heine and Hegel combined in one person—I say *combined*, not thrown together—and you have Dr. Marx," he wrote to a friend. The judgment is significant, the more so since the two men were temperamentally poles apart. More important, the choice of terms discloses the spiritual physiognomy of a Rhenish democrat, for whom the German Enlightenment and French materialism represented one and the same cause.[16]

Moses Hess (1812–75) is a more important figure in socialist history than might be imagined from the treatment he has commonly received by Marx's biographers, not to mention historians

for whom socialist theory is more or less synonymous with economics. Hess was not a systematic thinker, and among his many
interests economics came a long way behind philosophy, history,
and the natural sciences. Neither was he a success as a political
leader in the style of Lassalle (who may be counted among his
pupils). His significance is of a different sort. Having become a
socialist before 1840, he systematically converted an entire generation of youthful rebels to his views, which for his time were remarkably advanced. It was Hess who drew the attention of the
more radical among the Young Hegelians (the youthful Friedrich
Engels among them) to socialism as the concrete realization of the
Feuerbachian humanism they had adopted as their general philosophy. His own starting-point had been Spinozist, and there is a
sense in which his later differences with Marx may be said to have
originated in the fact that, unlike Marx, he never really assimilated
the Hegelian manner of reasoning about historical processes. Be
that as it may, Hess prepared the way for Marx by treating socialism as the political aspect of an anthropological doctrine for which
Feuerbach, with his critical analysis of religious "alienation," had
provided the philosophical basis. This became substantially the
message of the 1845 *Theses on Feuerbach*. It is irrelevant how far
Marx was then still influenced by Hess, whom in private he and
Engels were already beginning to treat with a certain irony, on
account of his naïve optimism about the approaching revolution
and his lack of political realism. The point is that so far as the
transformation of humanism into socialism is concerned, Hess was
Marx's precursor and, so to speak, his John the Baptist.[17]

If socialist doctrine were merely the record of more or less adequate theorizing about economic phenomena, Hess might be
ignored. But there was a radical philosophy, even (at any rate in
Germany) a humanist anthropology, before something like a socialist critique of bourgeois society made its appearance. Hess is
the link between the philosophical humanism of Feuerbach and the
revolutionary activism of Marx. This makes him important, even
though the "true socialism" he extracted from his favorite authors
was an eclectic doctrine that never made contact with political reality. "True socialism" was French socialism (of the Saint-Simonian

variety) translated into German: specifically into the philosophical jargon then current among those Left Hegelians who had come under the influence of Feuerbach. The weakness of the doctrine was its sentimental optimism; its strength lay in its rootedness within the central tradition of European philosophy. As a youthful Spinozist, Hess had originally felt confident that the discovery of universal principles guaranteeing social harmony lay within the unaided power of reason. What made him abandon this tranquil intellectualism was the painful discovery that the actual social reality confronting the men of his time was such as to necessitate a political revolution of the kind France had already undergone. This move away from the contemplative mode of thought inherent in Spinozism led him to Fichte, whose activist principle supplied just what was needed, even though his rather antiquated nationalism and liberalism did not. The upshot was an essay titled *Philosophy of Action* in which Hess made his bow to the cult of Fichte then prevalent among the Young Hegelians. "The time has come for the philosophy of spirit to become a philosophy of action."[18]

What Hess did in 1843 was to make "atheism and communism" (he expressly linked them together) philosophically respectable by representing them as necessary, albeit transitory, aspects of "the revolution." What revolution? Hess characteristically invoked "Fichte and Babeuf," the former having taught "atheism" in Berlin at about the same time that Babeuf tried to practice "communism" in Paris. But where was the inner link between these two principles? According to Hess it lay in an idea of freedom and autonomy incompatible with any kind of external determination, whether religious or social.[19]

> If I believe in a power outside or above myself, then I am externally determined. If, on the other hand, I conceive the object, consciously producing it in accordance with the law of my spirit, I determine myself without being determined from the outside. Likewise I am able to determine myself in social life, by being active in this or that manner, without recognizing an external barrier to my activity. . . . How now if all communism and atheism, all anarchy, had for its aim to transform external determinations into self-determination,

the external deity into the internal, material property into spiritual
property . . . ?

Hess conceded that the French Revolution, by emancipating the
individual, had for its immediate outcome an orgy of unrestrained
egoism, thereby provoking a reaction among whose representatives
he mentioned Saint-Simon and Fourier on the one hand, Hegel and
Schelling on the other. But now (in 1843) this phase was coming
to an end:

> At long last one begins to revert to the first heroes of the revolution,
> in France to Babeuf, in Germany to Fichte. . . . Proudhon starts
> from [the principle of] anarchy, German philosophy from self-
> consciousness. Atheism is once more taught in Germany, commu-
> nism in France. . . . Proudhon, like Feuerbach, has taken up the
> dialectical principle, without employing it for the purpose of re-
> storing the ancient, external, negated objectivity. It is along this
> path that one must proceed, it is thus that freedom will finally be
> won.[20]

The linking of Feuerbach and Proudhon reflects a constant
theme in the thought of Moses Hess, which in one form or another he was to pursue until his death in 1875: an alliance must
be formed between French and German thought; these two national
traditions must be synthesized if the European revolution is to get
under way. In an earlier pamphlet, *The European Triarchy,* he
had coupled Hegel and Saint-Simon as representatives of their
respective nations: the former an idealist whose philosophy embodied the traditional German habit of contemplating the past; the
latter a practical activist oriented towards the future. The problem,
as he saw it, lay in the attainment of a standpoint which would
relate philosophy and action, theory and practice. Hegel had given
birth to a universal system of thought which explained the past; the
Saint-Simonians meant to shape the future, but they lacked the
philosophical dimension. The French Revolution had been an
attempt to realize concrete ethical demands—something of which
the Germans only dreamed, having contented themselves since
the Reformation with mere freedom of speculation. Yet the Revolution had not attained its deeper aim, and had even provoked a

retrogressive movement in Germany. How then could these divergent tendencies be brought together? In 1841 Hess had a surprising answer ready: through the advent of a social revolution in England! The "European triarchy" of England, France, and Germany was the only means of overcoming the parochialism of their respective national cultures. This too was an element of the spiritual legacy which Marx and Engels inherited from their old teacher.[21]

In terms of social philosophy the originality of Hess lay in the manner in which he extracted the collectivist implications inherent in the line of thinkers beginning with Rousseau and ending with Feuerbach. Having rejected religion (he was to return to it at a later stage of his career, but this does not concern us), he was faced with the problem of defining a social morality based upon some alternative principle. Here Fichte was of no use, since his guiding ideas were purely individualist (in so far as they were not nationalist, and then limited to the German nation). For the Spinozist in Hess there had to be an ethical foundation of politics, a manner of deriving principles of action from objective insight into the veritable nature of reality. At this point he was helped out by Feuerbach: if there was no God, morality could only be grounded in the nature of man as a "species being" (*Gattungswesen*). But Feuerbach had neglected the social sphere, whereas the French had given their attention to it. "Theology is *anthropology*. That is true, but it is not the *whole* truth. The being of man, it must be added, is social, the cooperation of the various individuals toward a common aim . . . and the true doctrine of man, the true humanism, is the theory of human sociability. That is to say, *anthropology is socialism*."[22]

In principle there was nothing here that Marx could not accept, and indeed the *Paris Manuscripts of 1844* (jotted down by Marx before Hess had published his own essay on the subject) furnish proof that both men were then thinking along similar lines. This is hardly surprising, when one considers that it was Hess who in 1842–44 had constituted himself the bridge between Feuerbach and Marx. Yet within two years Hess began to furnish a target for Marx's sarcasms about "true socialism." Unpublished at the time, the *German Ideology* of 1845–46, in its later sections, takes the form of a sustained polemic against the "true socialists," and while Hess is treated rather more indulgently than Grün, he comes in for some tart remarks on the score of his sentimental humanism. For Hess had by 1845 committed himself to a distinction between "French communism" and "German socialism": the former a primitive inversion of the *status quo,* the latter a humanist doctrine transcending the class struggle. Communism appealed to the proletariat, "true socialism" to mankind as a whole. This was not to the taste of Marx, and his observations on the subject in 1846 already anticipate the well-known diatribe against "true socialism" in the *Communist Manifesto.* It is evident that he had by then abandoned the standpoint of the 1844 *Paris Manuscripts.* The paradox is that Hess for his part in 1846–47 moved closer to the Marxian position, e.g., in conceding the necessity of a "proletarian revolution." By the end of 1847 he was even reconciled to the notion of a temporary dictatorship. If there remained a divergence it was philosophical rather than political. For Hess the revolution was an unfortunate necessity which the ruling classes had rendered inevitable by their own selfishness and shortsightedness. To that extent his basic standpoint had not altered: the aim was social harmony and the overcoming of the class struggle.[23]

The development of Hess between 1841 and 1847 thus represents an analogue to that of Marx, even to the point of his becoming a member of the German exile colony in Paris and Brussels, from which by 1847 the German Communist League had emerged. It is no exaggeration to say that by 1848 Hess had come to regard himself as a follower of Marx. The subsequent relationship between the two men forms part of a complex story which in 1864 culminated in the founding of the First International. It lies outside our theme, as does the share taken by Hess in the subsequent rise of German Social Democracy, in its Lassallean and "Marxist" incarnations. Hess was to become, among others, the interpreter of French socialism to his German contemporaries: a role facilitated by his lengthy residence in Paris, his personal contacts in the Rhineland, and his abiding conviction that the European socialist movement must somehow proceed from a fusion of

French and German theorizing. None of this concerns us here. We simply register the fact that he was the first German socialist to fill the abstract concept of humanism with a specific doctrine derived from the ethics of Spinoza and the anthropology of Feuerbach. Socialism for him was both a philosophy of life and a politico-economic doctrine rooted in the "true" understanding of human nature, specifically in the perception that mankind was destined to establish a social order proper to the aims enshrined in traditional morality. Man's nature he conceived in terms of a pre-established harmony, and this was to become the line of division between the followers of Marx and those socialists who, in adopting Feuerbach's naïvely optimistic anthropology, had abandoned the tragic realism of Hegel.

10. The Marxian Synthesis

Theory and Practice

We have reached the threshold of our concluding chapter. Have we also for that reason reached the summit of our theme? The answer depends upon what one expects from an analytical account of socialist origins. Few people at the present time would deny Marx the status of socialism's greatest thinker—the one truly great mind associated with that complex movement. But this circumstance does not exhaust the enduring fascination of Marx as a writer or the relevance of Marxism as a system. Conceivably both will continue to be of importance to the historian of philosophy long after socialism has taken its place, with liberalism and conservatism, as one particular reaction to the two-fold upheaval of the industrial revolution and the French Revolution. We do not know. All we know is that Marx was unlike Comte or Mill or any other representative thinker of his age. He alone did what they all set out to do but failed to accomplish: he fused philosophy, history, and economics into a grandiose synthesis. The fusion may have been imperfect; it may have left some important problems unsolved or half-solved; here and there it may actually have misled his followers into an acceptance of thought patterns stemming from the "bourgeois revolution" and not really relevant to the theory and practice of socialism. All these and other valid arguments can be urged against the man and his creation. No matter—there he stands, a colossus in the midst of ordinary mortals. The critic of literature takes for granted the disparity between Shakespeare and the minor Elizabethans. The historian of socialism who has taken the measure of Marx need not trouble himself unduly over his rivals.

Self-evident though it may seem to be, an assessment of this

185

kind still needs to be justified in the light of continued attempts to present Marx as simply one among a group of theorists, Proudhon and Bakunin being the most familiar names commonly cited in this connection. Alternatively, for people who are capable of telling socialism and anarchism apart, there is another solution: Marx can be treated as the outstanding representative of *German* (as distinct from English, French, Russian, etc.) socialism. There is some evident justification for such an approach, and the external arrangement of Part III of this study bears witness to the necessity of treating the German contribution separately from the rest. But two qualifications impose themselves. In the first place, Marx's departure from Germany in 1843, and his subsequent residence in Paris and Brussels, is crucial for the understanding of the *Communist Manifesto* (not to mention the fact that from 1849 until his death in 1883 he lived permanently in London, where he did most of his real theoretical work as an economist). Secondly, the early Marx had already synthesized the most advanced currents of thought then coming to the surface in Western Europe, notably in France and England. What is nowadays called "Marxism" was from the start more than a German doctrine, although its author happened to be a German. This is precisely what distinguishes Marx from writers like Proudhon or Bakunin, not to mention Owen or Fourier, who were still firmly encased within their respective national traditions. It also distinguishes him from Hegelians like Bruno Bauer, or from writers like Stein, Rodbertus, or Lassalle, for whom in the last resort British and French conditions provided only a theme upon which to speculate in accordance with what they had learned from Fichte or Hegel. It is true that, as we have seen, Marx had a precursor in Hess, and it hardly needs to be remarked that he was to acquire a life-long friend and associate in Engels. But Hess—a born eclectic, and a learned publicist rather than a genuine theorist—lacked the capacity to translate his insights into a coherent doctrine. As for Engels, he was entirely candid, and wholly justified, in stressing the uniqueness of Marx and the secondary character of his own contribution to the finished structure.[1]

This is not to say that socialism as a doctrine depended upon one man. It is surely evident that, with or without Marx, there would have been a Central European variant of the intellectual and moral current of thought to which the name "socialism" had been given by British and French writers around 1830. But when one speaks of Marxism, one refers to something more than the application of German philosophizing to a West European debate already in progress for some decades. There exists, to be sure, a rather simple-minded notion (made more or less official, on the authority of Lenin, in East European literature on the subject) according to which Marx "combined" German philosophy with British economics and French socialism. One need only inquire how such disparate phenomena could have been brought together in order to realize that this formula explains nothing at all. The truth is that Marx did not have to "combine" these various systematizations—an impossible feat in any case. What he did was to go behind them to the central issue of his age: the genesis and functioning of modern society. To put it differently, when he turned his philosophical equipment to practical use by fusing certain rather novel theoretical notions then current in the leading West European countries, he was making use of intellectual tools already shaped by a particular historical experience: the "bourgeois revolution."

For the fact is, of course, that classical German philosophy, no less than French socialism and British economics, was the child of its age and reflected its problems. When—to resume very briefly an argument already developed at some length—Kant, Fichte, and Hegel pondered the role of the individual in society, they were wrestling with problems which in a more practical form had earlier presented themselves to Rousseau and the physiocrats in France, and to writers like David Hume, Adam Ferguson, and Adam Smith in eighteenth-century Scotland: problems arising from the character of the society which had begun to emerge from the maturation of the market economy. After 1800 the issue naturally presented itself differently depending on whether it was viewed in the light of traditional German metaphysics, Anglo-American empiricism and utilitarianism, or political theorizing in the wake of the French upheaval. But philosophy, economics, and

politics all possessed a common root in the great historical drama
which had brought about the emancipation of Western society from
its ancient medieval fetters. The revolutionary movement which
between 1776 and 1848 gave birth to modern society—the
"bourgeois revolution" in the Marxian sense of the term—was
among other things a movement in the realm of ideas. These ideas
included the philosophical concepts which the youthful Marx
brought to bear upon French politics and British economics. Had
it been otherwise, the system of thought retrospectively known as
Marxism could never have come into being.[2]

To approach the subject in this manner is to rid oneself at one
blow of a whole host of pseudo-problems which invariably arise
when the question is asked how and why Marx was able to
synthesize Hegelian dialectics or Feuerbachian naturalism with
French socialism and British economics. As we have seen, Hess in
his unsystematic fashion had already aimed at some such unification of German, French, and British theorizing. The notion of a
synthesis was "in the air," except that the Germans (notably the
Left Hegelians around Bruno Bauer) aimed at a "higher" standpoint from which to look down upon the crude materialism of the
French and the benighted empiricism of the British. Even Hess,
in his "true socialist" phase, shared this ambition, and it was never
abandoned by the more orthodox Fichteans and Hegelians, down
to and including Lassalle. The originality of Marx manifested itself among others in his resolute refusal to have anything to do
with "true or German socialism": then and later a considerable
temptation for any thinker eager to be applauded by patriots who
shared the Romantic urge to differentiate the *Reich* from the
decadent and materialist West. Profoundly Germanic though he
was in many ways, the youthful Marx had already soaked himself
so thoroughly in the French socialists and the British economists
as to have attained, almost without knowing it, a transnational
European consciousness. For a biographer this circumstance inevitably invites reflections upon the German-Jewish symbiosis—a
topic already mentioned in connection with Hess and his vision of
German-French reconciliation. But here we are not concerned with
Marx's spiritual ancestry, or even with his Rhineland culture,

although it is not irrelevant that he grew up in an environment sympathetic to French rationalism in general and Saint-Simonism in particular. This background must be taken for granted. The subject that concerns us is Marx's role in the evolution of socialist theory.

At this point, however, a reflection imposes itself: was Marx primarily a theorist? Was it not rather his aim to unify theory and practice, and did he not in large measure succeed? There can be no doubt that the unification of thought and action was his starting-point, but then it had been the starting-point of every German thinker since Fichte. If one wants to put the matter in terms relevant to an intellectual biography of the young Marx, one may say that his most urgent problem was to overcome the seemingly insuperable obstacle which Hegel's system presented to revolutionary idealism. Of all the vast quantity of nonsense that has been written on this subject, perhaps no single element has sunk deeper into the general consciousness than the notion that Marx "applied" Hegel's philosophy, or at any rate his "method," to the study of history and then came up with the triumphant discovery that socialism was both necessary and inevitable. The truth is that Marx encountered Hegel's philosophy on his way from Fichtean idealism to French materialism and—after a tormenting spiritual crisis—managed to surmount the gigantic barrier Hegel had erected in his path. That in the process he learned a great deal from him is undeniable; that he "applied" Hegel's doctrine to the study of history, or to the theory of society, is a notion whose inherent absurdity must be evident to anyone who has ever thought seriously about the topic. The youthful Marx (as his writings and letters testify) wrestled with Hegel in the spirit of one who experiences the fascination of a great antagonist. Hegel was the opponent who had to be overcome, albeit an opponent who had something to teach: primarily the lesson that history is a process which is kept going by its "negative" side.[3]

There are some equally tempting pitfalls that have to be avoided if one is to make sense of Marx's relationship to Feuerbach. The commonest is the belief that what Marx called his "materialism" (in contradistinction to the "idealism" of Hegel) was an ontological doctrine, or a general theory of the physical world, with "matter" substituted for "spirit" as a primary substance involved in the constitution of the universe. There is no trace of such a notion in Marx, whatever its significance for later Marxists from Engels on. His post-Hegelian standpoint, as set out in the *Theses on Feuerbach* and the *German Ideology,* was a development of French eighteenth-century naturalism, minus its Cartesian physics and the related problem of cognition, in which he took no interest. The basic orientation of this materialism was practical, and its application to social life led in the direction of socialism, for reasons having nothing to do with metaphysical ideas concerning the status of matter and spirit. Another fallacy to be avoided is the conclusion that, since Marx was evidently not a nominalist in the manner of Hobbes, he must have been an "essentialist" in the tradition of Plato and his successors. In fact he was neither. In his rather cautious approach to these matters, he steered clear both of the crude nominalism of the British, for whom general ideas were merely conventional labels, and the metaphysical idealism in which Hegel had gradually entangled himself by shifting from an Aristotelian to a Platonist approach. In practice this meant that Marx treated theoretical concepts as reports (or "reflections") of the inherent objective structure of things. To that extent he was a "realist" in the traditional Aristotelian sense of the term. Unlike Hegel he did not regard ordinary sensible reality as the "external" manifestation of an "inner" spiritual principle, but neither did he confuse "reality" with the "facts" of immediate experience. This kind of balance was difficult to maintain, but he did maintain it, and it was not his fault if his disciples fell back into one or the other of the misconceptions he had avoided.[4]

The *practical* significance of such *theoretical* problems was among the issues at stake in the gradual divorce of "Marxism" from Hegelianism—including the Hegelianism of the radicals, notably Bruno Bauer who in the 1840's made a significant contribution to the critique of theology. What in the end made it impossible for Marx to work with Bauer (in his own way an impressive writer who anticipated some of Nietzsche's conclusions) was Bauer's adherence to the speculative mode of thought which maintained an unbridgeable barrier between criticism and action, theory and practice, philosophy and the revolution. This was the spiritual heritage of German idealism (in the last analysis a secularized form of Lutheran Protestantism). In dissolving his ties with the Hegelians, Marx adopted the French naturalist standpoint, in contrast to the traditional German mode of approach, which for some years he had shared. For the Germans, theory and practice belonged to different orders of reality. For the French they were united, or in need of being united. But there was also a genuine philosophical dispute over the status of concepts. When Marx protested against the idealist "mystification" of reality, his target was the Hegelian procedure which interpreted the actual character of ordinary events in terms of timeless principles "unfolding" in nature and history. As a philosopher (not that he regarded himself as one) what Marx is saying is that from mere logic one cannot get to existence. Rather one must proceed from (material, natural, social) existence to logic. Thinking "reflects" the ordinary life process, in the sense that the mind is always engaged with some aspect of reality. The term "reflection" here does not imply that the mind passively mirrors an external world subsisting in itself. Mind or consciousness is always active—this was the great lesson Marx had inherited from Kant, Fichte, and Hegel—but it works upon the concrete material of an environment with which it interacts. This dialectic of being and thinking, existence and consciousness, cannot be compressed into an eternally valid formula, for the human mind is itself an historical product, and its interaction with nature is just what appears in history.

Marx's relationship to Hegel, in short, was "dialectical" in that he transcended the speculative standpoint, without for this reason surrendering the insights laboriously gained by Kant, Fichte, Hegel, and the idealist school generally. In advancing from contemplative metaphysics to practical, world-transforming practice, he did not relinquish either the idealist stress on self-motivated action or the principle that behind the "facts" there is an objective order of reality to be discovered by the thinking mind. This applies in particular to history, which is the record of mankind's experience. History is a social process and as such is subject to "laws," in as much as human collectivities behave in ways imposed upon them by their struggle with a particular environment and a given heritage. The process operates blindly because mankind as a whole is not conscious of what it is doing; hence the "logic of history" has to be reconstructed by philosophy after the event. How then can theory and practice be unified? The answer Marx gives is fundamental for the understanding of his mode of thought: history is the process whereby man changes himself in the act of changing the world. Men make their own history, but they do so under determined conditions which impose a particular character upon each successive stage of societal evolution. All manifestations of individual life are at the same time expressions of a particular social life. When Marx wrote (in his sixth *Thesis on Feuerbach*), "The human essence is no abstraction inherent in each separate individual. In its reality it is the ensemble of social relations," he deliberately undercut the time-honored distinction between society and the individual. Man *is* the sum total of his social relations, and this statement applies equally to the individual and the species. There is no unchanging "human nature" from which eternal principles of political and social organization can be abstracted. There is only a process of human auto-emancipation accomplished in the course of social evolution. This self-creation presupposes a certain degree of freedom, and indeed Marx (like Hegel) regarded freedom as being characteristic of man. But the replacement of one social order by another always occurs under definite limiting conditions, the past shaping the present even while new forms of existence are being worked out. The motor of the whole process is practical activity, *labor,* the production and reproduction of material existence:

> Men can be distinguished from animals by consciousness, by religion, or by anything else one chooses. They themselves begin to distinguish themselves from the animals as soon as they begin to *produce* their means of subsistence, a step which is conditioned by their physical organization. In producing their means of subsistence, men indirectly produce their actual material life.
>
> The manner in which men produce their means of subsistence depends in the first place upon the nature of the existing means of

subsistence which have to be reproduced. This mode of production is not to be viewed simply as the reproduction of the physical existence of the individuals. Rather it is already a definite form of activity on the part of these individuals, a particular way of expressing their life, a particular mode of existence. As the individuals express their life, so they are. What they are thus coincides with their production, both with what they produce and how they produce it. What the individuals are thus depends upon the material conditions of their production.[5]

Let us halt here for a moment and ask the question which inevitably imposes itself at this point: how far is this materialist standpoint compatible with a revolutionary "theory of action" which seeks to unify theory and practice? Does it not point towards a sociology which simply describes or analyzes the process whereby society periodically renews or transforms itself? Is not Comte rather than Marx the true inheritor of the French materialists? Or (granting the latter point), is there not an inherent paradox in the notion that a descriptive sociology can be joined to a practice of revolution? What, when all is said and done, is the real status of theoretical analysis in the Marxian system? How are theory and practice related to each other for a thinker who takes for granted the operation of objective laws of development, yet seeks to transform the society of his own day and age? Are these modes of thought compatible? Was Marx the author of a grandiose but untenable synthesis of political activism and scientific determinism, or did he somehow succeed in fusing these very different approaches into a coherent whole? We know the formulation he proposed at a later stage in the preface to the first volume of *Capital:* society, having at long last discovered its own *modus operandi,* cannot legislate the material process of development out of existence, but it can "shorten and lessen the birth-pangs" which inevitably accompany the advent of a new social order. But this was the mature Marx who had come to believe that the transformation of capitalism into socialism was inscribed in the logic of economic development. Moreover, the responsibility for "shortening and lessening the birth-pangs" was allotted to "society" (although in practice he relied upon the labor movement). What turned the youthful Marx into a revolutionary was a very different sort of faith: that expressed in the *Theses on Feuerbach.*

Yet it is true to say that even in 1845 Marx was not really a voluntarist like those of his former friends who in their growing exasperation with Hegel's complacency and conservatism had drifted back to Fichte. For all his revolutionary fervor he never lost his hold upon Hegel's insight that it is useless to confront the world with a Kantian or Fichtean "ought." The world simply will not listen to such sermons, any more than the French in 1794 were willing to obey Robespierre's and Saint-Just's command that they stop being Frenchmen and behave like ancient Romans. (Marx cites this example to illustrate the futility of idealist terrorism in politics.) What moves the world is its own logic, the logic of conflict and self-contradiction. History is kept going by its negative principle—the principle of strife. So far, Marx is in accord with Hegel. The world must be transformed, but it is no use trying to dictate to it. The self-activating principle must be discovered within the historical process itself, and so far as modern society was concerned Marx in 1844–45 believed he had located the unconscious agent of transformation: it was the proletariat.

On the assumptions worked out by Ruge, Bauer, Cieszkowski, Hess, and the Left Hegelians in general (not counting Feuerbach, who was not an activist and only doubtfully a Hegelian), there was in principle nothing wrong with this conclusion, although in practice Marx was the only member of the group to adopt it. Its validity might indeed be questioned. One might, for example, assert that the true instrument of world revolution was rather the *Volksgeist* or some particular nation (the Germans for choice, although Bakunin and his friends naturally allotted this role to the Slavs). But these were mere disputes over trifles. The basic question concerned the relation of theory to practice. If Marx was a Hegelian, then what sort of a Hegelian was he? Alternatively, if he had stopped being one, then what was Marxism? To Marx of course the problem posed itself differently: what was he doing as the theorist of a revolutionary movement? His reply is plain enough —he had stopped being a philosopher because philosophy was *by its nature* incapable of transforming the world. Yet some kind of theory was still necessary. What was that theory if it was neither philosophy nor science in the positivist sense? For Marx it was "criticism"—the analysis of the actual historical process. Criticism is powerless so long as it remains speculative. It becomes a material force when it sets men in motion by showing them how they can achieve their aims.

One is thus entitled to say that Marx had taken both Hegel and his critics seriously. Indeed, he took the critics more seriously than they took themselves. They—notably Ruge and Bauer—thought it possible to turn Hegel's system against the actual world, after having first purged it of its conservative and conformist traits. Marx was alone in realizing that such a purgation was impossible. Hegel's system was not simply conformist because its author had compromised with authority: it was useless as an instrument of revolution because as a "system" it was necessarily "total"—that is to say, it comprehended everything. But a system that comprehended everything could change nothing. Conversely, a philosophical critique could not well be "total," since whatever it criticized must necessarily be left out or abolished. This, however, meant that any attempt to actualize a "total" philosophy was bound to fail. Either the system comprehends the world, or it does not. If comprehensive, it is static; if critical, it is no longer total. What then was to be done? It was no use, after Hegel, trying to salvage philosophy. One had to launch out into a new element—the revolutionary actualization of critical theory. To do so was to leave behind forever the speculative mode of thought, yet Marx conserved the lesson he had learned from Hegel: the world must be confronted with its own logic. Moreover, history must be "ripe" for the change, and the transforming element must be located in the material substratum of social existence. "It is not enough that thought should seek to realize itself; reality itself must force its way toward thought."[6]

State and Society

The Marx of 1845–46, who thus traced the broad outline of what was later to become known as "historical materialism," had not only left Hegel's idealization of the state behind. He had also advanced beyond the Feuerbachian anthropology of the 1844 *Paris Manuscripts*, with their stress upon the "alienation of man" and their characterization of socialism as "man's positive self-consciousness." In 1842–44 Feuerbach had provided some of the intellectual tools required for the demolition of Hegel's system. After 1845 Marx was his own master and was soon to become the central figure of a "peer group" of revolutionaries drawn from the German exile community in Western Europe. This community centered upon Paris—then and for many years the unofficial head-quarters of an international movement whose watchwords pro-claimed their revolutionary origin: communism and the class struggle.

The literature on Marx's intellectual development has estab-lished beyond doubt that his adoption of what he himself described as a "communist" standpoint coincided with his stay in Paris be-tween the end of 1843 and the beginning of 1845. In this connec-tion we need not enter into the details of the increasingly scholastic dispute over the precise moment when it dawned upon him that his new-found convictions were incompatible with the sort of reasoning then fashionable among the Berlin Hegelians. It is un-likely that French and German Marxists will ever quite agree about the permanent relevance of Hegel's philosophy for "Marxism" as a doctrine or as a mode of viewing the world. For even if it were generally accepted that the mature Marx had in some sense re-mained a Hegelian (Engels remained one to the end of his days, as witness the quasi-philosophical writings he published after the death of Marx), it might be argued that this was merely a biographical circumstance, of interest to historians but not nec-essarily relevant for twentieth-century disciples of logical posi-tivism who have effected a rupture with traditional modes of reasoning. It could even be held that as a philosopher (if this term is properly applicable to the author of the *Theses on Feuerbach*) Marx only laid the cornerstone of a building that remains to be erected. Historically, both Social Democrats and Communists have tended to claim the mature Marx for positivism and faith in science. In recent years these conflicting interpretations have found learned and ingenious advocates among French and Central

European Marxists, though on the whole the former have stressed the originality of the post-1845 writings, the latter their concordance with the heritage of German idealism. What no one is ever likely to dispute is that Marx effected the fusion of German theorizing with French revolutionary practice of which others had merely dreamed. The precise moment when "Marxism" made its appearance may never be determined to the satisfaction of all concerned, but one thing is certain: whenever it was that Marx ceased to be a Left Hegelian, his new standpoint entailed the adoption of a very definite political orientation. This latter was "French" in that it involved an analysis of history in terms of class conflict, and the conviction that society was moving towards a confrontation between two fundamentally hostile classes: bourgeoisie and proletariat. Likewise there is no doubt that this mode of thought was not suggested to Marx by anything he had found in Hegel or Saint-Simon. Rather it was the outcome of an intensive preoccupation with the French Revolution and the radical movements to which it had given birth. At some stage between 1843 (when he began to immerse himself in this subject while preparing to leave Germany for Paris) and 1845, when he published the *Holy Family* and jotted down the *Theses,* he had turned from a democrat into a communist, from a left-wing Hegelian into a "materialist," and from an intellectual critic of established institutions into a revolutionary. In brief, he had become the man who not long thereafter was to take over and remodel the nascent Communist League.

In trying to establish the genesis of "Marxism" between 1843 and 1848, one is likewise obliged to take note of the fact that Marx during these years steeped himself in economics, specifically in the great British and French economists of the eighteenth and early nineteenth centuries. The immediate outcome of this intensive process of self-education was his pamphlet against Proudhon, to which reference has been made in an earlier chapter. This must be stressed because one can still hear it said that Marx did not seriously engage the topic of economics until he had moved to London, and more particularly until in 1852–53 he had withdrawn from active participation in politics and taken up his abode in the reading room of the British Museum. The grain of truth in this fable must not be permitted to blot from view the far more important circumstance that the author of *Misère de la philosophie* was already an economist, although one who still lacked the comprehensive grasp of the subject he was to acquire in later years. It is worth stressing that Marx during these years "synthesized" not merely two intellectual traditions, but three: the French, the German, and the British. It is likewise relevant that the notion of class conflict, which became his guiding idea in moving from the humanist socialism of the 1844 *Manuscripts* to the communism of the *Manifesto,* was inherent in the writings of the French historians and could also be extracted from the work of the "Ricardian socialists." After what has been said on this subject there is no need to emphasize once more that the Chartist movement (whose acquaintance the youthful Engels had made during his stay in Manchester in 1842–44) was a school of political education for anyone who came from backward Germany. It was thus quite in order that Marx should have had his eyes opened to the importance of the subject by the essay on economics which Engels contributed to the *Deutsch-Französische Jahrbücher* in 1844. Meantime his own acquaintance with French socialist and communist literature had brought him to the point of regarding the industrial proletariat as the class destined to inaugurate a new social order.

All this is familiar and presents no particular problem. What needs to be considered briefly is how this perspective appeared to one who had but recently emancipated himself from the "critical" standpoint of the Left Hegelians. Did Marx, as is frequently said, impose a philosophical scheme upon his reading of recent European history when he treated class conflict as the motor of social development? Did he (another popular interpretation) "combine" Hegel with Saint-Simon? Was he unconsciously guided by a "prophetic" view of mankind, an inherited quasi-religious version of world history in terms of an age-old dichotomy of oppressors and oppressed? Was he generalizing from the recent experience of the French Revolution and the literature to which it had given birth? To what extent was he influenced by the Scottish historians and economists of the eighteenth century in working out the "materialist conception of history"? Did the notion of class conflict serve to explain *both* the bourgeois revolution *and* the more recent impact of the industrial revolution? Finally, did Marx simply invert the Hegelian view of the relationship between state and society, or did he introduce a radically new approach? These topics have been endlessly debated. They cannot be considered in detail, but a brief general answer must be attempted if the originality of "Marxism" as a mode of thought is to be put in perspective.

Setting aside speculation about Marx's mental processes—a popular pastime, but not very illuminating in regard to the topic under discussion—one may say that he was during these years wrestling with a group of problems which had arisen from the interaction of three different but related currents: the aftermath of the French Revolution, the impact of British economic developments upon pre-industrial society, and the decay of absolutism and its religious sanctions in Germany. The corresponding movements of thought, as reflected in the literature of the age, had already given rise to a whole crop of writings for the most part devoted to suggesting specific solutions for particular problems. What Marx did was to fuse certain key elements of the most radical theorizing then current, the common theme being the nature of the society which had emerged from the crucible of the dual revolution. The method he employed was one that happened to suit his genius: namely, the critical analysis of the doctrines produced by German philosophers, British economists, and French historians, themselves responding to the upheavals of the past half-century. In analyzing these intellectual systematizations, Marx was struck by the fundamental similarity of certain key concepts employed by philosophers, economists, and historians alike. It appeared to him that, consciously or not, they were reasoning in ways which had gradually been evolved since the seventeenth century by the representative thinkers of one particular social stratum whose pre-eminence was no longer questionable: the bourgeoisie. And from this awareness he was led to the notion that all this complex theorizing constituted, as it were, the "ideological superstructure" of a particular social reality: "bourgeois society."[7]

Let us pause for a moment to see what this entailed. It did *not* imply that the thinkers in question were in some sense the hired spokesmen of their class: an absurdity hardly worth mentioning had it not acquired a certain unmerited popularity. Nor did it mean that their thinking was "ideological" in the sense of being remote from ordinary reality. What lent an "ideological" quality to their theorizing was rather that they believed themselves to be stating general truths about human nature when in fact they were describing one particular phase of societal evolution: the genesis of bourgeois society. This did not invalidate the truth of their observations, nor did it diminish the importance which these new modes of reasoning possessed in enabling people to understand their environment. The point was rather that in struggling with the theoretical and practical problems of individualism, they were imprisoned within the mental categories of a particular social order, an order founded upon the market economy. At the same time, however, in reflecting upon it they were also incidentally laying bare its "internal contradictions." With the advent of industrialism and democracy, the prime contradiction could now be analyzed in terms of class conflict: specifically, conflict between the economically privileged class (the bourgeoisie), and the class upon whose paid and unpaid labor the entire edifice had come to rest—the proletariat.

This having been said, the relationship of Marx to his precursors can now be stated rather more clearly. It was not simply a matter of employing the concept of "alienation" (which Feuerbach had borrowed from Hegel) for the purpose of expounding the philosophical thesis that history was the process of man's self-creation.[8] Nor was it sufficient to restate the socialist interpretation of the French Revolution in terms of class conflict, or to merge this notion with what the Ricardian socialists had begun to say about the industrial revolution in Britain. It was necessary to go behind these phenomena to their common origin—the growth of the market economy, and therewith the slow emergence of bourgeois society as such. In Hegel's *Philosophy of Right* (which had been Marx's prime target when in 1842–43 he began his critical revision of Hegel's system) bourgeois society appeared under the category of

"civil society" (literally, *bürgerliche Gesellschaft*), as distinct
from the state, which to Hegel was incarnate Reason struggling to
subdue the welter of blind material interests and conflicts which
made up the netherworld of ordinary existence. Years later, when
Marx had occasion to describe the mental process which led him
to the study of economics, he summarized his conclusions in the
well-known preface to the *Critique of Political Economy*. There he
laid it down that

> legal relations, as well as political relations [*Staatsformen*] are not
> to be comprehended out of themselves, nor from the so-called gen-
> eral development of the human mind, but rather are rooted in the
> material conditions of life, the totality of which Hegel—following
> the example of the eighteenth-century English and French—grouped
> together under the term "civil society"; and that the anatomy of
> civil society is to be sought for in Political Economy.[9]

The point is crucial for an understanding of what "Marxism"
is about. Political Economy—as developed by the physiocrats in
France and later by Smith and Ricardo in England—was directly
concerned with what Marx termed the "anatomy" of bourgeois
society: its material structure, the foundation of the majestic political, legal, and cultural edifice which the bourgeois philosophers
had invested with a spurious independence. This philosophy, from
Hobbes and Locke to Bentham, and from Spinoza to the French
materialists, had gradually established the elements of a political
doctrine. Its ultimate achievement, in the age of Rousseau and
Kant, was the idea of the emancipated individual: the citizen,
citoyen, Staatsbürger of political and legal theorizing. In making
the state rest upon "civil society" and describing the latter as a
"system of needs," Hegel in his fashion had taken note of the discoveries made by earlier British and French theorists. And yet,
writing after the great upheaval of the American and French revolutions, he was concerned to show that these socio-political earth-
quakes could still be comprehended within an intellectual tradition
he had inherited from Aristotle, a tradition that did not distinguish
clearly between state and society, save for the purpose of deni-
grating private life as an inferior realm of selfish material interests.

In taking his cue from Hegel (who was already conscious of "civil society" as an autonomous sphere, but still attached to the traditional Aristotelian view of politics as applied ethics), Marx went back to the source of the whole disturbance: the "bourgeois revolution," which had recently culminated in the industrial revolution. His conclusion then amounted to this: "civil society" was an ideological construct which half revealed and half concealed the reality of bourgeois society. The latter in turn rested upon the market economy, itself the creation of bourgeois entrepreneurs. It was a society riven by class conflict: not merely in the sense that it had come into being through a revolutionary struggle against feudalism and absolutism—this was something no democrat would have denied—but in the sense that it contained within itself the elements of a new cleavage: between the owners of the means of production and those excluded from their possession.

If it is not immediately obvious with what force these notions struck Marx's German contemporaries, the reason is that we have grown used to them. They seemed far from evident in the mid-nineteenth century—an age that witnessed the triumphant flowering of liberalism, both as a philosophical doctrine and as a politico-economic reality. Educated public opinion in those days was virtually synonymous with middle-class opinion, and the middle class had recently come to acquire a profound sense of self-satisfaction. This was particularly true after the storm of 1848–49 had spent itself. The 1840's had been a decade of strain, political and economic, whereas after 1850 liberalism entered upon a golden age of unimpeded progress. Marx arrived just in time to synthesize the intellectual travail of the critical transition period, and he had to pay for his consistent attachment to radicalism with long years of hostility and neglect. The notion of an ineluctable class struggle appeared discredited during the Victorian era. It had indeed been formulated by Marx under the impact of his recent conversion to French communism, and in the form he gave it in the *Manifesto* it did not survive the catastrophe of 1848—not even in his own mind, let alone in the consciousness of British and German socialists who had never quite shared his faith in the ability of the Paris proletariat to overthrow the established order.

Before engaging the topic of communism and the *Manifesto,* it may be useful to conclude this section with a brief glance at Marx's views on economics as he had worked them out by 1848. His mature work as an economist was done in the 1850's and 1860's, when—not accidentally—he abandoned or qualified some of his earlier political views. The problem in this respect is similar to that which we have already encountered in relation to Proudhon (whose death in 1865 preceded by only two years the publication of the first volume of *Capital* in 1867). In the case of Marx, who survived Proudhon by eighteen years, it is evident enough that his important work as an economist coincided with the age of the First International, when for all practical purposes he had ceased to be a communist in the sense of the 1848 *Manifesto* and transformed himself into the theorist of what came to be known thereafter as democratic socialism. Yet the logical structure of *Capital* (not to mention the unpublished *Grundrisse der Kritik der Politischen Ökonomie,* which although composed in 1857–58 only received due attention almost a century later) arose out of insights he had already gained in the 1840's. The dichotomy of class always remained crucial to the notion of exploitation as Marx understood it. Now this way of looking at things was certainly not peculiar to Marx—on the contrary, he had adopted it from the French socialists and communists of his age. What was peculiar was the manner in which he built it into the structure of his theorizing. Between 1843 and 1845 he had encountered the proletariat in his passage from (idealist) philosophy to (materialist) sociology and (revolutionary) politics. He then incorporated the concept of class in the first of his economic writings: his pamphlet against Proudhon, the main theme of which can be summed up by saying that in it Marx treated economics—or rather political economy—as *the theory of bourgeois society.* In this perspective, "economics" was not a politically neutral discipline which could be employed—as Proudhon had attempted to do—for the purpose of extracting socialist conclusions from liberal premises. The concepts of Political Economy were already so shaped as to reflect bourgeois property relations, and this quite irrespective of what the theorist in question was trying to accomplish. Thus we find

Marx in 1846–47 criticizing Ricardo for applying the notion of rent in an unhistorical manner to landownership in general. "This is the mistake of all the economists who represent bourgeois production relations as eternal categories."[10]

It is just as well to be clear about the significance of this sort of observation. For Marx, bourgeois society was historically determined by the way in which it had come into existence, and this unique process was bound up with the emergence of private property in the means of production: land, industry, and transport. But it was also bound up with a particular theoretical science, namely economics as formulated by the physiocrats and Smith, and subsequently by Ricardo (for whom—in his capacity as an analytical thinker—Marx always entertained the highest esteem). This essentially bourgeois science, which "reflected" the new "relations of production" in its formal structure, was the counterpart of liberalism as a political philosophy: Bentham's individualist concepts were also those of Adam Smith (or, for that matter, David Hume), and the individualism of the Scots in turn went back to Locke. If the idealist philosophy of Kant, Fichte, and Hegel was somewhat rudimentary on the socio-economic side, this was due to Germany's economic backwardness. *In principle,* their political thinking belonged to the same order of reality (except that Hegel was closer to Hobbes than to Locke). The problems they debated had their roots in the internal dilemmas of bourgeois society, and their horizon was that of bourgeois thought—taking the term to signify the entire intellectual development which had accompanied the rise of urban civilization since the Renaissance and Reformation. What was of special significance about Hegel's philosophy (and in a different sense about Ricardo's economics) was that it marked the dawning awareness of an insoluble contradiction within the social reality of which all this theorizing was the intellectual reflex. Hegel indeed in his later years had shown an inclination to revert to pre-liberal, i.e., authoritarian, forms of thought, whereas Ricardo was fully committed to the new world of political liberalism and capitalist economics. But these differences paled in comparison with what they had in common. Both Hegel and Ricardo accepted bourgeois society as it stood. They saw the emerging industrial proletariat only as a vague threat to the stability of the social order, or as an aspect of pauperism which indeed posed a "social problem" for those in authority.

They did not see it as the bearer of a new principle. Still less of course did they credit the notion that the industrial working class might acquire political power. Hegel indeed could not even conceive of a bourgeois form of democracy either in Germany or in England (as witness his critical comments on the British Reform Bill of 1831—practically the last thing he wrote, and thus in a sense his political testament). Ricardo, like any other utilitarian of his day and age, treated parliamentary government as the only rational form of political rule, but it is easy to imagine what he could have thought of the Chartists. After 1850, when Victorian society felt safe, democratic liberalism became respectable; that is to say, it became respectable for the more advanced liberals to argue that universal suffrage was not necessarily a mortal threat to civilization, now that the industrial working class had become reconciled to the operation of the new economic system. But in the 1840's this surprising discovery had not yet been made in any European country—not even in England, let alone France, where the proletariat followed the leaders of the various competing socialist and communist parties and sects.

The relationship of state and society, therefore, was an immediate practical problem for anyone who, like Marx, had discerned both the autonomy of "civil society" *and* its class character. If bourgeois society was riven by class conflict, then the state must reflect this cleavage. The *Manifesto* indeed affirms that "the bourgeoisie has at last, since the establishment of modern industry and the world market, conquered for itself, in the modern representative State, exclusive political sway." That this was not in fact the case even in Victorian England, Marx and Engels came to realize in later years, when they acknowledged that actual political power had been retained by the landed aristocracy, albeit in the interest of the economically stronger class which controlled Parliament. This was an inconvenience (as was the feudalization of the middle class in Bismarckian Germany), but it made no real dent in their basic approach. After all, the United States and France could be cited as proof of the contention that the democratic republic was the "classical" form of bourgeois rule. If British and German philistines showed a preference for non-classical variants, so much the worse for them and for their subservient spirit (which, however, they tended to transmit to the labor movement—another awkward circumstance not foreseen in 1848). So far as France was concerned, the *Manifesto* hardly exaggerated when it described "the executive of the modern State" as "a committee for managing the common affairs of the bourgeois class taken as a whole." A similar characterization of the Orléanist regime was suggested, after 1848, by Tocqueville, from an aristocratic standpoint which at any rate enabled him to treat the pretensions of bourgeois liberalism as the half-conscious make-believe they had by then become.

But the *Manifesto* also asserted something else—namely, that the industrial working class could and would win political power, as the bourgeoisie had done before. This hardly squared with the image of the proletariat as a downtrodden class of industrial helots comparable to the French peasantry in 1789, for the peasants had indeed been emancipated, but only in the wake of the bourgeois revolution. If the model of the latter was taken literally, the logical conclusion should have been that the workers would gain their *economic* freedom at the same time that a new stratum acquired *political* power. But Marx had no intention of drawing an exact parallel. For his immediate purpose it was sufficient to proclaim to the German public (for which after all the *Manifesto* was destined) what the communists had already made familiar in France: that the imminent democratic revolution would be the curtain-raiser of something far more grandiose—a conflict between bourgeoisie and proletariat for possession of power in the democratic republic both classes hoped to establish. It was this perspective that distinguished communists from socialists—not to mention the followers of Comte who had already adopted the bourgeois standpoint, or the numerous national-democratic movements of the period, which for the most part still relied upon the peasantry. For Marx, the attainment of socialism was bound up with the coming triumph of the proletariat.[11]

The Communism of 1848

In any history of communism as a movement, as distinct from an intellectual tradition, an important place would have to be reserved for the pre-history of the *Manifesto*. Even setting aside the biographical data concerning Marx and Engels during the period from 1846 to 1848, it would be necessary to trace the links between the German Communist League and the revolutionary movements—some of them socialist or communist, others simply democratic—in Britain, France, Italy, the Netherlands, Switzerland, etc., whose representatives gathered in London in November 1847, under the auspices of the Chartist leaders, to commemorate the Polish rising of 1830. One would then have to explain how and why it came about that Marx, who attended as a delegate of the Democratic Association in Brussels, went straight from a public meeting organized by the Fraternal Democrats to a private conclave of the German Communist Arbeiterbildungsverein (Workers' Educational Association), whose leaders—after ten days of discussion—invited him and Engels to draft a new party program and statutes. What needs to be retained for our purpose is that the *Communist Manifesto* to all intents and purposes emerged from lengthy debates among German exiles and was duly published in the German language (albeit in London) on the eve of a *French* upheaval. Unfortunately, the complex and fascinating circumstances surrounding the composition of the document lie outside our theme. They belong to the history of early communism, or to the biography of Marx, and the only point of recalling them here is to emphasize the close connection which the terms "democracy" and "communism" possessed on the eve of 1848. Much of the subsequent confusion surrounding this topic is due to the fact that in those days the notion of communism appeared to be more or less interchangeable with the idea of radical democracy.[12]

As if all this were not enough, there are some further historical and biographical hurdles to be taken. First, there is Marx's editorship of the *Neue Rheinische Zeitung* in 1848–49. This was a democratic paper founded with the help of bourgeois Rhineland sympathizers, some of whom indeed soon withdrew their support, although Marx ran the paper as an "organ of democracy" and even risked a quarrel with the Communist League's followers in Cologne who were unenthusiastic about what would later have been called his "united front" tactics. Specifically, they objected to the notion that the German revolution was a *bourgeois* one and that the workers should support the most advanced section of the democratic party. Marx's editorship of the paper reflected a long-range strategy quite unrelated to the immediate aims of the nascent workers' movement. "There was not a word about the special interests of the working classes, of the workers' special tasks in the German Revolution. Neither Engels nor Marx wrote a word about the position of the workers until the end of 1848."[13] Secondly, there is the important, if not very long-lasting, incident of Marx's temporary alliance with Blanqui in the spring of 1850, when he and Engels—along with the Chartist leader Julian Harney, who had previously organized the Fraternal Democrats—entered into a secret understanding with the Blanquist emissaries in London. The outcome of this strange association was a body called the Société Universelle des Communistes Révolutionnaires, which existed only on paper and only for a few months, but which left in its wake two written documents that were later to play a role in the genesis of Leninism: a brief declaration of principles including a reference to "proletarian dictatorship"; and the lengthy *Address of the Central Authority* (or Central Committee) which Marx and Engels composed in March 1850. This too was decidedly Blanquist in spirit, in that it looked forward to a proletarian (rather than a bourgeois-democratic) dictatorship on the next occasion when Germany might be expected to undergo a revolutionary upheaval. So far as Marx was concerned, the whole episode lasted only a few months and had no further consequences, the less so since he and Engels gradually abandoned the entire perspective of a worker-peasant rising, at any rate so far as Germany was concerned. But it marked the formulation of a viewpoint that was to become important elsewhere.[14]

In biographical and political terms all this is easily explained. On the one hand, secret societies were plentiful: Mazzini's liberal-national Young Italy being one of them. On the other hand, Marx and Engels—after they had laboriously transformed the secretive League of the Just into the "open" Communist League, and then virtually abandoned the latter for the sake of their alliance with the Democratic party in 1848–49—found themselves plunged back around 1850 into the familiar, if unwelcome, atmosphere of exile politics and subterranean conspiracy. Absolutism on the Continent being still in the saddle, it was not unreasonable to suppose that the next turn of the wheel would result in a temporary dictatorship on "Jacobin" lines, in which case a secret organization of the most determined revolutionary leaders might still have a part to play. This, more or less, was to remain the Blanquist view of the matter until the catastrophe of the Paris Commune in 1871 put an end to all such experiments, at any rate in Western Europe. It was briefly Marx's view in 1850, and he abandoned it rather reluctantly when it became evident that the preconditions for it no longer existed, and that a democratic labor movement was beginning to develop. To that extent Marx around 1865 had ceased to be a "communist" in the sense of the *Manifesto* and of the (secret) program of 1850. This revision of his earlier standpoint also entailed a departure from the notion that the role of the proletariat in the coming up-heaval in Central Europe was to help the bourgeoisie to power, whereas in France one might go further. It is necessary to be clear as to what "communism" in 1848–50 was about. On the one hand, the *Manifesto* put forward a theory of the "bourgeois revolution." On the other hand, it looked forward to a society transcending the bourgeois horizon. The notion of "proletarian dictatorship" served to connect the two levels of argument, but the link broke when it became evident that not even France (let alone Germany) could be expected to see a victorious proletarian uprising. As for the bourgeois revolution in the broader sociological sense of the term, it was certainly going forward (more or less as Marx had described it), but its immediate outcome was the establishment of liberal democracy on the one hand and the rise of an independent labor movement on the other. The 1848 upheaval was a decisive turning-point. When it was over, "communism" ceased for many years to be practical politics.

What has been said so far relates to Marx's theory of revolution in 1848 and to his practice as a revolutionary in the years immediately following. Both the theory and the practice were related to the *Manifesto,* whose date of appearance indeed was not accidental. But there is also the more general perspective of historical development set out in the document, a perspective that retained its relevance even after the hopes of 1848 had been disappointed. The most dramatic proof of this fact is furnished by the very real connection which Marx and Engels established, many years later, between their own generation and the precursors of the coming storm in Eastern Europe. For in 1882 they wrote a joint introduction to a new Russian edition of the *Manifesto,* and this preface (as every good Leninist knows) ends with the famous words: "If the Russian Revolution becomes the signal for a proletarian revolution in the West, so that both complement each other, the present Russian common ownership of land may serve as the starting-point for a communist development." In 1882, when Russian Marxism was just about to emerge from its populist chrysalis, this cautious formulation enabled the men and women who were to become Lenin's teachers to make the transition from their native faith to an "international" doctrine of socialism. There is no need to say more on a topic whose earth-shaking relevance has been drummed into the world's consciousness since 1917.

By comparison with the explosive effect the *Manifesto* eventually had in Russia and Eastern Europe, its political influence elsewhere has always been rather limited, although it did have some importance for revolutionary socialists in France, Italy, and Spain, who found it useful in countering the anarchist competition. So far as Central Europe was concerned, then and later, one may say that its short-run effect was nil and its long-term importance mainly literary. It familiarized Germans and Austrians with a doctrine and a way of looking at things that had come out of the French Revolution, and for this reason inevitably sounded outlandish, though also dramatic and exciting. Down to 1918, when the Hohenzollern and Habsburg dynasties fell, the democratic tradition was still surrounded by a romantic halo, in as much as its pathos was plainly derived from France—to be precise, from the kind of revolutionary radicalism that was the offspring of the French

Revolution. To put it differently, as long as the struggle for democracy was understood as a task whose burden had fallen upon the working class, the *Manifesto* conveyed a distinct political message even for Social Democrats in Central Europe, as a heritage from the heroic age and a distant foreshadowing of convulsions still to come. For the same reason, its political relevance in the English-speaking world was slight, even though some of the more radical Chartists in 1848 thought in similar terms. The kind of revolutionary movement with which Marx and Engels had involved themselves, in or about 1848, had been born in 1793. It traveled eastward from Paris by way of Berlin, Vienna, and Warsaw until in 1917–18 it reached Petrograd. It did *not* travel westward to Britain and North America.

So much for politics. But the *Manifesto* also had a theoretical content transcending the realm of immediate political practice. It set out both a long-term and a short-term historical perspective: a doctrine of class conflict as the motor of history; a rudimentary analysis of bourgeois society; and a brief summation of communism as a doctrine appropriate to a new and revolutionary class—the industrial proletariat. These various themes were fused together by an intellectual *tour de force* sustained by the powerful mind and the brooding passion of Marx. Is it possible in retrospect to do justice to the greatness of his achievement, without for that reason overlooking the logical flaws in the construction?

The *Manifesto* anticipates some of the socio-political concepts that are woven into the structure of *Capital,* but it would be pointless to judge Marx the economist on the evidence of the rather immature theorizing he put forward in that document. One need not, for example, worry unduly over the assertion that bourgeois society had already become ripe for revolution on economic grounds—because (as Marx put it in 1847) the bourgeoisie could no longer feed its slaves, who were sinking into hopeless poverty. As he himself recognized a few years later, this was to confuse the birth-pangs of a new social order with the death-throes of the old: an analytical mistake he shared with virtually every socialist of the 1840's and which he took pains to correct in his writings of the 1850's and in *Capital.* What was rather more serious was a fault in the argument which had to do with his quite realistic analysis of progress in terms of class conflict. Marx did not indeed make the elementary mistake with which he is sometimes charged—that of supposing there were only two classes: the exploiters and the exploited. He had, after all, read the British and French economists and was quite aware of the conflict dividing landowners from industrialists. Nor was he unsympathetic to the plight of small farmers and independent craftsmen. He did, however, tend to believe that the intermediate strata were on the point of merging with the proletariat, and that the latter in turn was sinking below subsistence level. On both counts he proved mistaken, a circumstance which did not matter greatly in 1848 but became troublesome later on. Furthermore, the parallel he drew between the antecedent rise of the bourgeoisie and the coming emancipation of the workers ignored the role of the private entrepreneurs in pioneering a new mode of production. On this analogy (if taken seriously) the rise to power of the industrial working class was likely to be slow and gradual, based as it was on its growing importance in managing and administering the new technological apparatus. In *Capital*—composed two decades later, after lengthy studies and prolonged experience of actual conditions in Victorian England—Marx took some steps in the direction of recognizing all this, but in 1847 he was still obsessed with the dichotomic picture of class conflict he had inherited from the French communists. The result was a theoretical muddle. On the one hand, the *Manifesto* made a bow to trade unionism and even mentioned the recent successful struggle for a ten-hours bill in England. On the other hand, the "proletarian revolution" it looked forward to was modeled on the French Revolution—in other words, on the *bourgeois* revolution. Notwithstanding subsequent revisions and modifications, Marx and Engels never quite managed to relate these very different perspectives to one another. In 1848 this did not matter, since the revolution—a democratic one—was plainly brewing anyhow, but it became a source of quite needless confusions later on.[15]

Behind the forecast of an imminent upheaval (which eventually turned out to have merely completed the bourgeois revolution) there lay a more general assumption about the historical process, namely the notion of class conflict as the motor of social development. This was a generalization which served to explain how bourgeois society had come into being, but it did not permit the conclusion that the emancipation of the working class would follow the same pattern. In fact the real development of industrial society and of the labor movement led away from the antagonistic model prominent in many people's minds around 1848. The model remained appropriate for Eastern Europe and for backward countries generally, but not for developed industrial societies. It is by now a truism that in advanced countries the working class has ceased to be a proletariat, for it is part of the definition of this term that the social stratum to which it relates is permanently held down to a subsistence level, unable to effect a gradual improvement in its condition, and obliged to conquer political power by violence. The abandonment of these notions is sometimes confused with the very different assertion that exploitation (in the Marxian sense of the term) has come to an end, but no such conclusion follows from the ascertainable fact that the "condition of the working class" in all industrial countries has steadily improved. What Marx meant by "exploitation" is not affected by statistical considerations, just as it would be meaningless to assert that what in 1844 he described as "alienation" has ceased to be a problem. The ethico-political assumptions underlying the *Manifesto*—and the communism of 1848 generally—have nothing to do with the question whether or not real wages have a tendency to rise. They relate to the proposition that the owners of capital and land constitute an "exploiting class" by virtue of their being monopolists of property. Marx was concerned with social relations, not with "economics" in the abstract. It never occurred to him to deny that land and capital were factors of production just as much as labor. What he denied was that they must of necessity be privately owned. This of course was the common faith of all socialists, including the most peaceable and reformist. But in 1848 Marx and Engels were "communists," not simply "socialists." The distinction had nothing to do with anticipations of a future stateless and classless order—all that came later. What was at stake was something more definite and concrete: the role of communism as the theory and practice of a proletarian class movement.

The Marx of 1848 was a communist not in some philosophical

sense, but in the sense of viewing himself as the theorist of an approaching revolution. "Le combat ou la mort; la lutte sanguinaire ou le néant; c'est ainsi que la question est invinciblement posée," George Sand had written, and Marx had concluded his *Misère de la philosophie* with this citation. To the extent that this vision was subsequently abandoned, the youthful Marx was not the founder of what in the 1880's came to be known as "scientific socialism." The transformation had begun as early as the 1850's. For that matter, 1848 proved a watershed for all the conflicting parties and programs of the age, from the romantic Toryism of the aristocracy, via the naïve Rousseauism of Mazzini and his Polish or Hungarian friends, to the proletarian faith of the first generation of communists. One and all were doomed to disappointment. Yet something survived this world-historical debacle—the vision of a new society. Defeated on the barricades and driven underground for more than a decade, the movement re-emerged in the 1860's, when its strands were pulled together once more by the founder of the International, who was also the author of *Capital*.

Conclusion

In the Preface to this study the reader was warned not to expect more than a reconsideration of socialist origins, down to the great divide of 1848, when Europe witnessed an upheaval unparalled since 1789 and not to be repeated until 1918. A summing-up at this point must start from the candid admission that these dates are somewhat arbitrary. It is, after all, quite legitimate to attempt a history of the bourgeois revolution from 1789 to 1871, or an account of democratic socialism from the founding of the First International in 1864 to the tacit acceptance of social-democratic laborism in Britain and Scandinavia a century later. It may even be possible to combine the two, although this cannot be easy, even if one adopts the Marxist perspective which has the advantage of relating these topics to each other. Be that as it may, the aim has been more narrowly defined: to review the circumstances under which socialism in general, and Marxism in particular, first took shape.

To say these circumstances were unique is merely to say they were historical, for history does not repeat itself. There will never be another revolution resembling the French or the Russian, if only because upheavals of this magnitude have the effect of shifting the angle of vision from which men (including revolutionaries) perceive the world. Similarly, there will never be another Romantic movement such as that which flourished in the first half of the nineteenth century, for Romanticism as a faith died on the barricades in 1848. It has had its heirs, existentialism among them. It may be said to have left a permanent imprint upon the mind of the Western world, much as the French or the American Revolution has altered for all time the manner in which Frenchmen or Americans react to the great issues of the day. But there can never again be a "springtime of the nations" such as that which swept

215

Europe in the early months of 1848, when for a brief moment nationalism, democracy, and socialism seemed to have formed an alliance under the aegis of the Romantic faith, itself the last flowering of the seed Rousseau had sown. Nor will the heirs of German speculative philosophy recapture the spirit of Hegel's grandiose synthesis: an achievement still possible in an age when, for the last time, one single mind could hope to encompass the entire universe of discourse.

It is because Marx bestrides this rift that he continues to matter to the world. Yet we have seen that he made the transition from one age to the next, and from one mode of thought to another, only at the cost of incorporating in his doctrine the unresolved tensions between philosophy and science, theory and practice, the universal and the particular, then at work in the minds of lesser men, Comte and Mill among them. Marxism was kept in balance by a ceaseless effort to include within its framework both the philosophical suppositions from which it had sprung and the scientific investigations imposed upon its author by the effort to comprehend the totality of recorded history. The resulting fusion of philosophical, historical, sociological, and political reasoning laid the foundations for what was to become the enduring monument to Marx's greatness: his analysis of what he termed the "capitalist mode of production." But for all its grandeur the achievement remained fragmentary when measured against the original plan of his work: nothing less than a critical theory of bourgeois society as a whole, including its political institutions and its intellectual "superstructure." The immensity of the task proved too much for Marx, but even had he been able to complete it, his followers would still have been plagued by the heritage of ideas taken over from the bourgeois revolution: the only one of its kind.

For what occurred in the Western world between the middle of the eighteenth and the middle of the nineteenth century was unique and unprecedented. Never before had there been such a conjunction of a democratic upsurge and a technological gear-change that radically altered men's environment and their way of life. The consequential change in the structure of inherited institutions and modes of thought was more profound than anything mankind had experienced since the rupture with tribal society which made city life possible. And it was all compressed into less than one century. No wonder a great deal of theorizing went hopelessly astray. Even where thought came to grips with reality, the outcome was inevitably flawed by the inheritance of outmoded concepts. Rousseau, Saint-Simon, Comte, Hegel, Ricardo, and Marx forged the intellectual tools that made both socialism and sociology possible, but the full extent of the transformation was not entirely grasped even by Marx: the last in this line of thinkers and in some ways the greatest of them all.

It is natural to experience some regret that the socialist movement should have emerged into the light of day without an adequate conception of its own role; natural but also a trifle foolish. For a movement, like an individual, cannot discount in advance the circumstances that are going to shape it, the setbacks it is going to suffer, the lessons it is going to learn. Above all, it cannot from the start comprehend its relationship to earlier generations of men who have lived and thought, and passed their experience on to their descendants. The principle that men make their history under definite conditions, imposed upon them by their surroundings and by the structure of their society, holds good for us all, including those of us who believe that acceptance of this truth paradoxically offers a means of evading its full consequences. Freedom is indeed the recognition of necessity—if that term is understood to signify that we are never free to make a completely fresh start. What we can do is to distinguish between those features of reality that are unalterable and the variables whose alteration makes it possible to extend the boundaries of human freedom.

Notes

Notes to the Introduction

1. In French literature the term *"socialisme"* made its first known appearance in print on February 13, 1832, in the Saint-Simonian periodical *Le Globe,* then edited by Pierre Leroux. Some years earlier, in November 1827, the *Co-operative Magazine,* founded by Robert Owen's followers in England, had already employed the word "socialist" to designate adherence to Owen's doctrine. The latter implied that industrial wealth should be owned not individually but in common, on a cooperative basis, and those who held this view were styled "Communionists" or "Socialists" by the *Co-operative Magazine.* While it is uncertain whether the concept originated in France or in England, early English socialism was generally impregnated with French notions. It is worth observing that Saint-Simon's French followers in the 1830's were more concerned with collective regulation of industry than with cooperative ownership of wealth: there was thus from the start an ambiguity in the use of the term. See G. D. H. Cole, *A History of Socialist Thought,* Vol I, *The Forerunners: 1789–1850* (London, 1955), pp. 1–10; M. Beer, *A History of British Socialism* (London, 1953), I, 185 ff.; and Alexander Gray, *The Socialist Tradition* (London, 1963), pp. 197 ff.

2. For the interplay of the French Revolution and the industrial revolution, see E. J. Hobsbawm, *The Age of Revolution: Europe 1789–1848* (London, 1962), Part II, pp. 149 ff.; see the same author's *Industry and Empire* (London, 1968) for the impact of the industrial revolution on British society after 1750. So far as France is concerned, the most comprehensive study of the relevant literature is to be found in H. J. Hunt, *Le Socialisme et le romantisme en France* (Oxford, 1935). For the general history of the early socialist movement in France and its connection with prerevolutionary radical and Rousseauist currents, see J. L. Talmon, *Political Messianism: The Romantic Phase* (London and New York, 1960), *passim.* For biographies of Turgot, Condorcet, Saint-Simon, Fourier, and Comte and analytical treatment of their doctrines, see Frank E. Manuel, *The Prophets of Paris* (Cambridge, Mass., 1962), *passim.* A good brief account of the link between French radical democracy and the early socialist movement is to be found in Arthur Rosenberg, *Democracy and Socialism* (New York, 1939). The advent of the industrial revolution in Britain and the formation of the early labor movement are impressively

described in E. P. Thompson, *The Making of the English Working Class* (London, 1964).

3. For the urban and agrarian roots of British democracy in the age of Jacobinism and the early Chartists, see Thompson, *op. cit., passim.* This covers the period down to 1832. For the first stirrings of the industrial working class in England see, in addition to Thompson, E. J. Hobsbawm, *Labouring Men: Studies in the History of Labour* (London, 1964), pp. 5 ff. For the corresponding phenomenon in France see Edouard Dolléans, *Histoire du Mouvement Ouvrier,* Vol. I (Paris, 1947). The French development got under way a generation after the British but was distinguished by greater political awareness. In an account of the labor movement, these differences would have to be gone into. They are an essential aspect of the history of socialism considered in its totality but can be discussed only marginally in a study dealing with the filiation of concepts. For the same reason it is impossible to go into details about radical movements antedating the industrial revolution; see E. J. Hobsbawm, *Primitive Rebels* (Manchester, 1959; New York, 1963). The conservative and Christian socialist currents in France and England prior to 1848 must also be ignored here. They are alluded to in Talmon, *op. cit.,* pp. 229 ff.; Beer, *op. cit.,* I, 271 ff., and Cole, *op. cit.,* pp. 189 ff. For William Godwin, Thomas Paine, Thomas Spence, and the early British democratic radicals generally, see Cole, *op. cit.,* pp. 23 ff.; Beer, *op. cit.,* pp. 106 ff.; and Gray, *op. cit.,* pp. 114 ff. The emancipation of the nascent socialist movement from its agrarian democratic forerunners (Jacobin or populist, depending on circumstances) was a gradual process which in Western Europe was substantially completed in 1848, whereas in Russia it only began at this date and lasted until the 1890's. The statement that socialists were substantially committed to acceptance of the new industrial order does not hold good for Proudhon, but this topic will have to be examined separately.

4. Hobsbawm, *The Age of Revolution,* pp. 209 ff. The term "working class" (as distinct from the looser and more general "the working classes") makes its first appearance in England shortly after 1815, while its French equivalent dates from about 1830. The English term clearly reflects the infiltration of what has been called "Jacobin consciousness." The political upheaval in France in the 1790's impinged upon a rudimentary proletarian movement in England which was ahead of its French counterpart in the measure that Britain was industrially more advanced. Conversely, the methods of the democratic struggle for the franchise in and after 1830 (political rallies, newspaper campaigns, pamphlet distribution, demonstrations, etc.) stemmed from the British politics of the later eighteenth century and in turn helped to mold the character of the emerging labor and social-democratic movement. See George Rudé, *The Crowd in the French Revolution* (Oxford, 1959), *passim;* and the same author's *Revolutionary Europe: 1783–1815* (Cleveland, 1964) and *The Crowd in History: 1730–1848* (New York, 1964), *passim.*

Eighteenth-century Britain was significantly freer than the Continent, in that popular movements possessed recognized outlets, if they did not conflict seriously with the interests of the ruling class. Dissident members of the latter might even on occasion work up a popular clamor against the parliamentary oligarchy, thus preparing the way for the gradual democratization of the system. But there was also a good deal of reactionary "mob oratory," as there always is. It is just as well to remember that in 1780 the populace of London distinguished itself by a furious outburst of anti-Catholic violence, the so-called Gordon riots. It was the same "Church and King mob" that in July 1791 (with the tacit connivance of the Tory magistrates) rioted in Birmingham against the very moderate, and very bourgeois, pro-French liberals headed by the eminent scientist and Unitarian minister Joseph Priestley. The notion that the working class is invariably in the van of progress belongs to the realm of fantasy.

5. R. H. Tawney, *Religion and the Rise of Capitalism* (London, 1926; 2d. ed., 1937, reprinted 1961), pp. 271 ff. The presence of individual Christians (or for that matter Buddhists, or adherents of other faiths) in a socialist movement is clearly a different matter from the assertion that such a movement is inherently Christian (or Buddhist)—whatever such a claim may signify. Historically, the Christian Church has accommodated itself to every conceivable social system, from the slave empires of antiquity, via the feudalism of the Middle Ages, to modern capitalism. There is no obvious reason why religion cannot co-exist with a socialist order (though on the Marxian assumption it will presumably dwindle away under full communism, along with other "alienations"). But this is evidently something different from the assertion that Christianity as such possesses a socialist bias or that socialism is in some sense a secularization of Christian values. It is only the acceptance of some such claim that entitles a writer, or a school of thought, to be styled "Christian socialist." For an example one might cite Tawney, *op. cit.,* p. 280: "Compromise is as impossible between the Church of Christ and the idolatry of wealth, which is the practical religion of capitalist societies, as it was between the Church and the State idolatry of the Roman Empire." Whether or not one regards this as a sensible observation, it is certainly expressive of what may be termed a Christian socialist outlook. From the historian's viewpoint it has to be noted that, unlike the Roman Empire, contemporary civilization has shown itself remarkably tolerant of Christianity, though not perhaps very eager to live up to its other-worldly precepts.

6. Tawney, *op. cit.,* p. 48:

The medieval theorist condemned as a sin precisely that effort to achieve a continuous and unlimited increase in material wealth which modern societies applaud as meritorious. . . . The essence of the argument was that payment may properly be demanded by the craftsmen who make the goods, or by the merchants who transport them, for both labour in their vocation and service the common need. The unpardonable sin is that of the speculator or the middleman who snatches private gain by the exploitation of private necessities. The true descendant of the doctrines of Aquinas is the labour theory of value. The last of the Schoolmen was Karl Marx.

This seems questionable. The labor theory of value distinguishes between the production of material wealth and the creation of exchange value, but this distinction differs from the medieval doctrine. What both have in common is the belief that the expenditure of human physical energy (labor) constitutes a unique cost element and thus demands a remuneration proportionate to the effort involved, as distinct from the economic benefit to the purchaser.

7. For the problem of Christian ethics in relation to social morality, see Alasdair MacIntyre, *A Short History of Ethics* (New York, 1966), pp. 110 ff. The principal difficulty (as the author does not fail to point out) arises from the fact that religious morality has shown a remarkable talent for accommodating itself to different forms of social life. Early Christianity represented an ethic of otherworldliness for a brief interim period before the inauguration of the Messianic kingdom, while medieval Christendom was thoroughly integrated into the feudal order. The egalitarian bias remained, and it was precisely the modern age which brought it to the surface. "In fact, the distinctive values of equality, and of the criteria of need which Christianity in large part begot, could not possibly commend themselves as general values for human life until it began to appear possible for the basic material inequalities of human life to be abolished." *Ibid.*, p. 115.

There are three comments to be made upon this important statement. First, the doctrine that all men are created equal is of Stoic origin and has no Biblical foundation. While this need not trouble Roman Catholics overmuch, it raises a difficulty for Protestants. Secondly, the millenarian sects of the later Middle Ages who kept alive something of the primitive ascetic morality of the early Christian community received no mercy from the Church. See Norman Cohn, *The Pursuit of the Millennium* (London, 1957), *passim.* Thirdly, what is sometimes (by Roman Catholics) termed the "anti-capitalist" bias of certain modern papal pronouncements—e.g., *Rerum novarum* (1891) or *Quadragesimo anno* (1931)—is better described as an appeal for a more equitable share-out. In all such pronouncements, "capital" and "labor" figure as equal partners, which is indeed not orthodox liberalism but not socialism either. When Leo XIII in *Rerum novarum* affirmed that capital could not subsist without labor nor labor without capital (*non res sine opera nec sine re potest opera consistere*), he was stating a doctrine which could seem alarming only to the most benighted employers in Latin countries. He also by implication accepted the notion that means of production necessarily assume the form of "capital," which was just what socialists were concerned to disprove, even if they did not define "capital" precisely in the Marxian sense. In these respects, *Mater et Magistra* (1961) represented a cautious accommodation to what might perhaps be termed a "Christian socialist" standpoint.

8. For a polemical and rather unsatisfactory discussion of this topic, see Gray, *op. cit.,* pp. 76 ff. For Rousseau's relationship to the radical egalitarians of his age (principally Mably and Morelly), see J. L. Talmon, *The Origins of Totalitarian Democracy* (London, 1952; New York, 1961), pp. 38 ff. The most thorough and enlightening analysis of this complex subject known to the present writer is by Iring Fetscher, *Rousseaus Politische Philosophie* (Neuwied, 1960), where the humanist and democratic core of Rousseau's doctrine is clearly differentiated from later accretions. The French standard work is Robert Derathé, *Le rationalisme de J.-J. Rousseau* (Paris, 1948). See also the article on Rousseau in Vol. XII of the *International Encyclopedia of the Social Sciences* (1968 edition), pp. 563 ff., where both the works and the supplementary bibliography are listed. Students curious to pursue this theme will do well not to neglect the corresponding entries in the Encyclopedia under the headings "Aquinas," "Aristotle," and "Natural Law." They may also find matter for rumination in Joseph A. Schumpeter's *History of Economic Analysis* (New York, 1954), Chap. 2, "The Scholastic Doctors and the Philosophers of Natural Law," pp. 73 ff., where Rousseau, Morelly, and Mably are briefly discussed under the sub-heading "The Semi-Socialist Writers." It is arguable that all three are better described as pre-socialists, but the point cannot be pursued here. What matters in our context is the link between the Scholastic tradition (itself rooted, at least partly, in Aristotle) and that strand of Natural Law doctrine which at a later date made it possible for the early socialists to look back to Rousseau as a critic of at least one aspect of bourgeois society: its indifference to certain permanent and authentic human needs which had been satisfied in earlier and more primitive times. None of this implies that Rousseau was a socialist in the modern sense. Neither does it imply that the labor theory of value can be deduced from the Thomist concern with the doctrine of the "just price." The latter does emphasize production cost rather than demand, and it also preserves the Aristotelian distinction between "use value" and "exchange value" which later recurs in Smith, Ricardo, and Marx, and which enthusiasts for "free enterprise" and the market economy have always found so tiresome. But this does not suffice to turn it into an exploitation theory in the Marxian sense. For the difference, see Schumpeter, *op. cit.,* pp. 588 ff.

9. For the Natural Law derivation of utilitarianism, see Schumpeter, *op. cit.,* pp. 130 ff. There is no point in pretending that Jeremy Bentham (1748–1832) was an original mind, but his influence has been immense, not least in fathering the intellectual tradition which eventually culminated in the Fabian school of socialism. Since this development falls out-

side the range of our survey, the circumstance is simply noted. Bentham of course held that the only interest an individual can be relied upon to consult is his own, and this conviction (itself inherited from David Hume and the Scottish philosophers in general) made him the oracle of English liberalism between 1820 and 1850, when that ideology took the shape it has retained until the present day. But it was only necessary for Robert Owen to apply the Benthamite pleasure-pain calculus to men in general (as distinct from owners of private property) for the first English socialists to be armed with a propagandist weapon which, for rhetorical purposes anyhow, proved irresistible. For the rest, the utilitarians held that legislation ought to be based upon a proper understanding of "human nature." What was this if not Natural Law in a new form? The principal difference, compared to the medieval doctors on the one hand and the Romantics on the other, lay in the fact that the Benthamite pleasure-pain calculus was supposed to embrace not merely the inferior order of current daily business, but human existence as a whole. Trite and shallow though it undoubtedly was, this doctrine did represent something like a coherent philosophy of life. That is to say, it supplied an answer to the question: what is man's nature, and what sort of politico-social order is best adapted to this nature? The reply the utilitarians gave to this question was not that which Rousseau had given, and it differed in decisive respects from both the French and the German doctrines of early socialism; but by and large it satisfied the first generation of British socialists (and their Fabian successors later in the century). This is all that needs to be said here. We are not concerned with Bentham and his system. Its analysis can safely be left to people who are by nature disposed to operate at this particular level of ratiocination.

10. MacIntyre, *op. cit.,* pp. 182 ff.; Franz Neumann, *The Democratic and the Authoritarian State* (Glencoe, Ill., 1957), pp. 22 ff. While not a communist in the technical sense, Rousseau in his projected Corsican constitution made room for an extensive socialization of property which conflicted with his favorable estimate of the small independent property-owner in other passages of his voluminous writings. "Far from desiring that the state be poor, I prefer on the contrary that it should possess everything and that individuals share in the common wealth only in proportion to their services." (C. E. Vaughan, ed., *The Political Writings of Rousseau* [Cambridge, 1915], II, 337.) The "state" here is the idealized polis of classical antiquity, not the modern despotic or bureaucratic state. This has not prevented some contemporary critics of Rousseau from holding him responsible for totalitarian doctrines he would have abhorred. In actual fact, the distinction between state and society hardly exists for Rousseau, which is one reason why his Jacobin followers were unable to make his doctrines work in practice: he and they were imprisoned in the cult of antiquity, with its superstitious belief in the omnipotence and omnicompetence of an all-wise legislator. This is the side of Rousseauism against which both the liberals and Hegel reacted, though for different reasons: the liberals because they

wanted as little interference with private initiative as possible, Hegel because, although he placed the state above society, he had no use for the "state of nature" as a model for the actual state. The German philosopher closest to Rousseau in the domain of moral philosophy was Kant, in that he too did not believe that the "ought" can be derived from the "is," that is to say, from things as they are. But Kant had no substantive social philosophy: the "general will" for him is merely the sum of individual wills. See Neumann, "Types of Natural Law," in *op. cit.,* pp. 69 ff.; MacIntyre, *op. cit.,* pp. 190 ff.

PART ONE

HEIRS OF THE FRENCH REVOLUTION

Chapter 1: The Egalitarians

1. For a brief introduction to the subject, see G. D. H. Cole, *A History of Socialist Thought,* Vol. I, *The Forerunners, 1789–1850* (London, 1955), pp. 11–22. For a critical account of utopian communist literature see Talmon, *Political Messianism: The Romantic Phase* (London and New York, 1960), pp. 157–76. The principal sources are Victor Advielle, *Histoire de Gracchus Babeuf et du babouvisme* (Paris, 1884); Georges Morange, *Les Idées Communistes dans les sociétés secrètes et dans la presse sous la Monarchie de Juillet* (Paris, 1905); Maxime Leroy, *Histoire des idées sociales en France* (Paris, 1950; 2d ed., 1962), Vol. II, *De Babeuf à Tocqueville,* especially pp. 55 ff.; Maurice Dommanget, *Babeuf et la conjuration des Égaux* (Paris, 1922); *Les Idées politiques et sociales d'Auguste Blanqui* (Paris, 1957); Alan B. Spitzer, *The Revolutionary Theories of Louis Auguste Blanqui* (New York, 1957). Standard works on the Revolution itself include Georges Lefebvre, *La Révolution française* (2d rev. ed., Paris, 1957), and *Études sur la Révolution française* (Paris, 1963), and *Napoléon* (5th rev. ed., Paris, 1965); to which Jacques Godechot, *La Contre-Révolution 1789–1804* (Paris, 1961) might be added. The Rousseauist sources of early French communism are discussed in Leroy, *op. cit.,* Vol. I, *De Montesquieu à Robespierre* (Paris, 1946), especially pp. 154 ff., where the question is raised whether Rousseau's condemnation of private ownership as the source of all social evil (in the *Discours sur l'Inégalité* of 1755) was intended by its author in the sense later given to it by Sylvain Maréchal in his *Manifeste des Égaux,* the only coherent manifesto of the Babouvist sect before the attempted rising of 1796. For details, see Albert Soboul, ed., *Babeuf et les problèmes du Babouvisme* (Paris, 1963), *passim.*

2. For the Abbé Meslier, see Leroy, *op. cit.,* I, 238 ff. This mysterious figure (even the dates of his birth and death are uncertain, although he probably died around 1730) is among the precursors of utopian French communism. Babeuf's associate Sylvain Maréchal in 1789 published the so-called *Catéchisme du curé Meslier,* but some extracts from his religious writings had already been edited by Voltaire in 1762, and a further selection was published by Holbach in 1772. A full text of Meslier's *Testament* appeared in Amsterdam in 1864, edited by Rudolph Charles.

3. The Abbé Bonnot de Mably (1709–85) was another contemporary of Rousseau with a hankering for a Spartan form of government, conceived as the rule of austere equality. See Talmon, *The Origins of Totalitarian Democracy* (London, 1952), pp. 50 ff.; Leroy, *op. cit.,* I, *passim.* The notion that private property (specifically in land) is the original source of all social inequality is one that Mably shares with Rousseau, though the latter's utterances on the subject are better known; see Mably, *Doutes proposés aux philosophes économistes sur l'ordre naturel et essentiel des sociétés politiques* (Paris, 1768). Unlike the physiocratic school, which favored agriculture but had no desire to tamper with private ownership, Mably is an early forerunner of the "free land" doctrine, in the sense that he attacked the monopolization of the soil by private owners. This need not have made him a communist, but he also assailed private property in general, although he did not advocate its abolition once it had come into existence. For Mably's odd synthesis of Catholicism and rationalism, see Talmon, *The Origins of Totalitarian Democracy,* p. 55. Unlike Rousseau, who was fundamentally an optimist about human nature (and thus failed to explain why men had ever abandoned their original state of harmony), Mably seems to have retained the notion that this fall from grace was in some sense due to the workings of original sin. Nonetheless he also held that society could be purified and reformed, if not exactly brought back to its primitive innocence. This intermingling of pessimism about human nature and qualified optimism about the future is very typical of one branch of the French Enlightenment, which after all had to make its way within a Catholic culture. The more determinedly rationalist and humanist strain is represented by writers like Diderot and Helvétius and by their political pupils, e.g., the Girondist politician J. P. Brissot de Warville (1754–93), whose *Recherches philosophiques sur le droit de propriété et sur le vol* (1780) anticipated by sixty years the slogan later made famous by Proudhon: *la propriété c'est le vol.* So far from being Proudhon's discovery, this was an eighteenth-century commonplace on which Rousseau, Brissot, and Mably were in full agreement, although they did not think there was much that could be done about it in practice.

4. Morelly's *Code de la nature* (1755, at first erroneously attributed to Diderot) probably had more influence on the radical egalitarians of the 1790's than the writings of Mably, but it is noteworthy that his admirers under the *ancien régime* also included the Marquis d'Argenson, a former

minister of Louis XV. Morelly may have been the first to give currency to the basic idea of collectivism, the notion that social equality must rest on common ownership of wealth and central regulation of all productive labor. He had of course been anticipated by Thomas More and Tommaso Campanella, but he was less of a pure utopian and more of a practical legislator. See Talmon, *The Origins of Totalitarian Democracy,* pp. 52–54, and Leroy, *op. cit.,* I, 243 ff.

5. The revolt of 1795–96 against the Directory united left-wing Jacobins (that is, Robespierrist followers of Rousseau) and the "communist" adherents of Babeuf. In the later development of the radical movement, these tendencies went separate ways. After 1830 the terms Babouvism and communism were employed as synonyms, for by then it was generally accepted that Babeuf had aimed at some form of common ownership. For the bourgeois republicans who backed the Directory in its struggle against radical tendencies in 1796–97, the terms "communism" and "anarchism" seem to have signified much the same thing: principally disregard for private property, or even the general confiscation of all wealth belonging to the bourgeoisie. See Leroy, *op. cit.,* II, 80.

6. In the confusion of the moment this was easily overlooked. Hébert, Chaumette, and other radicals (all guillotined at Robespierre's instigation in 1794) had pushed their clamor for a massacre of the rich, and confiscation of their property, to such an extreme that they might easily pass for primitive communists; and indeed they were so described by Michelet in the preface to his *Histoire de la Révolution* (Paris, 1868). Buonarroti, likewise, in his account of the Babouvist conspiracy, for all his loyalty to the cult of Robespierre, treats these extremists as forerunners of the post-Restoration sects.

7. There would also have been no distinction between government and the governed, at any rate if the advice of Sylvain Maréchal had been followed. The *Manifeste des Égaux* is not altogether specific on this point, but in his other writings Maréchal comes forward as an anarchist, for whom even a Republique des Égaux was only a stepping-stone to the stateless order of the future. When on trial for his life in 1797, Babeuf understandably minimized these notions, but in private he too seems to have identified communism with anarchism, i.e., the absence of any form of political power, however democratic. See Maurice Dommanget, "Les Égaux et la Constitution de 1793," in Soboul, *op. cit.,* pp. 98–99; also Dommanget's *Sylvain Maréchal* (Paris, 1950), *passim.*

8. Georges Lefebvre, "Les Origines du communisme de Babeuf," in *Études sur la Révolution française,* pp. 415 ff.; and J. Suratteau, "Les Babouvistes, le péril rouge et le Directoire (1796–1798)," in Soboul, *op. cit.,* pp. 147 ff. The Babouvists were in effect the radical wing of a "united front" combining former Robespierrists, surviving Hébertists, and a handful of genuine "communists," in common opposition to the republican Directory (whose five members figured prominently on the list of those

to be eliminated). At the trial in 1797, the chief accusation against Babeuf related to these terrorist designs and to his plans for restoring the Constitution of 1793, rather than to speculative notions about common ownership. This did not prevent Jaurès, more than a century later, from claiming him as a forerunner, on the grounds that his conception of democracy was already implicitly socialist. See Jean Jaurès, *Histoire socialiste de la Révolution française*, rev. ed. by Albert Mathiez (Paris, 1922–24), VIII, 179. But then Jaurès also cites Chaumette's proposal (made in October 1793) to requisition factories so as to overcome the failure of the merchants to observe official price regulations. (*Ibid.*, pp. 271 ff.) This was hardly intended as more than a crisis measure and in any case was never adopted, but it can perhaps be regarded as an early manifestation of socialist principles.

9. Maurice Dommanget, *Pages choisies de Babeuf* (Paris, 1935), esp. pp. 207–221, 250–65.

10. See Nos. 34 and 35 of his journal *Le Tribun du Peuple*, published in 1796; Dommanget, *Pages choisies;* and Lefebvre's comment in *Études*, pp. 423–25. Babeuf's position on the *loi agraire* was complicated by tactical considerations, since the notion was at once very popular and highly subversive, but on the whole he seems to have regarded it as impractical. In his *Cadastre perpétuel* of 1787, i.e., before the outbreak of the Revolution, he had suggested that land might be owned communally though worked individually. Does this make him a communist in the modern sense? It is difficult to say. Statements suggesting that the land belongs to all and that all have an equal right to its fruits are too vague to permit a conclusion.

11. See Samuel Bernstein, *Buonarroti* (Paris, 1949); Armando Saitta, *Filippo Buonarroti* (Rome, 1951); and Paul Robiquet, *Buonarroti et la Secte des Égaux* (Paris, 1910). The primary source for Buonarroti's link with Babouvism in his own account of the matter, *Conspiration pour l'Égalité, dite de Babeuf, suivie du procès auquel elle donna lieu et des pièces justificatives,* first published in two volumes in Brussels in 1828; it was reprinted in Paris after the July Revolution of 1830 (and again in 1850 and 1862); it was translated into English by the Chartist leader Bronterre O'Brien and appeared in London in 1836. For Buonarroti's links with Blanqui see Spitzer, *op. cit.,* pp. 126 ff.; for his involvement with Freemasonry and the Carbonari see E. J. Hobsbawm, *Primitive Rebels* (Manchester, 1959; New York, 1963), pp. 164 ff. Buonarroti was *inter alia* the dominant figure of a secret society known as the Sublime Perfect Masters (perhaps a fusion of two Masonic groups, the Adelfi and the Filadelfi), to which Italian Carbonari, French Republicans, German Tugendbuendler, and Russian "Decembrists" are thought to have adhered in the 1820's. This was part of the conspiratorial underworld of the post-Napoleonic age and had no inherent connection with communism. Both Blanqui and Mazzini had links with these societies, notably the Carbonari.

12. Édouard Dolléans, *Histoire du mouvement ouvrier* (Paris, 1947), I, 175 ff.; see also Maurice Dommanget, "Buonarroti et Blanqui," in Soboul, *op. cit.,* pp. 241 ff. The Société des Saisons, founded by Blanqui and Barbès in 1837, still had the character of a ritual brotherhood—ulti- mately a medieval heritage, conserved also by the Carbonari and the other secret societies in the 1830's and 1840's. The distinction between these creeds remained fluid for some time. In the Société des Droits de l'Homme, active in the 1830's, some sections were named after Babeuf and Buonar- roti, but the transition from democracy to communism was a gradual affair. According to Étienne Cabet, it occurred largely in the prisons of the July Monarchy, where middle-class republicans made the acquaintance of revolutionary workers for whom the Babouvist tradition formed a bridge to the secret societies. Leroy, *op. cit.,* II, 458.

Chapter 2: The Utopians

1. Jean Charles Léonard Simonde de Sismondi (1773–1842) is per- haps a borderline case, in that, if not a socialist, he was certainly a critic of liberal economics. His major work, *Nouveaux principes d'économie politique: Ou, de la richesse dans ses rapports avec la population* (Geneva, 1819) was aimed at David Ricardo and J. B. Say, the French apostle of Adam Smith and the Manchester school. Previously Sismondi had been an ad- herent of Smith, but the spectacle of pauperism in Britain (where after 1815 he spent some time) shocked him and made him wonder whether liberal economics was really compatible with the welfare of the poor. He thought competition would gradually give way to monopoly; also that economic crises (which he attributed to lack of purchasing power) would get worse and lead to general pauperization. On these grounds, Elie Halévy, in his *Histoire du socialisme européen* (Paris, 1948), has claimed him for the socialist school (pp. 48 ff.). But if worry about under-consumption constitutes socialism, how is one to classify Constantin Pecqueur, who in 1839 advocated state control of all means of communication yet, unlike Sismondi, took an optimistic view of the industrial future? In this he re- sembled Saint-Simon, generally regarded as the fountainhead of socialist doctrine in France. For details of Sismondi's work, see Joseph Schumpeter, *History of Economic Analysis* (New York, 1954), pp. 493 ff. On Lamen- nais, see H. J. Hunt, *Le Socialisme et le romantisme en France* (Oxford, 1935), *passim;* and Maxime Leroy, *Histoire des idées sociales en France,* Vol. II, *De Babeuf à Tocqueville* (Paris, 1950; 2d ed., 1962), *passim.* On Philippe Buchez, another "Christian socialist" in the France of the July Monarchy, see Halévy, *op. cit.,* pp. 62–63; and Hunt, *op. cit.,* pp. 83 ff. and *passim.*

2. For details, see G. D. H. Cole, *A History of Socialist Thought,* Vol. I, *The Forerunners, 1789–1850* (London, 1955), pp. 75 ff.; Hunt, *op. cit.,* pp.

161–63, 245–46; Leroy, *op. cit.,* pp. 415 ff.; and Carl Landauer, *European Socialism: A History of Ideas and Movements from the Industrial Revolution to Hitler's Seizure of Power* (Berkeley, Calif., 1959), I, 41 ff. For the Icarian experiments in America, see T. D. Seymour Bassett's article in D. D. Egbert and Stow Persons, eds., *Socialism and American Life* (Princeton, 1952), I, 155 ff., where the link with Owenism is stressed. Cabet has some affinities with Wilhelm Weitling, the German apostle of primitive communism in the 1830's and 1840's, but his political outlook, modified by his studies in England and his acquaintance with Owen's ideas, forms part of the radical egalitarian stream released by the French Revolution. It is fair to say that he had few original notions of his own, being an organizer rather than a theorist, but *Voyage en Icarie* nonetheless counts among the classics of communist literature. For sources on Icaria, see the detailed bibliography in Egbert and Persons, *op. cit.,* II, 137 ff. For a biography of Cabet see Jules Prudhommeaux, *Icarie et son fondateur Etienne Cabet* (Paris, 1907). That Cabet believed himself to be in the Jacobin tradition would appear to be obvious from a passage in his writings (quoted by Prudhommeaux, p. 121) where he asserts "The doctrine of true equality and community was . . . the doctrine . . . of Robespierre, of Saint-Just . . . of Buonarroti, before it was that of Babeuf." In general Cabet tends to praise the Jacobins for their (largely verbal) egalitarian sentiments, while deploring the crudities of the Babouvists and their terroristic utterances, which in his opinion had frightened the bourgeoisie and driven it into the arms of Bonaparte. He was most decidedly not in favor of bloody violence, yet he was a thorough-going authoritarian when it came to the constitution of his Icaria. In France he tended to moderation and disclaimed any intention to interpret democracy as "the oppressive rule of the most laboriously toiling . . . class over the richer classes; I mean by democracy the principle of fraternity and equality without exclusion or oppression of anyone." (Landauer, *op. cit.,* p. 42.) Nonetheless Engels, in his preface to the 1888 English-language edition of the *Communist Manifesto,* unhesitatingly numbers Cabet with Weitling among the proponents of what he describes as "Utopian Communism," while classing Owen and Fourier among the "Socialists." He goes on to say: "Thus, Socialism was, in 1847, a middle-class movement, Communism a working-class movement. Socialism was, on the Continent at least, respectable; Communism was the very opposite." Cabet had a working-class following in France, while Fourierism attracted the intelligentsia, and this association of "communism" with the proletariat accounts for the title chosen by Marx and Engels for their *Manifesto.* Needless to say, they had no use for Icarianism. What they liked about Cabet was his commitment to the egalitarian tradition, which indeed reflected working-class sentiment, although by social origin Cabet was no more proletarian than the reformist socialists of the period.

3. In their *German Ideology* (1845–46), Marx and Engels exercised their wit at the expense of the then fashionable attempt to make communism

seem respectable by claiming the ancestry of celebrated writers who, in the traditional manner, had thundered against the worship of riches. At the same time, however, they expressed a favorable opinion of Cabet's work, albeit with some qualifications. For Marx's critique of primitive egalitarianism, see Karl Marx, *Economic and Philosophic Manuscripts of 1844*, ed., Dirk J. Struik (New York, 1964), pp. 132 ff. What Marx here describes as "crude" and "thoughtless" communism is plainly the Babouvist doctrine, insofar as it was then known to him from his first-hand studies and impressions in Paris. What French working-class communists in the 1840's regarded as true egalitarianism (half a century after Babeuf, but at the height of Cabet's popularity) may be inferred from Marx's animadversions upon crudities such as negation of culture (i.e., intellectual differentiation) or "the community of women"—neither of these, it is fair to say, advocated by Babeuf or Buonarroti. Marx may have been thinking of Maréchal's *Manifeste des Égaux,* which contained exclamatory phrases such as "Let all the arts perish, if need be, provided true equality be attained!" But this never became Babouvist doctrine, though it may have confirmed the more primitive members of the sect in their naïve materialism. It is not altogether clear where Marx obtained the notion that "this as yet completely crude and thoughtless communism" advocated "the community of women, in which a woman becomes a piece of communal and common property," a notion he denounced as "universal prostitution," just as in the same text he condemned general levelling and "the abstract negation of the entire world of culture and civilization." (*Ibid.,* p. 133.) Cabet can hardly be said to have been responsible for such notions, but Marx may have felt that he was implicitly giving currency to them by failing to counteract the implications of primitive working-class Babouvism. At a higher intellectual level, there was an approach toward what would today be called "free love" and the dissolution of marriage in Théodore Dézamy's *Code de la Communauté* (Paris, 1842), but since Marx elsewhere expressed a favorable opinion of Dézamy, he cannot have been referring to his proposals.

4. A brief but incisive account of Fourier's career is to be found in Frank E. Manuel, *The Prophets of Paris* (Cambridge, Mass., 1962), pp. 197 ff. Manuel's bibliographical notes (pp. 334–37) should satisfy the most exhaustive curiosity. There is no point in reproducing them here, but it may be noted that Hubert Bourgin, *Fourier* (Paris, 1905); Charles Gide, *Fourier précurseur de la coopération* (Paris, 1922–23); and Celestin Bouglé, *Socialismes français* (Paris, 1932), are the main secondary sources. The principal German work on the early socialist tradition, Thilo Ramm, *Die Grossen Sozialisten als Rechts- und Sozialphilosophen* (Stuttgart, 1955), has a chapter on Fourier, and the bibliography (pp. 315–17) lists a selection of international literature on Fourierism (mainly French and German) from 1839 to 1946. The subject is briefly discussed in Cole, *op. cit.,* I, 62 ff. On the Fourierist experiments in the United States, see

Egbert and Persons, *op. cit.,* I, 173 ff.; II, 132 ff. There is a summary account of Fourier and his school in Landauer, *op. cit.,* I, 35 ff. On Victor Considérant, who continued the Fourierist tradition, see Leroy, *op. cit.,* II, *passim;* and J. L. Talmon, *Political Messianism: The Romantic Phase* (London and New York, 1960), pp. 134 ff., 529 ff. The American branch of the movement achieved some popular success through the propagandist activity of Albert Brisbane and Horace Greeley, whose colleague Charles Dana appointed Marx as London correspondent of their journal, the New York *Tribune.* Fourierist influence extended to most Western countries before 1848 but dwindled thereafter, though in France the school continued to have a small following down to 1870.

5. For the best general discussion of the utopian tradition in French socialist thought, see Georges Duveau, *Sociologie de l'Utopie et autres essais* (Paris, 1961) who *inter alia* places Fourier's eccentricities within a broader context. For his role as an early proponent of sexual freedom and life-enhancement in general, see Norman O. Brown, *Life Against Death* (New York, 1959), pp. 34 ff. and *passim.* The notion that, in a future social order, work can and will be transformed into play goes back to Fourier, though in this as in other respects he ran too far ahead of the actual material circumstances of his time to make an immediate impact on the emerging socialist consciousness. For the influence of his moral libertarianism on Marx, see *The Holy Family* (1845), which is full of Fourierist sentiment, notably in the critical passages dealing with Eugène Sue's then very popular novel, the *Mystères de Paris.* Marx particularly disliked Sue's moralism, though he lauded those of his figures in whom an emerging, post-Christian and nonbourgeois, humanist and life-affirming attitude had been briefly concretized. For a discussion of this theme, see Pierre Naville, *De l'Aliénation à la jouissance* (Paris, 1957), pp. 161 ff.

6. See Friedrich Engels, *Socialism: Utopian and Scientific,* in *Marx-Engels Selected Works* (Moscow, 1951), II, 113–14. In addition to praising him as a social satirist, Engels also credits him with the discovery that civilization (i.e., bourgeois society, the last of the four historical stages recognized by Fourier) exhibits internal contradictions which it reproduces without being able to solve them, and thus moves in a vicious circle. On these grounds Engels suggests that Fourier "uses the dialectic[al] method in the same masterly way as his contemporary Hegel." This is perhaps going rather far. One may surmise that Marx would have been more restrained. Engels likewise sees considerable merit in the fact that Fourier "introduced into historical science [the idea] of the ultimate destruction of the human race." Fourier's grounds for doing so are, however, rather different from Engels' own addiction to a variant of the ancient cosmological myth that makes universal creation and destruction alternate in cycles.

7. Talmon, *Political Messianism,* p. 127, notes Fourier's belief (itself a development of Rousseau's famous statement: "Tout était bien, sortant des mains de l'auteur des choses; tout dégénéra entre les mains de l'homme.")

that man's estate displayed an original harmony so long as the passions had not been thwarted by coercive social and moral institutions. The task of the future lay in reconstituting this harmony at a higher level. "Le génie devait retrouver les voies de ce bonheur primitiv et l'appliquer à la grande industrie." For a similar suggestion by the early Marx, see *Das philosophische Manifest der historischen Rechtsschule* (1842), where Marx comments on the eighteenth-century belief in the superior wisdom and virtue of primitive people, adding: "All such eccentricities rested on the correct notion that crude conditions are, as it were, naïve Dutch paintings of *true* conditions." See Karl Marx–Friedrich Engels, *Werke* (Berlin, 1961), I, 78.

8. Alexander Gray, *The Socialist Tradition* (London, 1963), p. 174. The author is unsympathetic to Fourier (and to socialism in general), but even so his account of the matter is rather heavily weighted on the side of cosmogonic fantasy. The reader would hardly infer that Fourier had something to say about the link between cultural history and education. However, this lack is more than balanced by Gray's detailed description of Fourier's weird system of cosmic harmonies, not to mention his forecast of the coming transformation of the oceans into lemonade, the emergence of anti-lions, anti-rats, and anti-bugs (to replace the noxious creatures now in existence), and his views on the supposed connection between the orbits of the planets and the genesis of various animals and herbs. There is also a fairly circumstantial account of Fourier's analysis of the passions (pp. 175 ff.).

9. Manuel, *op. cit.*, p. 199. Proudhon, like Fourier a native of Besançon, was born in 1809 and became a printer in 1826, so the work he typeset must have been the 1829 version of the *Théorie* (published under the title *Le Nouveau monde industriel*), from which the eccentric cosmogony of 1808 had sensibly been omitted.

10. Thereby incurring the censure of Jenny Marx (*née* von Westphalen) who refused to entertain his women friends, even when they had become his life-long companions. It was perhaps the only point on which Engels was more radical than Marx, who in this domain adhered fairly closely to bourgeois convention.

11. Gray, *op. cit.*, pp. 189 ff.; Manuel, *op. cit.*, pp. 215 ff.; Hunt, *op. cit.*, pp. 121 ff. Most of Fourier's animadversions on the institution of bourgeois marriage are set out in his *Traité de l'association domestique-agricole* (1822; see *Oeuvres Complètes* [Paris, 1841–45], Vol. II) and *Théorie de l'unité universelle* (*Oeuvres Complètes*, Vol. IV). The organization of the phalanstery is touched on in various places, down to *Le Nouveau monde industriel et sociétaire* (1829; see *Oeuvres Complètes*, Vol. VI), perhaps the least eccentric of his writings. No genuine phalanstery was ever quite literally modeled on his prescriptions, but some of the Jewish communal settlements in Palestine-Israel may be described as approximations. For the Fourierist settlements in America, see above, note 4. For a brief outline of the proposed model, see Manuel, *op. cit.*, pp. 224 ff. For the literary off-

shoots of Fourierism (including Eugène Sue), see Hunt, pp. 143 ff., where
the romantic cult of the fallen woman is traced to its Fourierist source.
Speaking generally, the Fourierist streak in women writers like George
Sand and Flora Tristan is an aspect of that alliance between socialism,
romanticism, and feminism which became a reality in the 1840's.

12. Historians have noted that, for all his Rousseauism, Fourier is not
hostile to technical progress as such or indifferent to the contribution industry and science can make toward lessening the burden of toil. He is also
reconciled to the general notion of progress. "It is Nature's wish that
barbarism should tend toward civilization and attain to it by degrees; tHat
civilization should tend toward guarantism [*garantisme*], that guarantism
should tend toward . . . association." (*Le Nouveau monde industriel,* in
Oeuvres Complètes, VI, 418; cited by Landauer, *op. cit.,* I, 1031.) To the
extent that Fourier believes that in the final "harmonist" stage of association, the need for a central authority will disappear and people will cooperate freely in phalangist communes, he sounds the anarchist note, which
is indeed inherent in all forms of Rousseauism. But he is careful to specify
that this desirable goal cannot be attained by a simple return to primitive
conditions or by doing without the arts and sciences.

13. *Théorie des quatre mouvements* (1808; see *Oeuvres Complètes,* I,
195). For Marx's view of the subject, see the *Paris Manuscripts of 1844,*
and *The Holy Family* (1845), where Fourier's remarks are approvingly
cited (chap. VIII). Marx gave an additional dimension to Fourier's idea
that the emancipation of woman is an index of general emancipation, in
the sense of the gradual overcoming of primitive brutality. The assumption
here is that the subjection of woman was originally due to her physical
weakness, but this is qualified by the suggestion that the specific form of
modern oppression is a consequence of private property leading to monog-
amy. In the *Paris Manuscripts* these notions are not clearly distinguished;
see "Private Property and Communism," in Karl Marx, *Early Writings,* ed.,
T. B. Bottomore (London and New York, 1964), pp. 152 ff.

14. This is an aspect of a subject which would be worth pursuing in a
different context: that of pre-1848 European romanticism in general. A
typology of this influential movement could hardly fail to stress the
curious family resemblance linking Charles Fourier with some contemporary German literary figures of whom assuredly he was quite unaware,
e.g., Jean Paul (Johann Paul Friedrich Richter) and E. T. A. Hoffmann,
both characteristically the inventors of a form of grotesque fantasy that
would have found additional nourishment in Fourier's weird cosmogony.
Again, Fourier's "law of universal attraction," which by a happy coincidence governs both the passions and the planets, has evident affinities
with the biological speculations of those German romantics who tried to
refute Newton and Descartes (Schelling is a case in point). In this context it is immaterial that Fourier had a high regard for Newton. Consider,
e.g., his analysis of the human passions (the basic instinctual drives) which

—like the signs of the Zodiac, the Olympian gods, and the Apostles—were exactly twelve in number! This was the sort of thing contemporary German disciples of Hamann, Swedenborg, and Böhme would have found to their liking. What in the end connects them all is the organismic model: the vision of human society on the analogy of a natural entity, preferably a tree. The tree of course is the tree of life, and the repression of the instincts, which unhappily constitutes the basis of civilization, is synonymous with man's expulsion from Eden. In this regard the romantics and Fourier anticipated some of the discoveries of modern psychology.

Chapter 3: The Saint-Simonians

1. The literature on Saint-Simonism, if less overwhelming than that on Marxism, is still bulky enough to daunt all but the specialists. It ranges from the forty-seven volumes of the *Oeuvres de Saint-Simon et d'Enfantin* (Paris, 1865–78; new ed., reprinted from the original with an introduction by A. Pereire, 1925) to a more recent edition of Saint-Simon's writings alone, a six-volume collection published by Editions Anthropos under the title *Oeuvres de Saint-Simon* (Paris, 1966), which includes a volume of previously unpublished texts while ignoring Enfantin, the disciple who in the first edition had come to overshadow the master. Such earlier compilations as the three-volume selection made by Lemonnier, *Oeuvres choisies de C. H. Saint-Simon* (Brussels, 1859), have now been relegated to the status of bibliographical curiosities. Jean Dautry's *Saint-Simon: Textes choisis* (Paris, 1951) comprised excerpts from manuscripts unpublished at the time which can now be consulted in the 1966 edition.

The standard introduction to the history of the school is Sébastien Charléty, *Histoire du Saint-Simonisme* (Paris, 1931). For the first presentation of Saint-Simonian doctrine (as distinct from Saint-Simon's own writings), see the *Exposition de la Doctrine de Saint-Simon,* originally published by his disciples in 1830 and 1831 (new ed. with introduction and notes by Celestin Bouglé and Elie Halévy, Paris, 1924). Bouglé's *L'Oeuvre d'Henri de Saint-Simon* (Paris, 1925) is an anthology of extracts. For a biography of Saint-Simon, see Maxime Leroy, *La Vie véritable du Comte Henri de Saint-Simon* (Paris, 1925). Henri Gouhier, *La Jeunesse d'Auguste Comte* (Paris, 1933–41), Vol. III, gives an account of Comte's relations with Saint-Simon.

Critical and historical discussions of Saint-Simonism as a movement and a doctrine are numerous, ranging from Emile Durkheim's *Le Socialisme, sa définition, ses débuts, la doctrine saint-simonienne* (Paris, 1928) to Georges Gurvitch's brief but pregnant discussion of the subject in *Les Fondateurs français de la sociologie contemporaine* (Paris, 1955), a lecture course in the series "Les cours de la Sorbonne." See also Maxime Leroy, *Histoire des idées sociales en France,* Vol. II, *De Babeuf à Tocqueville* (Paris, 1950;

2d ed., 1962), pp. 324 ff.; Georges Duveau, *Sociologie de l'Utopie* (Paris, 1961), *passim;* Elie Halévy, *Histoire du socialisme européen* (Paris, 1948), pp. 54 ff. For the fusion of Saint-Simonism and romanticism, see H. J. Hunt, *Le Socialisme et le romantisme en France* (Oxford, 1935), pp. 10 ff. For the influence of Saint-Simonism on German literature since the 1830's see E. M. Butler, *The Saint-Simonian Religion in Germany* (Cambridge, 1926). For a thoroughly hostile account of Saint-Simonism and of the French socialist tradition in general, see F. A. Hayek, *The Counter-Revolution of Science* (New York, 1955). The Messianic and theocratic aspects of Saint-Simonism are extensively discussed in J. L. Talmon, *Political Messianism: The Romantic Phase* (London and New York, 1960), pp. 35 ff. The most useful general English-language study of the subject is Frank E. Manuel, *The New World of Henri Saint-Simon* (Cambridge, Mass., 1956). For a briefer introduction, see the same author's *The Prophets of Paris* (Cambridge, Mass., 1962), pp. 103 ff.; also G. D. H. Cole, *A History of Socialist Thought,* Vol. I, *The Forerunners, 1789–1850* (London, 1955), pp. 37 ff. For a scholarly German discussion of the topic see Thilo Ramm, *Die Grossen Sozialisten als Rechts- und Sozialphilosophen* (Stuttgart, 1955), pp. 210 ff.; the author supplies an extensive bibliography. The Saint-Simonian school continued in existence until about 1870, and a list of its principal writings would burst the bounds of this survey. For a brief note on Pierre Leroux, see Cole, *op. cit.,* p. 320. For an interesting comment on Michel Chevalier, see Joseph Schumpeter, *History of Economic Analysis* (New York, 1954), pp. 496–97 n.; also Hayek, *op. cit.,* pp. 146–55. The spread of Saint-Simonism in the 1830's was indirectly promoted by the American writer and traveler Albert Brisbane, then not yet a Fourierist, from whom German sympathizers first learned of Saint-Simon (Hayek, *op. cit.,* p. 160). For Brisbane's Fourierist activities, see D. D. Egbert and Stow Persons, eds., *Socialism and American Life* (Princeton, 1952), II, 133 ff., which supplies an extensive critical bibliography compiled by T. D. Seymour Bassett and also gives many biographical data.

2. See Manuel, *The Prophets of Paris,* pp. 105 ff.; Hayek, *op. cit.,* pp. 117 ff.; and Alexander Gray, *The Socialist Tradition* (London, 1963), pp. 136 ff. There is no space for detail about Saint-Simon's early writings, but one may note in passing that the *Lettres d'un habitant de Genève* proposed the creation of a "Council of Newton" (composed of twenty-one eminent scientists and artists) to take over the government of the world—eliminating both the churches and the philosophers, whom Saint-Simon regarded as useless metaphysicians. Apart from being a manifestation of the Voltairean cult of Newton, this was an interesting anticipation of Comte's scientism. A celebrated passage in the *Lettres* already foreshadows much of the later doctrine: "All men will work; they will regard themselves as laborers attached to one workshop whose efforts will be directed to guide human intelligence according to my divine foresight. The supreme Council of Newton will direct their works." See *Oeuvres de Saint-Simon et d'Enfantin*

(new ed.), XV, 55 (as cited by Hayek, *op. cit.*, p. 121). This is followed by a passage discreetly omitted from the first edition of the *Oeuvres* but found in Pereire's separate 1925 edition of the *Lettres* and quoted by Hayek: "Anyone who does not obey the orders will be treated by the others as a quadruped." Illiberal sentiments of this kind, though frequent in Saint-Simon, hardly warrant the suggestion that he looked forward to the age of concentration camps. In his writings of the years 1807–8, when he lived in Paris under straitened circumstances, the Council of Newton assumes a less extravagant shape: it becomes the editorial committee of a new Encyclopedia which is to unify and systematize all knowledge. For some reason, the *Introduction aux travaux scientifiques du XIXe siècle,* where this quite sensible proposal occurs for the first time, was not included in the *Oeuvres* of 1865–78, though it appears in the *Oeuvres choisies* of 1859. See Hayek, *op. cit.*, pp. 122, 227.

3. For the above, see the writings of his later period, notably *L'Industrie* (1816–18), *L'Organisateur* (1819–20); *Du système industriel* (1821–22), and the *Catéchisme des industriels* (1823–24). These were periodical publications issued at irregular intervals, in part edited or even written by Auguste Comte (who broke with Saint-Simon in 1824) and subsequently included in the various editions of Saint-Simon's collected works. For the quarrel between Saint-Simon and Comte, see Manuel, *The Prophets of Paris,* pp. 251–60. The precise extent of Comte's participation in the jointly edited productions of these years has never been made clear. What is certain is that the two men had no serious differences about the "industrial system," and that Comte, then and later, was wholly opposed to public ownership (though authoritarian enough in his own fashion). If anything, Saint-Simon was the more liberal of the two, as he was certainly less respectful of organized religion. Comte therefore cannot rank among the precursors of socialism, though attempts have inevitably been made to enlist him, on the grounds that some of his doctrines anticipated what later became known as "state socialism" or "national socialism" in Germany (see Hayek, pp. 183–84). Comte's distaste for democracy clearly removes him from the central stream of the socialist tradition. As Hayek himself notes, Comte adopted and made his own the political philosophy of L. G. Bonald, the theorist of the Catholic counterrevolution. His denigration of individualism anticipates the "organicist" ideology of writers like Othmar Spann, and has affinities with the Italian, Spanish, and Austrian varieties of fascism. There is no space here to deal with Comte's sociology or with the influence exercised by his disciples. In general it may be said that, depending on the prevailing intellectual climate, they tended to be politically liberal (e.g., in England), populist (in Russia), or authoritarian (as in Brazil, where Comte achieved the distinction of being officially recognized as the author of the national motto "Order and Progress").

4. See Manuel, *The Prophets of Paris,* pp. 111–13; Hayek, *op. cit.*, pp. 129–32; Gray, *op. cit.*, pp. 151–53. For the text of the "Parabole" (1819),

see *L'Organisateur,* in *Oeuvres choisies* (1859), Vol. II. The parable that drew the wrath of the authorities was by no means the most important piece of writing published in *L'Organisateur*. From a theoretical viewpoint it was less significant than Saint-Simon's (or Comte's) sketch of a new political system. This would dispense with an elected parliament, such as France now possessed under the Charter of 1814, and instead be based on three corporate bodies: a *chambre d'invention* of 200 engineers plus 100 artists (poets, painters, writers, sculptors, architects, and musicians); a *chambre d'examination* of 300 mathematicians, physicists, and biologists; and a *chambre d'exécution,* or executive body made up of leading bankers and industrialists, who would have the final say. The reorganization of the laws, so as to render them "most favorable to production," was to be entrusted to these three assemblies. It is not altogether clear why this modest proposal should have frightened the eminent bankers and economists who had backed Saint-Simon, but memories of the Revolution and the Napoleonic regime were still fresh, and they may have sensed an authoritarian undertone. To their timid minds, the "Parabole" and Saint-Simon's trial in 1820 merely confirmed his already established reputation as a dangerous firebrand.

5. For details see Leroy, *op. cit.,* II, 206 ff. Saint-Simon seems to have coined the term *industriel* in 1817, as a noun replacing the familiar *industrieux,* the latter denoting a disposition rather than a social category. The distinction is significant. Did he also invent the concept of "individualism"? Not long after his death in 1825, the word made its appearance in the journal edited by his followers, *Le Producteur.* What is certain is that after 1830 Leroux gave currency to the term "socialism." The implications of the doctrine unveiled themselves only gradually. Talk of founding "le système social le plus avantageux à la production" was too vague and general to lend itself to any interpretation other than that already hinted at in the "Parabole": namely, that people useless from the standpoint of industrial production were to be classed as "fainéants" (do-nothings). This need not have alarmed the industrial bourgeoisie, but quite clearly the only groups likely to feel directly flattered would be engineers and scientists. Under the Napoleonic regime one of Saint-Simon's few patrons had been Lazare Carnot, the Republic's "organizer of victory" in 1793–96 and an engineer by profession. (It was thanks to him that Saint-Simon was briefly employed in 1815, during the Hundred Days.) Engineers and scientists were to become important in the spread of Saint-Simonism after 1830, but in his own lifetime it was the bankers who mattered, and he had managed to alarm them. As Leroy puts it, "Saint-Simon a repoussé la formule: respect à la propriété et aux propriétaires, la remplaçant par celle-ci: respect à la production et aux producteurs." Production was what counted. No wonder the Restoration bankers thought him dangerous.

6. For the above quotations, see the *Catéchisme des industriels* in Rodrigues, ed., *Oeuvres de Saint-Simon* (Paris, 1841). See also the sketch

of the future society in one of Saint-Simon's last writings (drafted in cooperation with the poet Léon Halévy, the physiologist Bailly, the lawyer Duveyrier, and other members of the school), *Opinions littéraires, philosophiques et industriels* (Paris, 1825), where he goes into some detail about the ruling triumvirate he hoped to see established: "L'artiste, le savant et l'industriel."

In contradistinction to Saint-Simon, and to the Saint-Simonians who had turned to the proletariat, Comte (in his *Cours de philosophie positive* of 1830–42) developed a different perspective: that of a stable hierarchical order in which an elite drawn impartially from all social classes would govern in the interest of the majority, but without abolishing social differences and privileges distinguishing the various strata. He too looked forward to the disappearance of social conflict, but this was to come about by way of state regulation harmonizing the interests of entrepreneurs and workers. All social activities would be organized as public services, with rights and (particularly) duties attached to them. These conclusions were derived from what Comte regarded as a dispassionate analysis of the tendencies inherent in the social system. Sociology and socialism may thus be said to have emerged simultaneously from the dissolution of the Saint-Simonian school. For an incisive analysis of Comte's contribution to sociology, see Raymond Aron, *Les étapes de la pensée sociologique* (Paris, 1967), pp. 79 ff.; cf. *Main Currents in Sociological Thought* (New York and London, 1965) for an abbreviated version, not including the lengthy and important Notes appended to the French text. The same applies to the sections dealing with Montesquieu, Tocqueville, and Marx.

7. Hayek, p. 165. For a different view see Schumpeter, *op. cit.,* p. 462. The Pereires and their associates financed railway construction in Austria, Switzerland, Spain, and Russia, "employing as engineers on the spot other Saint-Simonians to carry out their directions," to cite Hayek (p. 166). It is likewise of interest that Enfantin eventually became a railway director and helped to construct the system linking Paris with the Mediterranean. Schumpeter's suggestion that, with or without Saint-Simonism, the Crédit Mobilier would "have been founded and managed exactly as it was" stands at the opposite extreme from Hayek's belief that Saint-Simonism was instrumental in pioneering the Continental type of finance capitalism, i.e., the close interpenetration of industry and banks. This feature was certainly absent in England, but was the difference due to the spread of Saint-Simonism or, rather, to the different tempo of industrialization and the need for larger agglomerations of capital? There was also on the Continent, notably in France, a tradition of state intervention in the economy which had no roots in England. (On this point see Andrew Shonfield, *Modern Capitalism* [London and New York, 1965], esp. pp. 71 ff.) Saint-Simonism fitted easily into this background, but the long-run consequences of exposure to Saint-Simonian ideas could also work in the liberal direction, as may be seen from the Cobden-Chevalier treaty. It simply is not

possible to identify Saint-Simonism with one school rather than the other. At most it can be said that former Saint-Simonians were prominent in the middle years of the century over a wide range of activities designed to speed the rate of industrial progress. It was industrialism, not liberalism or socialism, that mattered to them. (Equally, it is quite irrelevant that Emile and Isaac Pereire were Jews—as were Olinde and Eugène Rodrigues, both among the earliest and most faithful disciples of the master. The fact has some cultural significance against the general background of French society in the nineteenth century, but it does not concern the historian of socialism. Talmon, *op. cit.*, pp. 77 ff.)

8. *Système industriel*. See Hayek, *op. cit.*, citing *Oeuvres de Saint-Simon et d'Enfantin*, XXII, 257–58.

9. For *Le Producteur* and the *Exposition*, see Hayek, *op. cit.*, pp. 143 ff.; Cole, *op. cit.*, I, 31 ff. For Rodrigues, Enfantin, and the Messianic strain, see Talmon, *op. cit.*, pp. 70 ff., and Hunt, *op. cit.*, pp. 50 ff. The principal figure in the early phase of the movement was Saint-Amand Bazard (1791–1832), a founder of the Charbonnerie, whose early death deprived the group of its best intellect, while confirming the ascendancy of Barthélemy-Prosper Enfantin (1796–1864), the future *Père Suprème* and effective gravedigger of Saint-Simonism, The son of a banker, Enfantin (like Comte and Considérant) had attended the Ecole Polytechnique but did not complete the course. While his mystical eroticism, which eventually brought the sect into conflict with the authorities, can hardly be blamed on his training as an engineer, he was largely instrumental in making Saint-Simonism synonymous with scientism and the cult of technology. A number of *polytechniciens* joined the movement in his wake, notably Abel Transon and Jules Lechevalier, both of whom afterward became Fourierists (Lechevalier having in 1829–30 attended Hegel's lectures in Berlin). Other important recruits between 1826 and 1829 included Michel Chevalier, Henri Fournel, and Hippolyte Carnot, son of the great Lazare Carnot and brother of the famous physicist Sadi Carnot. (For a time before 1829 the Paris apartment of the Carnots was the meeting-place of the group.) For the role of the *polytechniciens* in the spread of scientist and socialist ideas see Hayek, *op. cit.*, pp. 105 ff., 143 ff. The lectures of 1828–30, later assembled in the *Exposition*, were delivered publicly. For their texts see *Doctrine de Saint-Simon, Exposition, Première Année* (Paris, 1830); *Deuxième Année* (Paris, 1831). New ed., with introduction and notes by Celestin Bouglé and Elie Halévy, in *Collection des Économistes et réformateurs français* (Paris, 1924).

10. Bouglé and Halévy, eds., *Exposition*, pp. 243 ff., 253 ff.

11. Abel Transon, *De la religion Saint-Simonienne: Aux Elèves de l'École Polytechnique*. First published in the (second) *Organisateur* (July–September, 1829) and later appended to some editions of the *Exposition*.

12. For *Le Producteur* and the (second) *Organisateur*, see Hunt, *op. cit.*, pp. 21 ff. The original editors of *Le Producteur* included A. Cerclet, who

at one time had been associated with the Nestor of revolutionary conspiracy, Buonarroti. His departure marked the beginning of the later split dividing liberals from socialists. In 1825–26 the line of division was rather between rationalists and romanticists, with Comte and Cerclet heading the former and Rodrigues (later joined by Enfantin and Barrault) the latter. Not all the future socialists were romantics or religious mystics, but it is relevant that a new prospectus of May 1826 (issued by Enfantin, Bazard, and Buchez, after the departure of Comte and Cerclet) abandoned positivist scientism in favor of a more comprehensive and philanthropic humanism. Cerclet eventually became editor of the bourgeois-republican organ, the *National,* which down to 1848 carried on a two-front war against the Orleanist regime on the one hand and the socialists on the other. In the 1820's these future dissensions were still hidden behind philosophical disputations over the respective roles of science and the humanities.

13. Bouglé and Halévy, eds., *Exposition,* p. 255.

14. *Ibid.,* p. 261.

15. *Ibid.,* pp. 272–73.

16. Manuel, *The Prophets of Paris,* pp. 151 ff.; Hunt, *op. cit.,* pp. 37 ff.; Talmon, *op. cit.,* pp. 75 ff. For details see Charléty, *Histoire du Saint-Simonisme.* Since Saint-Simon himself was a free-thinker, in other words a secularist (despite the title *Le Nouveau Christianisme,* the message of which, after all, had been that religion must become worldly), the conversion of his school into a religious sect could only be effected by splitting it and thus obliging the rationalists to withdraw. Hence the schism at the end of 1831, when Leroux, Carnot, Bazard, Lechevalier, and others seceded, to be followed shortly by Rodrigues. It was after their departure that Enfantin and Barrault launched their campaign of moral (that is, erotic) liberation which eventually landed the principal members of the sect in jail. (For this climax, and the preceding episode of Ménilmontant, when the Saint-Simonians tried to practice their doctrine by engaging in physical labor, while briefly enforcing celibacy after publicly preaching something close to free love, see Manuel, *ibid.,* pp. 185 ff.; Hunt, *op. cit.,* pp. 71 ff.; Leroy, II, 362 ff.) The public trial and condemnation of Enfantin and his associates in August 1832 had the effect of discrediting the sect in the eyes of the respectable bourgeoisie, but it also gained them new sympathies among the semi-proletarian art world then beginning to form in and around Paris. For the rest it resulted in the departure of Michel Chevalier, the group's chief organizer and fund-raiser, thus striking a heavy blow at their activities. *Le Globe* had already closed down in April 1832, not long after Joncières (another apostle of liberation) had alarmed his fellow-editors by delivering an open apology of incest. (Hunt, *op. cit.,* p. 70.) For the association of Sainte-Beuve with the *Globe* in its earlier, semi-socialist, semi-romantic phase, and the general theme of Byronism and literary romanticism in France during the late 1820's and early 1830's, see Hunt, *op. cit.,* pp. 37 ff.

17. The relevant facts can be briefly stated. Carnot and Leroux, both former editors of the *Globe,* abandoned Saint-Simonism at the close of 1831 and launched the *Revue encyclopédique,* whose general orientation remained socialist but without the specific coloration given to Saint-Simonism by Enfantin. Buchez, formerly one of the editors of the *Producteur,* had already broken with Enfantin and Bazard at the end of 1830. Among the Saint-Simonians a struggle for supremacy then ensued between Bazard and Enfantin. A compromise, installing Bazard as *chef du dogme,* Rodrigues as *chef du culte,* and Enfantin as *Père Suprême,* broke down, and by the end of 1831 Bazard seceded, shortly followed by Rodrigues. The split had been provoked by Enfantin's and Barrault's campaign for the emancipation of the flesh and by Enfantin's discovery that the new Church needed a *Mère* as well as a *Père.* Since Bazard was married, this revelation would by itself have been enough to wreck the cooperation between the two *Pères,* Mme. Bazard not being a suitable candidate for the position of *Mère Suprême.* The schism was followed by the episode of the withdrawal to Ménilmontant, where Enfantin (now sole *Père*) and his followers labored the ground but did not otherwise seek to mortify the flesh. Enfantin, Chevalier, and Duveyrier were put on trial in August 1832, on charges of political subversion and moral impropriety, ending with a collective sentence of one year in prison. Later, the sect split up, some of its members following Barrault's lead in searching for the *Mère* in Turkey, while Enfantin led the faithful remnant to Egypt, with the object of uniting East and West by a canal through the Isthmus of Suez—an undertaking intended to symbolize, among other things, the spiritual union of the Supreme Father (the West) and the Supreme Mother (the East).

Enfantin's later career included business enterprises in Algeria (recently become a French colony) and a project for Franco-Arab cooperation (once more to promote the union of Orient and Occident). Back in France he resumed his Suez Canal project, but was shouldered aside by Ferdinand de Lesseps who had earlier joined the Saint-Simonians in Egypt. Enfantin later turned to the promotion of railway building, ending his days as a director of the Paris-Lyon-Marseilles line. Despite his somewhat checkered career he remained faithful to Saint-Simonism, his last writings—*La Science de l'homme* (1858) and *La Vie éternelle* (1861)—still expounding the original gospel. His death in 1864 removed one of the last survivors of the original group. A man of great energy and considerable charm, Enfantin exercised a magnetic hold over his followers and by all accounts was entirely sincere, though possibly somewhat deranged. He must unfortunately take the prime responsibility for the split of 1831–32 which separated the more intellectual socialists from the religious and erotic mystics. (His works are embedded in the forty-seven-volume *Oeuvres de Saint-Simon et d'Enfantin.* See also Sébastien Charléty, *Enfantin* [Paris, 1931], which presents some selections. For a brief account of the decay of Saint-Simonism see Cole, *op. cit.,* I, 53 ff.; Talmon, *op. cit.,* pp. 108 ff.; Hunt, *op. cit.,* pp. 94 ff.)

18. *Exposition,* pp. 235 ff. "Voilà le droit nouveau qui remplace celui de la conquête et de la naissance: l'homme n'exploite plus l'homme, mais l'homme associé à l'homme exploite le monde livré à sa puissance. . . . Nous sommes arrivés à cette conclusion que l'avenir vers lequel [l'espèce humaine] s'avance est un état ou toutes les forces seront combinés dans la direction pacifique." In their lighter moments the members of the school were not above parodying these famous utterances. Thus on October 30, 1830, Enfantin informed Chevalier of the coming transformation of Leroux' *Globe* into a socialist organ in these terms: "Saint-Simon te dit par ma bouche qu'à l'exploitation de l'homme par l'homme doit succéder l'exploitation du *Globe.*" Hunt, *op. cit.,* p. 46.

19. The Pereire brothers, Chevalier, and de Lesseps have already been mentioned. In general, the "Saint-Simonism of the Ecole Polytechnique" accommodated itself easily enough to the reign of Napoleon III, himself a former sympathizer, though hardly an effective ally once he was installed in power. It was indeed during his reign that the "technocratic" and "managerial" aspects of Saint-Simonism fully revealed themselves. Significantly, the school did not survive the collapse of the Empire and the inauguration of the Third Republic in 1871.

20. For a detailed account of the literary scene between 1830 and 1848, see Hunt, *op. cit.,* esp. pp. 108 ff. It was largely due to George Sand that socialist influences became dominant among advanced literary circles in the 1840's. At a lower level, Eugène Sue was quite effective, although Marx was severely critical of his sentimentalism. Victor Hugo, torn between his romantic, Fourierist leanings and his liberal (or Orléanist) inclinations, was a less reliable ally, while Sainte-Beuve, once an associate of Enfantin, gravitated steadily toward liberalism and bourgeois conformism. Balzac remained resolutely hostile to the socialists (contrary to Hayek's assertion, *op. cit.,* p. 157), and on a celebrated occasion in 1847 almost came to blows with Sue when the subject came up at a dinner party arranged by Heinrich Heine. The sequel included an attack on Balzac in the Fourierist journal *La Démocratie pacifique,* culminating in the prediction that as a novelist he would soon be forgotten. This turned out to be a notable misjudgment. It also had no effect on Marx, who continued to regard Balzac as a critic of capitalism *malgré lui.* (Hunt, *op. cit.,* pp. 213–16.) Among composers, Franz Liszt was a frequent attendant of the early Saint-Simonian gatherings, and Berlioz composed his *Chant d'Inauguration des chemins de fer* with the intention of setting Saint-Simonism (as he understood it) to music. On the whole, the Romantics were divided in their sympathies between Byronism, i.e., individualism, and the new socialist creed, but for a while both tendencies went together—notably among feminists like Sand for whom socialism was a vehicle of personal emancipation. (Hunt, *op. cit.,* pp. 339 ff.)

21. Manuel, *The Prophets of Paris*, p. 157. It is well to bear in mind that the Saint-Simonians were among the first European thinkers to reject the Christian dichotomy of spirit and flesh. Saint-Simon himself had already pointed the way, but it was his disciples who said in so many words that the sexes were equal, that sexual desires were legitimate, and that their fulfillment was a necessary condition of human self-emancipation. They thus at one blow rid themselves of two deeply ingrained perversions: the ascetic degradation of the flesh, and its Nemesis, the despairing cynicism and Satanism of libertines like Sade. It was an immense and long overdue liberation, and for the sake of it one may well forgive them their absurdities: e.g., Enfantin's doctrine that God's nature is androgynous, and the consequent resolve of his disciples to die with the words *"père-mère"* on their lips. Manuel, *The Prophets of Paris*, p. 164.

Chapter 4: The Socialism of the 1840's

1. The history of ideas during this period is traced in Vols. II and III of Maxime Leroy, *Histoire des idées sociales en France* (Paris, 1950; 2d ed., 1962). The respective subtitles, *De Babeuf à Tocqueville* and *D'Auguste Comte à P. J. Proudhon,* fail to do justice to the originality of an enterprise which also covers the intellectual history of liberalism and Catholicism. The reader should not, however, expect a systematic presentation of the ideas of, e.g., Lamennais, Buchez, Leroux, or Proudhon. He is more likely to find stimulus for further thought than detailed exegesis. The internal relationship of romanticism and socialism during this period is discussed by H. J. Hunt, *Le Socialisme et le romantisme en France* (Oxford, 1935), *passim.* Anyone curious to know what Balzac, Victor Hugo, George Sand, Michelet, Flaubert, Comte, and others made of the 1848 upheaval and its sequel, the Bonapartist dictatorship, may profitably divide his time between Leroy and Hunt. For Tocqueville there exists a first-hand source in his *Souvenirs,* composed in 1850–51, first published in 1893, republished in 1942, and more recently re-issued in a new edition with a useful introduction and notes (Paris, 1964). Remarkable for their acid pen-portraits of Louis Philippe, Guizot, Thiers, Lamartine, Louis Blanc, Buchez, Blanqui, and Louis Bonaparte, the *Souvenirs* are also distinguished for a brutally realistic analysis of the 1848 revolution in terms of class conflict between bourgeoisie and proletariat, the author quite consciously treating the events of June 1848 as a civil war comparable to the bloodbaths of the later Roman Republic. Tocqueville's open partisanship and his Ciceronian style (the effect of which is lost in translation) make the *Souvenirs* required reading for anyone trying to understand the mentality of the "Party of Order" and the spiritual lineage of French conservatism. But all this belongs to the political history of the period and has no direct relationship to our theme, save in so far as Tocqueville treats the Orléanist regime as

the political caretaker of the bourgeoisie—a class he despised. In this respect, however, he did not anticipate Marx (as has sometimes been suggested), for the bourgeois nature of the regime was generally recognized at the time, as was the class character of the June insurrection. See Leroy, *passim*. It is remarkable how rapidly the early socialists grasped the point. Bazard had an interview with the aged Lafayette during the night of July 29–30, 1830, which left him and his friends in no doubt as to the social blindness of the liberals, now at long last installed in power. In a letter dated August 1, 1830, Enfantin drew the appropriate moral: the people had fought on the barricades, but the real victory had gone to the possessing class:

> Qui a vaincu? C'est la classe pauvre, la classe la plus nombreuse, celle des prolétaires . . . le peuple, en un mot. . . . Le peuple n'avait pas de chefs; les bourgeois pouvaient encore dormir en paix. . . . La révolte sainte qui vient de s'opérer ne mérite pas le nom de révolution; rien de fondamental n'est changé dans l'organisation sociale actuelle; quelques noms, des couleurs, le blason national, des titres, quelques modifications législatives . . . telles sont les conquêtes de ces jours de deuil et de gloire.

L'Organisateur, August 15, 1830. See Edouard Dolléans, *Histoire du mouvement ouvrier* (Paris, 1947), I, 44.

2. That the protest movements of the early 1830's were simple starvation riots was recognized by sympathetic observers and occasionally by the employers, who argued that they could not afford to pay a living wage or to reduce the working day (then averaging twelve to fourteen hours). The workers and their leaders at first displayed a good deal of simplicity on this subject, as well as a touching faith in King and Church. However, the government soon took pains to cure them of these illusions. The November 1831 strike movement at Lyon was spontaneous and had no political character, although it led to a clash with the Army and the National Guard. In December the Société des Amis du Peuple, then dominated by old-style Jacobins, published a pamphlet paying homage to the men and women who had assembled at Lyon under black banners bearing the famous inscription "Vivre libres en travaillant ou mourir en combattant." Revolutionary republicanism was still quite distinct from socialism (and a good deal more violent).

By 1834 the illegal workers' corporations, which were beginning to transform themselves into regular trade unions, had in part fallen under republican leadership. The republican secret societies, notably the Société des Droits de l'Homme which organized the Paris insurrection of April 1834, were led by youthful intellectuals with a following of workers, but their aims were democratic rather than specifically socialist. For the savage suppression of these risings by Thiers and Guizot, see Dolléans, *op. cit.,* pp.

105–7. Socialism, as represented by Leroux and Buchez, was still reformist and opposed to violence. Buchez even dreamed of a social transformation under the aegis of the Catholic Church; see Elie Halévy, *Histoire du socialisme européen* (Paris, 1948), p. 62. For the reaction of the intellectual elite to the events of 1830–34, see Leroy, *op. cit.*, II, 402 ff. In general it may be said that the advanced republicans, or some of them, came to socialism by way of democracy, then still a revolutionary creed. The ideological inspiration of the secret societies (and of a "republican socialist" such as Louis Blanc) was Robespierre, whose name had become synonymous with the cult of popular sovereignty. But even moderate republicans were appalled by Guizot's brutal statement in the Chamber of Deputies that the working classes could only be kept under control if they were obliged to labor. Leroy, *op. cit.*, II, 400.

3. Some of the literary sources relevant to Blanquism have already been noted in connection with Babeuf and Buonarroti. For a more comprehensive assortment see the bibliography in Alan B. Spitzer, *The Revolutionary Theories of Louis Auguste Blanqui* (New York, 1957), a useful study that does not exhaust the subject but should satisfy the curiosity of beginners. Maurice Dommanget, *Blanqui* (Paris, 1924) is regarded as authoritative, and the same applies to A. Zévaès, *Auguste Blanqui* (Paris, 1920). Blanqui's own writings appeared for the most part in periodicals during his lifetime. They were partly collected in *Critique sociale* (Paris, 1885) and *Ni Dieu ni maître* (Paris, 1925). On his unpublished manuscripts, see Spitzer, *op. cit.* On the subsequent fortunes of the Blanquist movement, see, *inter alia,* Claude Willard, *Les Guesdistes: Le mouvement socialiste en France (1893–1905)* (Paris, 1965), especially pp. 392 ff. The Blanquist tradition survived the catastrophe of the Paris Commune in 1871 for another three decades before merging completely with the Marxist stream. For some of the later implications of this fusion, see Robert Wohl, *French Communism in the Making* (Stanford, Calif., 1966), pp. 6 ff.

4. On the secret societies, see Dolléans, *op. cit.*, pp. 172–77. The Société des Amis du Peuple launched the Paris insurrection of June 1832, when the republicans for the first time tried to capitalize on working-class unrest (also on Bonapartist sentiments directed against Louis Philippe). Blanqui migrated from this group to Barbès' Société des Familles. Police persecution having resulted in a further transmogrification, the Société des Saisons took over in 1837. Its membership was predominantly working-class and its propaganda plainly Babouvist, i.e., communist. It was this organization which in 1839 very nearly succeeded in seizing the Hotel de Ville and the Police Prefecture in Paris. By 1848, Blanqui and the more moderate Barbès had become enemies. See Spitzer, *op. cit.;* also G. D. H. Cole, *A History of Socialist Thought,* Vol. I, *The Forerunners, 1789–1850* (London, 1955), pp. 158 ff. Democratic republicans adhering to the extreme wing of the Société des Droits de l'Homme transformed themselves

into communists in the prisons of the July Monarchy, where they came into contact with Babouvist proletarians. Dolléans, who makes this point, also refers to a formally constituted Société Communiste founded in 1840. *Op. cit.,* pp. 174–75.

5. Cole, *op. cit.,* I, 158 ff. For a detailed account of Blanqui's general philosophy see Spitzer, *op. cit.,* pp. 28 ff. His thinking has to be reconstructed in part from unpublished manuscripts and partly from scattered journalism and pamphleteering, but the general trend is clear enough. Blanqui was philosophically an amateur and his education was narrowly classicist, but he cannot be described as self-taught. His principal defect as a theorist stems rather from a rigid adherence to the French rationalist tradition; he was only vaguely aware of Feuerbach and other contemporary German materialists.

6. This is not to say that Blanqui's classicism had no political significance: it was related to his militant republican patriotism, which in 1870–71 made him and his followers outstanding among the bitter-enders. The defense of Paris against the besieging German army during that winter brought Blanqui to the forefront, and the fierce spirit he aroused among the National Guard—300,000 men hastily enrolled by the Provisional Government after Sedan and the fall of the Empire—led directly to the great insurrection of March 1871 and the adventure of the Paris Commune. This (like the antecedent reluctance of the Blanquists to join their Proudhonist rivals in the International Workers' Association) was inherent in the peculiar Blanquist fusion of Jacobinism with a primitive form of communism— a fusion destined to have lasting consequences. Blanqui's classicism was an aspect of his republicanism. But it was just this which linked him with neo-Jacobins like Clemenceau.

7. The same applies to their crude antisemitism, their constant railing against the Rothschilds, and their evident conviction that the Jews were, if not wholly responsible for, at any rate unduly prominent in the growth of capitalism, which they identified with banking and finance. In this respect both Proudhon and Blanqui differed from the Saint-Simonians, who welcomed Jewish adherents even if they happened to be bankers (not that Saint-Simon had much use for Judaism as a religion, but this was an attitude he had inherited from Voltaire and the Enlightenment in general). The Proudhonist and Blanquist forms of antisemitism go back to Fourier, whose disciple Toussenel in 1847 published a pamphlet against the financiers prominent during the Orléanist regime under the suggestive title *Les Juifs rois de l'époque.* Blanqui's associate Tridon later distinguished himself with a similar production, and Blanqui himself filled his letters and manuscripts with scattered references to "Jewish usury." This form of socialist antisemitism endured in France until the 1890's, when it was washed away by the Dreyfusist flood. The only interest of Blanqui's contribution to this murky stream lies in the fact that he combined it with a naïve bullion-

ism, i.e., distrust of paper money, and a conviction that the banks were exploiting the producers. This last was not an irrational belief, but too primitive to form the basis of a socialist critique of capitalism. See Spitzer, *op. cit.*, pp. 80 ff.; R. F. Byrnes, *Anti-Semitism in Modern France* (New Brunswick, N.J., 1950); and Edmund Silberner, "The Attitude of the Fourierist School towards the Jews," *Jewish Social Studies*, IX (1947), 339–62. For Marx's attitude on this subject (a topic on which a quite inordinate amount of nonsense has been written), see Solomon F. Bloom, "Karl Marx and the Jews," *Jewish Social Studies*, IV, No. 1 (1942). The theme of socialist antisemitism is treated at greater length in Edmund Silberner, *Sozialisten zur Judenfrage* (Berlin, 1962). See also Helmut Hirsch, "Marxiana judaica," and Roman Rosdolsky, "La Neue Rheinische Zeitung et les Juifs," in *Cahiers de l'Institut de Science Economique Appliquée* (*Etudes de Marxologie*) (Paris), No. 140 (August 1963).

8. Harold Draper, "Marx and the Dictatorship of the Proletariat," *Cahiers de l'Institut de Science Economique Appliquée* (*Etudes de Marxologie*) (Paris), No. 129 (September 1962). The document in question, a programmatic platform for an international Société Universelle des Communistes Révolutionnaires founded (on paper) in April 1850, when Marx was in London, was signed by Marx, Engels, and August Willich for the German Communist League, George Julian Harney for the Chartists, and two Blanquist emissaries named Adam and Vidil. It refers briefly to the need for establishing a "dictatorship of the proletariat" ("dictature des prolétaires") for the purpose of "maintaining the revolution in permanence until the achievement of communism, which is to be the last organizational form of the human family." For the original French text, see Boris Nicolaevsky and Otto Maenchen-Helfen, *Karl Marx: Man and Fighter* (London, 1936); for a German translation, see the official East German edition of the collected (but incomplete) writings of Marx and Engels, *Werke* (Berlin, 1960), VII, 553. The brief alliance between Marx and the Blanquists lasted for only six months, until the Communist League split in September 1850, with the Blanquists backing the Willich-Schapper faction, whereupon Marx dissolved the association he had formed with them. The interest of the document lies in the fact that it introduced the concept of "proletarian dictatorship" into communist literature.

9. For details of her life see Dolléans, *op. cit.*, I, 192–95. J. L. Puech, *La Vie et l'oeuvre de Flora Tristan* (Paris, 1925), is the standard work. It may be worth citing an extract from *l'Union ouvrière* whose spirit prefigures the founding of the First International in 1864:

L'Union ouvrière, procédant au nom de l'Unité universelle, ne doit faire aucune distinction entre les nationaux et les ouvriers et ouvrières appartenant à n'importe quelle nation de la terre. Ainsi pour tout individu, dit étranger, les bénéfices de l'Union seront absolument les mêmes que pour les Français.

For the links between Flora Tristan, George Sand, and the Romantic movement of the 1840's, see Hunt, pp. 262n, 277n, 289n; for a brief summary of the 1843 project, see Cole, *op. cit.,* I, 185–86.

10. For Considérant's political role in 1848, see among others Tocqueville, *Souvenirs,* pp. 155, 180, 219. Though hardly an impartial witness, Tocqueville had the advantage of seeing his antagonist in action. The intensity of the political hatred dividing these two distinguished men finds a distant echo in the *Souvenirs,* with their constant evocation of the days of Jacobin rule, a reminiscence facilitated by the ominous label *Montagnards* which the radical democrats of 1848–49 had pinned to themselves. This hardly accorded with their modest aims and their (on the whole) quite peaceful behavior, but it served to frighten their opponents. For an aristocratic conservative like Tocqueville, Considérant was not merely "l'élève et le successeur de Fourier" (*ibid.,* p. 219), but above all a chief of the self-styled neo-Jacobins. For a more balanced appreciation see Leroy, *op. cit.,* II, *passim.* For the role of Fourierist propaganda after 1836 see Hunt, *op. cit.,* pp. 121 ff.

Considérant's main works (apart from his writings in *Le Phalanstère* and *La Phalange*) are *La Destinée sociale* (Paris, 1835–44); *Principe du socialisme: Manifeste de la démocratie au XIXème siecle* (Paris, 1847); *Le Socialisme devant le vieux monde, ou le vivant devant les morts* (Paris, 1848). The standard biographies are Hubert Bourgin, *Victor Considérant* (Paris, 1909), and Maurice Dommanget, *Victor Considérant, sa vie et son oeuvre* (Paris, 1929). For Considérant's American followers see D. D. Egbert and Stow Persons, eds., *Socialism and American Life* (Princeton, 1952), II, 136–37. Having left France after the failure of the 1848 movement and emigrated to the United States at the invitation of Albert Brisbane, he won the latter's support for a Fourierist experiment at Reunion, near Dallas, which lasted from 1855 to 1875. Its launching involved Considérant in some promotional tracts, e.g., *Au Texas* (Paris, 1854), and *European Colonization in Texas: An Address to the American People* (New York, 1855). Long before the failure of the enterprise Considérant withdrew to San Antonio and later returned to France, where he lived until his death in 1893 at the age of eighty-five.

11. Hunt, *op. cit.,* pp. 150 ff. This orientation had a twofold aspect: sympathy for illness (including mental illness) and the exaltation of morbid tendencies. To the Romantics, the criminal was not merely an outcast, and as such to be pitied, but also an instinctive rebel against a repressive social and moral order. But this was dangerous ground, for if they were to retain their respectability (not to mention the claim to being taken seriously), they had to steer clear of the antinomianism always lurking just below the surface of such attitudes. Satanism was a real and present danger. Lucifer might figure as a mythical embodiment of liberation from an oppressive moral law, but the collapse into moral nihilism was a distinct possibility. This was one reason why socialists like Marx, who were imbued

with the classical tradition, favored the Promethean image, while instinctive rebels against Christianity (like Bakunin and most of the anarchists) reckoned themselves "of the Devil's party."

12. Hunt, *op. cit.*, pp. 261 ff. The European crisis of 1840–41 had its origin in a conflict between France and England. Its later stages involved a chauvinistic campaign in Paris for the re-annexation of the Rhineland, a campaign in which the republican socialists took the lead and which Considérant did his best to resist. Most of the fashionable poets, with Victor Hugo and Alfred de Musset in the lead, supported a war of conquest; the unspoken assumption was that such a war would revive the revolutionary tradition and sweep the Left into power on a wave of nationalist fervor. It was precisely this revival of Jacobin chauvinism which the Fourierists disliked.

13. Considérant, *Exposition abrégée du système phalanstérien de Fourier* (Paris, 1845), pp. 90–91.

14. Considérant, *La Destinée sociale*, p. 2 .

15. Cole, *op. cit.*, I, 177–79; Halévy, *op. cit.*, pp. 62–63. For *L'Européen* and Buchez' other literary and editorial activities, see Hunt, *op. cit.*, pp. 83 ff. and *passim*. Buchez had been among the founders of the Société des Amis du Peuple, and his subsequent adherence to more orthodox politics did not dim his Jacobin fervor. His principal work, the *Histoire parlementaire de la Révolution française* (edited in collaboration with Roux-Lavergne) (Paris, 1834–38), is shot through with tirades against the Girondins, those Voltairean individualists and enemies of national unity whom Robespierre (in Buchez' opinion quite properly) had dispatched to the guillotine. Buchez impartially admired Richelieu, Robespierre, and Napoleon as founders of French national greatness and at the same time combined religious faith with fervent belief in progress, democracy, and popular sovereignty.

16. For details see Cole, *op. cit.*, I, 179–82; Halévy, *op cit.*, pp. 51–54. On Pecqueur's Fourierist phase see Hunt, p. 116n. In 1834 he was one of the editors of Jules Lechevalier's *Revue du progrès social*. Lechevalier, who had become a Fourierist after abandoning Saint-Simonism, was instrumental in launching the first Fourierist journal, the *Réforme industrielle*, also known as the *Phalanstère*. One may therefore surmise that Pecqueur had Fourierist sympathies, but since his first important work, *Économie sociale des intérêts du commerce, de l'industrie et de l'agriculture* . . . (the full title is too lengthy for citation) appeared in 1839, the point is of minor importance. For further information on Pecqueur see Benoît Malon, *Constantin Pecqueur, doyen du collectivisme français* (Paris, 1887). Malon, a survivor of the 1871 Paris Commune, represented what was left of the Proudhonist school after that catastrophe, and his book on Pecqueur was an attempt to show that collectivist socialism was not the invention of Marx, but possessed a respectable French ancestry.

17. For details see Cole, *op. cit.*, I, 168 ff.; Gray, *op. cit.*, pp. 218 ff.

For Blanc's political and journalistic activities in the 1830's and 1840's, see Hunt, *op. cit.,* pp. 165 ff. For his role as a precursor of democratic socialism, see Arthur Rosenberg, *Democracy and Socialism* (New York, 1939), pp. 36 ff. Rosenberg notes that Blanc influenced Ledru-Rollin, the leader of the democratic party (the so-called Montagne) in 1848–49, and that the democrats adopted some of his ideas. In the 1840's their journal, *La Réforme,* combined republican propaganda against Louis Philippe with vaguely socialist proposals inspired by Blanc. The subsequent alliance of the two factions in 1849 gave rise to a phenomenon that caused Marx (then at the height of his commitment to Blanquist communism) some exasperation: "The social and the democratic part[ies], the party of the workers and that of the petty bourgeoisie, united to form the *social-democratic* party, that is, the *Red* party." *Class Struggles in France* (1850), reprinted in *Marx-Engels Selected Works* (Moscow, 1958), I, 191. In this passage (written after the defeat of the revolution) the socialists are treated as representatives of the working-class movement, which was new for Marx and represented a step toward his later position. In the *Manifesto* he had described Proudhon (and by implication Blanc) as a bourgeois socialist, whereas in 1850 he consented to treat them as spokesmen of the workers, though he deplored their political tactics. Rosenberg misstates the issue. For him "Blanc's historical significance lies in the fact that he personified the connexion between revolutionary democracy and socialism, and thus continued successfully the tradition of Babeuf" (p. 36). What Blanc really personified was the fusion of Robespierrist rhetoric and the new reformist socialism. The "republican socialism" of the 1840's was democratic, not Babouvist. Its chief progenitor was Leroux, from whom Blanc had inherited the socialist part of the Saint-Simonian message. See Hunt, *op. cit.,* p. 165.

18. For the events of 1848 see Leroy, *op. cit.,* III, 33 ff.; and Dolléans, *op. cit.,* I, 227 ff. For the conservative viewpoint, see Tocqueville, *op. cit., passim.* Tocqueville, who detested all socialists without exception, gives a characteristically acid account of the *journée* of May 15, when an armed mob tried to storm the Chamber of Deputies, while Blanc attempted to restore calm. His popularity may have saved the lives of a few conservative deputies that day, but he got no thanks for it. The June insurrection was a spontaneous rising provoked by the sudden and savage suppression of unemployment relief—probably with the intention of hastening the inevitable collision between the workers and the Army. Whatever its immediate cause, it ruined Blanc's reputation, apart from obliging him to go into exile, where he was joined a year later by Ledru-Rollin. The panicky middle class saw in the wordy Ledru a reincarnation of the Jacobin terror, but Tocqueville was not taken in by the rhetoric of the new *Montagne,* and his disdain for Ledru-Rollin equaled Marx's contemptuous treatment of the democrats (*op. cit.,* p. 128). Tocqueville and Marx, for different reasons, agreed that the issue in 1848 could only be settled

by force and that men like Blanc and Ledru-Rollin were wasting their breath. For the social-democratic propaganda campaign launched in 1843 by Blanc, Ledru-Rollin, Arago, Flocon, and George Sand in *La Réforme,* see Halévy, *op. cit.,* p. 64. *L'Organisation du travail* first appeared in the republican-socialist journal Blanc had founded in 1839, *La Revue du progrès,* and was published in book form in 1841.

Chapter 5: Proudhon and the Origins of Anarchism

1. Proudhon was a prolific author, and only the best known of his writings can be listed here. Very few have been translated. His most important works are *Qu'est ce que la propriété?* (1840–41); *De la Création de l'Ordre dans l'humanité* (1843); *Système des Contradictions économiques, ou Philosophie de la misère* (1846); *Le Droit au travail et le droit de propriété* (1848); *Les Confessions d'un révolutionnaire* (1849); *Idée générale de la Révolution au XIXème siècle* (1851); *Philosophie du progrès* (1853); *La Révolution sociale démontrée par le coup d'État du 2 décembre* (1852); *De la Justice dans la Révolution et dans l'Église* (1858); *La Guerre et la Paix* (1861); *Du Principe fédératif* (1863); *Théorie de la propriété* (1865); *De la Capacité politique des classes ouvrières* (1865); *Césarisme et Christianisme* (posthumous, 1883); *Jésus et les origines du christianisme* (posthumous, 1896). Proudhon's writings were first collected between 1867 and 1875. A new edition of the *Oeuvres complètes,* begun in 1923 under the joint editorship of Celestin Bouglé and H. Moysset, is not yet finished.

Authoritative critical studies include Édouard Droz, *P.-J. Proudhon* (Paris, 1909); Émile Faguet, *Proudhon* (Paris, 1900); Celestin Bouglé, *La sociologie de Proudhon* (Paris, 1911); Jeanne Duprat, *Proudhon, sociologue et moraliste* (Paris, 1930); Édouard Dolléans, *Proudhon* (Paris, 1941); and Georges Gurvitch, *Proudhon. Sociologue* (Paris, 1955); *Dialectique et sociologie* (Paris, 1962), esp. chap. VII, "La dialectique chez Proudhon"; *Pour le centenaire de la mort de P.-J. Proudhon* (Paris, 1964); and *Proudhon. Sa vie, son oeuvre* (Paris, 1965). See also Georges Sorel, *Matériaux d'une théorie du prolétariat* (Paris, 1926), esp. "Exégèses proudhoniennes"; and Pierre Naville, *De l'Aliénation à la jouissance* (Paris, 1957), esp. chap. VIII, "Les bons et les mauvais côtés." For brief introductions to the subject in English see Cole, *op. cit.,* I, 201 ff.; Gray, *op. cit.,* pp. 230 ff.; James Joll, *The Anarchists* (London and Boston, 1964), pp. 61 ff.; and George Woodcock, *Anarchism* (London, 1963).

2. Gurvitch, *Proudhon. Sa vie, son oeuvre,* pp. 1–4. The two parts of *Qu'est-ce que la propriété?* and the *Avertissement* (1842) were followed by *De la Création de l'Ordre,* in which Proudhon broadened his approach from economics to history and philosophy. It was the subtitle to the

Système des Contradictions économiques—Philosophie de la misère—to which the punning title of Marx's rejoinder related. Marx composed his learned diatribe in French, which he wrote and spoke fluently. For the original text see *Marx-Engels Gesamtausgabe* (Berlin, 1932), Section I, Part 6, 117 ff.: *Misère de la philosophie. Réponse à la philosophie de la misère de M. Proudhon.* See also *The Poverty of Philosophy* (Moscow, 1956); this translation misses the pun and is altogether rather wooden. The American edition (by International Publishers [New York, n.d.]) carries Engels' prefaces to the first and second German editions and a number of appendixes, notably Marx's letter to P. V. Annenkov and one to J. B. Schweitzer of January 24, 1865, in which he undertook a critical estimate of Proudhon's work. The tone of this obituary has occasionally been held against Marx, though the critics have failed to notice that Proudhon was a far more vituperative writer. For a brief analysis of the dispute between the two men, see H. P. Adams, *Karl Marx in his Earlier Writings* (London, 1940, 1965), pp. 183 ff. Proudhon was extremely incensed by Marx's polemic of 1847 and covered the pages of his copy with marginalia (reproduced in the 1923 edition of the *Système des Contradictions*), but he did not reply in print. Whether Marx was unfair to Proudhon in 1847, and whether Proudhon in turn understood Marx's critique, continues to be debated. See Gurvitch, *Proudhon. Sa vie, son oeuvre,* pp. 23 ff.; and Naville, *op. cit.,* pp. 311 ff. Possibly Proudhon was less naïve than he appeared to be, but his standpoint was incompatible with Marx's conviction that the concepts of economic theorizing were, historically speaking, the creation of the bourgeois mind and could not simply be turned around in the hope of extracting socialist conclusions from them. See Engels' preface to the first German edition (1885) of Marx's rejoinder.

3. For details see Gurvitch, *Proudhon. Sa vie, son oeuvre,* pp. 6 ff. Proudhon's quasi-philosophical writings do not enter into consideration here, but one may note that *De la Justice dans la Révolution et dans l'Église* (1858) became the sacred book of the anticlericals. This work, an enormous and rather bizarre compilation, made a deep impression upon the generation of French intellectuals who rose to prominence after 1870 as leaders of the Radical and Socialist parties under the Third Republic. It also gained favorable mention from Marx, who preferred Proudhon's anticlericalism to the mystical religiosity of other French socialists, e.g., Louis Blanc. For Proudhon's diatribes against the Saint-Simonians under Napoleon III see his *Manuel d'un spéculateur à la Bourse* (3d ed., 1857), where he refers to the *féodalité industrielle* (a term invented by Fourier and brought into prominence by Enfantin in his promotional writings on Algerian colonization) as having come into being with the help of the Saint-Simonians. He particularly named the Pereire brothers, with whom he had a personal quarrel. As noted above, a socialist version of antisemitism (the Jews being held specially responsible for the predominance of finance

capital in France) was already established in Proudhon's day and was later inherited by Georges Sorel, who shared Proudhon's loathing of the banks and the Saint-Simonian technocracy. The latter had an influential advocate during the reign of Napoleon III in the person of Cournot, then inspector-general of public education. Cournot is the author of the notion that human history can be summed up in the phrase: "Du roi des animaux au concessionnaire de la planète." See Georges Duveau, *Sociologie de l'Utopie* (Paris, 1961), p. 63.

4. *Les Confessions d'un révolutionnaire* (1851 edition), p. 88.

5. *General Idea of the Revolution* (an English translation published in 1923), p. 120.

6. Proudhon's anti-feminism went with his high estimation of the family, especially the rural family. His mother having been a peasant woman, he chose his own wife with a view to obtaining a good housekeeper who would defer to her patriarchal husband. None of this is very original or surprising when one considers his background. What is more remarkable is that in his writings he never lost an opportunity to affirm that women were congenitally inferior to men. In general, woman—in Proudhon's view—is a kind of link between man and the animal creation: "une sorte de moyen terme entre lui et le reste du règne animal" (*De la Justice*, IV, 135). Women are both physically and intellectually handicapped, and their moral condition is no better: "Par sa nature, la femme est dans un état de démoralisation constante." He even offers an algebraical formula: the "total value" of man to woman is in the ratio of 27 to 8. On the subject of women and the sanctity of the (male-dominated) home, Proudhon sounds like an early Church father. This was one of the sources of his furious opposition to the communists (i.e., Cabet and his followers) and the Fourierists, with their amoral notions about free love and sexual equality. If the preservation of the traditional rural family was the touchstone, there was undoubtedly a certain consistency about all this, but it has made it difficult to cast Proudhon in the role of an exemplary libertarian.

7. See also *Jésus et les origines du christianisme*, pp. 526–27. This is a late work. Most of Proudhon's reflections on the topic are to be found in *De la Création de l'Ordre*, in the *Système des Contradictions économiques*, the *Confessions*, and *De la Justice*. In general he follows the tradition of the French eighteenth-century materialists: that is, he treats the deity as a fanciful representation of humanity and religion as a confused groping toward a rational apprehension of man's place in the universe. This was also Feuerbach's view, but Proudhon's tone is more bellicose, as befitted a critic of the Catholic Church. Religion for Proudhon signifies Christianity, and Christianity signifies Catholicism. Here and there he anticipates the sociology of the later nineteenth century which sees religion as a fantastic reflex of the human collectivity. "En deux mots: religion et société sont termes synonymes; l'homme est sacré pour lui-même comme s'il était Dieu. Le catholicisme et le socialisme, identiques pour le fond, ne diffèrent que

pour la forme: ainsi s'expliquent, à la fois, et le fait primitif de la croyance en Dieu et le progrès irrécusable des religions." *(Confessions,* pp. 59–60.)

8. H. P. Adams, *op. cit.,* p. 185. The resemblance extends even to Proudhon's patriarchal notions about family life, which after all were not so very different from Tolstoy's. As for Carlyle it is hardly necessary to stress the point that his anticapitalism went with a decidedly authoritarian cast of mind and a positive admiration for military heroes. But the common frame of reference is another matter: it has to do with the fact that all these writers reacted against an individualism which divorced communal ethics from what was "practical." In this context it is immaterial that Tolstoy saw the solution in a return to religion, whereas Proudhon loathed the very thought of the deity. What matters is that both were agreed about the essential immorality of modern society.

9. *Théorie de la propriété,* pp. 135 ff.

10. *Ibid.,* p. 211.

11. *Système des Contradictions économiques,* II, 328.

12. In general Proudhon operates with the labor-time theory of value he took over from Owen and the Ricardian socialists in England. On occasion, however, he introduces ideas of his own. Thus he argues that the workers are necessarily underpaid if the employer fails to remunerate them for that part of their product which is the result of their combined effort. Combined labor is more productive than individual labor, hence the employer, in paying each worker separately, makes a profit from that "immense force which results from the union and the harmony of the laborers." This union is an additional source of wealth-creation, and this "collective force" goes unpaid. See *Qu'est-ce que la propriété?,* pp. 117 ff. This was the germ of an exploitation theory different from the Marxian, but Proudhon did not follow it up.

13. *Système des Contradictions économiques,* I, 284, II, 258, 266.

14. "On ne remédie pas à la rage en faisant mordre tout le monde." *Ibid.,* II, 223. "Quiconque, pour organiser le travail, fait appel au pouvoir et au capital, a menti parce que l'organisation du travail doit être la déchéance du capital et du pouvoir." *Ibid.,* II, 310. Proudhon had already developed the anti-communist theme in *Qu'est-ce que la propriété?,* where he assailed the Babouvists for wanting to generalize property by way of the community of goods. After 1848 he sharpened his criticism of Louis Blanc's reformist socialism as being irrelevant to the real needs of the workers; see his *Lettres à Louis Blanc.* The argument is always the same: no good can come from reliance on the state, and a socialist state would be the worst of all. The source of this attitude is to be found in Proudhon's anti-Jacobinism, which blinded him to the realization that an ancient "pluralist" system might have to be swept away by force before anything new could be put in its place. See Gurvitch, *Proudhon. Sa vie, son oeuvre,* pp. 45–46.

15. Gurvitch, in *Dialectique et sociologie,* pp. 110–12, sees the main

weakness of Proudhon's argument not where Marx found it (namely, in his Platonizing idealism), but rather in his tendency to seek an equilibrium between the extremes. He is thus led to treat the synthesis as the medium term between thesis and antithesis. This criticism corresponds fairly closely to Marx's view that Proudhon aimed at a social compromise, but Gurvitch makes the point that after 1848 he identified himself much more clearly with the "party of labor" against the "party of capital." In the *Système* he is still trying to find a solution lying midway between their antagonism, whereas in the 1850's and 1860's he comes forward as the spokesman of the working class.

16. Marx, *The Poverty of Philosophy*, p. 36.

17. *Système des Contradictions économiques*, I, 66, 68.

18. Marx, *The Poverty of Philosophy*, p. 45.

19. *Ibid.*, p. 43.

20. *Ibid.*, p. 55.

21. For the above see *ibid.*, chap. II, *passim*. For a qualified defense of Proudhon's approach see Gurvitch, *Pour le centenaire de la mort de P.-J. Proudhon* (pp. 47 ff.); for a critique delivered from the Marxist standpoint see Naville, *De l'Aliénation à la jouissance*, pp. 312 ff. Proudhon's annotations on his copy of Marx's book show plainly enough that the point of Marx's critique had escaped him, although not necessarily (as Marx supposed) because he was unable to make use of Hegel's method.

In one respect Marx was factually mistaken: Proudhon had obtained a fairly detailed knowledge of Hegel's philosophy not (as Marx thought) from private conversation with the German emigrant Karl Grün, but from the *Cours de Psychologie* published by a German lecturer at the Collège de France, Ahrens, in 1836–38. See Gurvitch, *Dialectique et sociologie*, pp. 96 ff., where the subject of Proudhon's relationship to Hegel is discussed at some length.

22. *Organisation du crédit et de la circulation, et solution du problème social sans impôt, sans emprunt* (1848). This pamphlet together with two others (*Banque d'Echange* and *Banque du Peuple*) was published in some editions of Proudhon's writings under the joint title *Solution du problème social;* the English translation is *Solution of the Social Problem* (London, 1927).

23. For details of the scheme, see *ibid.*, p. 90 ff. In technical terms, what Proudhon proposed was not the abolition of money, but the introduction of token money based on property values. The bank (which would have behind it merely the authority conferred upon it by the associated producers) would advance credit to borrowers in the form of coupons to the value of two-thirds or three-quarters of their property, and these coupons would become legal tender. Proudhon claimed that this was merely a generalization of the existing system of letters of exchange. The emission of credit would be governed by the principle that paper could be issued only against "bonnes valeurs de commerce."

PART TWO

CRITICS OF THE INDUSTRIAL REVOLUTION

Chapter 6: The Heritage

1. For the general background, see E. J. Hobsbawm, *The Age of Revolution* (London, 1962), especially pp. 27, 114 ff., 241 ff. and the same author's *Industry and Empire: An Economic History of Britain since 1750* (London, 1968); T. S. Ashton, *The Industrial Revolution 1760–1830* (London–New York, 1948); and Paul Mantoux, *The Industrial Revolution in the Eighteenth Century* (London, 1928). For the political history of the period see S. Maccoby, *English Radicalism 1786–1832* (London, 1955). For the early labor movement and its links with the older democratic traditions of the pre-industrial age, see E. P. Thompson, *The Making of the English Working Class* (London, 1964). For the last of the plebeian movements antedating the industrial age, see George Rudé, *Wilkes and Liberty: A Social Study of 1763 to 1774* (Oxford, 1962). There was in Britain a heritage of popular radicalism going back to the Puritan movement and the English Revolution of the seventeenth century, but (contrary to legend) no significant anticapitalist tradition; see Christopher Hill, *The Century of Revolution 1603–1714* (Edinburgh, 1961); and C. B. Macpherson, *The Political Theory of Possessive Individualism* (Oxford, 1962). In what follows, the term "socialism" is reserved for doctrines or movements stemming from the industrial transformation of the late eighteenth and early nineteenth century. Earlier forms of (agrarian or merchant) capitalism evoked a different response. For this reason, some interesting historical studies of democratic stirrings on the left wing of the Puritan movement, before and after the collapse of the Commonwealth in 1660, do not enter into consideration here.

This is not a terminological quarrel: the specific content of socialism as a protest movement reflected the fact that European capitalism had entered its industrial phase; or (if one prefers it) that the industrial revolution was taking place under capitalist direction, i.e., under the control of a new class of private entrepreneurs. The ideology was provided by the utilitarians or, as they came to be called, the "philosophic radicals." In its origins this group was composed of the small circle of friends gathered around Bentham and James Mill. Later it came to include notable parliamentarians as well as moderate labor leaders like Francis Place. The latter acquired his early political education in the democratic movement of the 1790's and terminated his long career as the principal ally of the Whigs in pushing the 1832 Reform Bill through Parliament. The Bill enfranchised the middle class, but not the urban working class, which had to wait until 1867 to get the vote. Yet Place in 1831–32 was all for peaceful change and would have nothing to do with the left wing of the radical movement which pressed for revolution. See Thompson, *op. cit., passim,* for Place and for the roots of this liberal-radical tradition (which had a counterpart in the United States, but not in France). For a critical analysis of utilitarianism and its relevance to economics, see Joseph Schumpeter, *History of Economic Analysis* (New York, 1954), pp. 407 ff. When combined with faith in parliamentary democracy and economic *laissez-faire,* Benthamite utilitarianism made up the sum and substance of liberalism, as the term was then understood. What is today known as "conservatism" in Britain and the United States is a debased form of this early liberalism, whose doctrines took shape in England between 1820 and 1850. This is all that needs to be said on this tedious subject. Students in search of detailed information about Benthamite legislative projects and Whig-liberal politics, before and after 1830, are advised to consult Élie Halévy's six-volume *History of the English People in the Nineteenth Century* (rev. ed., London, 1961), especially Vols. II and III, where the liberal triumph is celebrated at considerable length. See also Halévy's *The Growth of Philosophic Radicalism* (rev. ed., London, 1952), *passim.*

2. Thompson, *op. cit.,* pp. 95–96. Formally, *The Rights of Man*—composed and published in 1791–92, after Paine's return to England from the United States in 1787—was a defense of the French Revolution against Burke's attack. Its welfare-state proposals were incidental to the main theme.

3. For Thelwall and the Spenceans, see Thompson, pp. 157 ff. For the impact of the early industrial revolution on living conditions in towns and countryside, see E. J. Hobsbawm, "The British Standard of Living, 1790–1850," in *Labouring Men: Studies in the History of Labour* (London, 1964), pp. 64 ff.; the notes appended to this essay furnish an introduction to the voluminous literature on the subject. See also M. Beer, *A History of British Socialism* (London, 1953), I, 106 ff.; and Alexander Gray, *The Socialist Tradition* (London, 1963), pp. 257 ff. In addition to Spence, William Ogilvie (1736–1819) is usually mentioned in this context for his *Essay on the Right of Property in Land* (1782) which has been described as an application of physiocratic doctrines to British conditions. Ogilvie, a professor at Aberdeen, was philosophically not far removed from Adam Smith, although more sharply critical of private property, on the familiar Natural Law grounds that the earth belongs to all men. His practical proposals do not amount to much more than the settlement of landless farmers on holdings to be assigned to them in perpetuity, against payment of a nominal rent to the landlord, who is not to be dispossessed; nor are the tenants to become freeholders. It is difficult to see why this modest proposal has come to figure in some textbooks as a forerunner of socialism. John

Thelwall's *The Rights of Nature* (1796) is a different kettle of fish, but then Thelwall was a "Jacobin" writing under the impact of events in France. Even so, his revolutionary program does not get significantly beyond "a right to the share of the produce . . . proportionate to the profits of the employer," and free education whereby the laborer's child might rise to the "highest station of society." He also inaugurated the description of the eight-hour day as the traditional "norm" for the laboring man, a term which in his day signified artisans rather than factory workers.

4. See Asa Briggs, ed., *Chartist Studies* (London, 1962). The fortunes of the movement, from the publication of the Charter on May 8, 1838, to the collapse of 1848 and the gradual decline of the 1850's, form part of the general history of the period. The topic is not germane to a study of socialism, any more than would be an account of factory legislation. This is not to say that socialists at the time could ignore either. It was Marx who described the adoption by the British Parliament of the Ten Hours Bill in 1847 as an epoch-making event, on the grounds that "it was the first time that in broad daylight the political economy of the middle class succumbed to the political economy of the working class." (*Inaugural Address of the Working Men's International Association,* in *Selected Works* [Moscow, 1958], I, 383.) But labor legislation was, in principle at least, compatible with capitalism, even though it constituted an infringement of property rights and *laissez-faire.* The subsequent distinction between laborism and socialism is already inherent in this circumstance.

5. Paine, *Agrarian Justice,* cited in Maccoby, *op. cit.,* p. 468. In general, Paine's argument in this pamphlet is derived from the familiar notion of the earth as the Creator's gift to all mankind. This sounds archaic, but here is Marx on the same subject:

> From the standpoint of a higher economic form of society, private ownership of the globe by single individuals will appear quite as absurd as private ownership of one man by another. Even a whole society, a nation, or even all simultaneously existing societies taken together, are not the owners of the globe. They are only its possessors, its usufructuaries, and like *boni patres familias,* they must hand it down to succeeding generations in an improved condition. (*Capital,* III [Moscow, 1960], p. 757.)

The authority for such a judgment could scarcely be other than ethical in a Natural Law sense. If this reflects an inconsistency in Marx's thought, it is also a pointer to the kind of morality he took for granted.

6. See John Locke, *Two Treatises of Government* (1690), especially the *Second Treatise,* Chap. V, where the individual's claim to (private) ownership is developed in language equivocal enough to serve the purposes of agrarian reformers and socialists alike: the former because of the assumption that land had once been held in common, the latter because Locke

describes labor as the source of wealth. See also *The Wealth of Nations,*
Book 1, chap. VIII, where Smith applies Lockean *ius naturale* to a pre-
sumptive state of affairs antedating the institution of private ownership:

> In that original state of things, which precedes both the appropriation of
> land and the acquisition of stock, the whole produce of labour belongs
> to the labourer. He has neither landlord nor master to share with him.
> Had this state continued, the wages of labour would have augmented
> with all those improvements in its productive powers, to which the divi-
> sion of labour gives occasion. . . . But this original state of things, in
> which the labourer enjoyed the whole produce of his own labour, could
> not last beyond the first introduction of the appropriation of land and
> the accumulation of stock.

Smith saw no reason to regret this, since he held that private ownership of
"stock" (capital) was favorable to the growth of wealth. But he had no
illusions about such a state of affairs being "natural." It was a social con-
trivance and could presumably be altered. On either Lockean or Smithian
principles it might thus be inferred that common ownership was "natural"
and private property "unnatural." This was just why Burke attempted to
formulate an alternative to *ius naturale* which he correctly associated with
Rousseau and his Jacobin progeny. See Beer, *op. cit.,* I, 50 ff. and 101 ff.
As Beer notes (p. 103):

> The course of the French Revolution made it impossible to adhere to
> natural law, and thinking men were searching for a new social theory.
> Philosophically, the French Revolution appeared as a great experiment
> in *ius naturale;* all its declarations were written in its spirit and terms,
> and its inspirer was Rousseau. The terroristic acts and wars into which
> that social earthquake degenerated had the effect of discrediting the
> whole system of natural law. Robespierre and Bonaparte destroyed the
> halo of Rousseau.

This describes the conservative reaction, but not the reason why the early
socialists had trouble with Rousseau's spiritual legacy, which was attuned
to the pre-industrial age. Natural Law continued to guide the socialist
critique of inequality, notably in England, where such considerations
formed a bond between humanist radicals descended from Paine and others
who adhered to some form of Christianity. On the other hand, it was not
necessary to adhere to Natural Law doctrine to arrive at the conclusion
that the social order was capable of improvement, when measured by some
such standard as "the greatest happiness of the greatest number."

Chapter 7: The New Commonwealth

1. See Godwin's *An Enquiry Concerning Political Justice* (London, 1793,
revised 1796); *The Enquirer* (1797); and *Thoughts on Man* (1831); also

George Woodcock, *William Godwin* (London, 1946). Godwin's influence on the Romantics is described in H. N. Brailsford's *Shelley, Godwin, and their Circle* (London, 1913). It may be noteworthy that Coleridge and Robert Southey, then respectively students at Cambridge and Oxford, were inspired by *Political Justice* to write hymns on the coming dawn of liberty. So, at a later date, was Shelley. Godwin is also the source of Coleridge's proposal to Southey in 1794 to found a pantisocracy, or communist colony, where perfect equality should reign. (Coleridge, *Letters* [1895], I, 81.) Southey, as the only prospective pantisocrat who owned some property, was not forthcoming, whereupon Coleridge proclaimed him "lost to Virtue." (*Ibid.,* I, 137–51.) Both men in later years were among the fathers of the new anti-revolutionary (and anti-capitalist) conservatism, as was Wordsworth whose *Prelude* had already chronicled the growing loss of faith in Rousseau and Godwin. All three are likewise among the ancestors of "Tory democracy," a romantic attempt by the so-called Young England group (in the 1840's joined by Benjamin Disraeli) to establish a bond between the aristocracy and the proletariat over the heads of the manufacturing class with its faith in Manchester economics. Southey's *Letters from England* (1807) paint a gloomy picture of manufacturing industry as a source of misery and depravity threatening England with destruction, and Wordsworth to the end of his life professed sympathy for the Chartists. What was later, in the age of John Ludlow (1821–1911) and Frederick Denison Maurice (1805–72), known as "Christian socialism" had its source in this kind of sentiment, a conservative reaction to the industrial revolution. A distant echo of these doctrines, intermingled with contemporary antisemitism, is to be found in the writings of T. S. Eliot. For literature see C. E. Raven, *Christian Socialism* (London, 1920); G. D. H. Cole, *A History of Socialist Thought,* Vol. I, *The Forerunners 1789–1850* (London, 1955), pp. 290 ff.; Beer, *op. cit.,* I, 271 ff.

2. For the citation from Mill see his *Dissertations,* I, article on "Coleridge"; and the *Autobiography* (1873), pp. 160–62. For an authoritative discussion of Carlyle's position see René Wellek, "Carlyle and the Philosophy of History," in *Confrontations* (Princeton, 1965), pp. 82 ff., where the notion of Carlyle's spiritual affinity with Saint-Simonism (from which he borrowed a few concepts) is dismissed as the absurdity it is. In so far as he made systematic use of philosophical notions, Carlyle's view of history was rooted in the doctrines of the German Romantics, with their stress on the mysterious and unpredictable course of human history. The German obsession with cultural evolution—e.g., in the relentless quest for an *Urvolk,* or primitive race at the origins of history—must not be confused with the naturalistic humanism of the French, including those writers of the early nineteenth century (Victor Hugo and the Saint-Simonians among them) who had been powerfully affected by the Romantic current. As a thinker, Carlyle is wholly in the Germanic tradition, a tradition founded by J. G. Herder in the late eighteenth century and partly anticipated by

Leibniz, with his patriotic belief in German as the *Ursprache*—at once the purest and the most primitive of all languages, nearest to the beginnings of things and to God. This sort of stuff is much closer to Carlyle's outlook (in some ways a throwback to the mentality of the seventeenth century) than is the naturalism and positivism of the French *philosophes* and their socialist successors.

3. The wording diverges from the revised text found in *A New View of Society, and other Writings by Robert Owen*, ed., G. D. H. Cole (London, 1927); it is taken from the First Essay (p. 20); see also the Third Essay, where it is affirmed (p. 45) that "the character of man is, without a single exception, always formed for him. . . . Man, therefore, never did, nor is it possible he ever can, form his own character." To Owen's way of thinking (which in this respect does not differ from that of Godwin), education is the path to progress. This is really all there is to be said on the subject, and it follows for Owen that religion, with its demand that the individual undertake a personal moral reformation, is totally misguided and indeed harmful, in that it burdens men with an obligation to which they are necessarily unequal.

4. A good short account of Owen's career is furnished by G. D. H. Cole, *Life of Robert Owen* (London, 1925, rev. ed., 1930). A brief polemical treatment of the subject may be found in Alexander Gray, *The Socialist Tradition* (London, 1963), pp. 197–217. The intellectual and social background is discussed with admirable lucidity by M. Beer, *A History of British Socialism*, I, 160 ff. There is no lack of literature on Owenism, starting with Owen's autobiography, *The Life of Robert Owen* (London, 1857–58; republished in New York, 1920, without the supplementary volume of 1858). His early writings include *Observations on the Effect of the Manufacturing System* (1815); *An Address delivered to the Inhabitants of New Lanark* (1816); *Two Memorials on behalf of the Working Classes* (1818); *Lectures on an Entirely New State of Society* (1820); and *Report to the County of Lanark* (1821). Later writings, mostly concerned with ethical themes, include *The Book of the New Moral World* (1836–44) and *The New Existence of Man upon the Earth* (1854–55). The crucial phase of Owenism as a movement is best studied from its periodicals, notably *The Pioneer* (1833–34), *The Crisis* (1832–34), and *The New Moral World* (1835–45). For the great labor upsurge of the early 1830's, see among others Sidney and Beatrice Webb, *History of Trade Unionism* (London, 1894, revised 1920). For the Owenite experiments in America, see D. D. Egbert and Stow Persons, eds., *Socialism and American Life* (Princeton, 1954), I, 161 ff.; II, 47–49, 128–32, and *passim*. Owenite ideas appear to have first reached the United States about 1817, while Owen himself launched the movement on American soil in 1824–25, when the settlement of New Harmony, Indiana, was founded. The reasons why American communitarians at this time preferred Fourierism to Owenism are set out in Egbert and Persons, *op. cit.*, II, 132 ff.

5. See Beer, *op. cit.,* pp. 163 ff.; Gray, *op. cit.,* 198 ff.; Cole, *The Life of Robert Owen, passim.* There is no point in going into the details of Owen's numerous propagandist and philanthropic activities during this period, which may be said to have lasted until about 1820. New Lanark in these years was a Mecca for visitors curious to see what an enlightened manufacturer could do in the way of combating drunkenness and disorder, improving labor conditions, and teaching the rudiments of education to a primitive working class. New Lanark, in Owen's words many years later, was "literally a self-employing, self-supporting, self-educating and self-governing population." (*The Revolution in the Mind and Practice of the Human Race* [1849], p. 29.) New Lanark won the approval of prominent public figures, including the elder Sir Robert Peel who joined Owen in pressing for the first effective Factory Act in 1819. The subsequent change in Owen's friendly relations with the governing class dated from a public lecture he gave in London on August 21, 1817, when for the first time he disclosed his anti-religious views. Nonetheless he remained a prominent figure, calling upon the European monarchs and statesmen assembled at Aix-la-Chapelle in 1818 to lay his philanthropic schemes before them. His *Report to the County of Lanark* was followed in 1824 by a stay in the United States, at the start of which, in February–March 1825, he addressed both Houses of Congress and was introduced to the new President, John Quincy Adams. (Egbert and Persons, *op. cit.,* I, 162.) He spent more than four years in America, most of his energy going into the establishment of New Harmony, on the site of an older settlement founded by religious sectarians from Germany, the Rappites. While dwelling in what he described as the "comparatively uncorrupted atmosphere" of the United States, he lost touch with his British disciples, some of whom founded the Orbiston community in Lanarkshire, an enterprise soon wrecked by the death of its principal organizer, Abram Combe. In 1829 Owen, tired of the constant bickering at New Harmony, returned to England, leaving his sons in charge of the settlement. See Frank Podmore, *Robert Owen: A Biography* (London, 1906; New York, 1924).

6. Beer, *op. cit.,* p. 178. Owen seems to have drifted into socialism (as distinct from educational reform and general philanthropy) under the impression of the economic crisis of 1816–19, which followed years of wartime prosperity. Wealth creation now assumed a place of importance in his thinking. This was natural, for after 1815 industrial unemployment became a real problem in Britain. That Owen's concern with pauperism was shared in high places is evident from the fact that in 1819 a committee was formed by the Duke of Kent, Sir Robert Peel, David Ricardo, and others, to inquire into the practicability of Owen's schemes for combating unemployment, and to raise funds for an experimental "parallelogram." Subscriptions failed to come in, and the committee dissolved after a few months. Southey blamed this upon Owen's tactless remarks about religion, holding that if he "had not alarmed the better part of the nation by proclaiming, upon the most

momentous of all subjects, opinions which are alike fatal to individual happiness and the general good," he might have obtained more support. "For the connection between moral truth and political wisdom is close and indissoluble; and he who shows himself erroneous upon one important point, must look to have his opinions properly distrusted upon others." (Robert Southey, *Sir Thomas More, or Colloquies on Society* [London, 1829], I, 130–32.) In short, since Owen was an atheist, the Church could not be expected to take an interest in the plight of the workless. By contrast, Ricardo (whom Owen had denounced in 1817, along with Malthus, James Mill, and Robert Torrens, as a purveyor of false and harmful doctrines) showed real willingness to help, but without success.

The later fortunes of Owenism as a doctrine gradually merged with the Secularist movement launched by G. J. Holyoake and continued by Charles Bradlaugh. Indeed "Secularism" (a term conceived by Holyoake in 1851, after the political movement had collapsed) was the direct descendant of Owenism, though by the 1880's, when it became influential, Bradlaugh's leadership had dissociated it from its socialist origins and turned it into a vehicle of respectable middle-class radicalism.

7. Not, however, Charles Hall, who in some textbooks figures alongside them. Hall, whose only book (*The Effects of Civilisation on the People in European States*) appeared in 1805, was a social critic, but hardly a socialist. His affinities are with Adam Ferguson, the author of a celebrated *Essay on the History of Civil Society* (1767), and even more with Rousseau and the physiocrats. For Hall, as for the physiocratic school founded by Quesnay, agriculture is a "natural" occupation, while trade and manufacture are "sterile." If so many of the poor are employed in factories, the reason is that the rich have driven them off the land or attracted them to the towns to manufacture useless luxuries. Hall was an agrarian, and thus a radical (in our terminology) rather than a socialist. His place in the prehistory of socialism is with writers such as Paine, Spence, and Ogilvie. For a different view see Beer, *op. cit.,* I, 126 ff., where Hall is classed as an early socialist on the grounds that he treats profit as an illegitimate deduction from the produce of labor. Hall's book was noticed by Thomas Spence, with whom he corresponded, and mentioned by George Mudie in the Owenite journal *The Economist* (1820–21, No. 4), though mainly in order to draw the moral that cooperation (rather than return to the land) was the remedy for the evils of pauperism to which Hall had drawn attention. It is questionable whether this suffices to establish Hall as a socialist, but he certainly made much of the class antagonism between the poor and the wealthy. He also has the distinction of being among the early pacifists, and of having asserted that wars are caused by the desire of the ruling class to increase its wealth and power.

8. *Co-operative Magazine* (November 1827), p. 509 n. See Beer, *op. cit.,* I, 186–87. Of course the matter was not quite so simple, as this editorial

footnote did not fail to point out: there also had to be a theory of value. If the value of a commodity consisted of both present and past labor (i.e., capital), then the question arose "whether it is more beneficial that this capital should be individual or common." To this question there might be different answers, the economists—notably Malthus and James Mill—holding it "beneficial" that capital should be owned by the employer who had contributed it (never mind how he came to acquire it in the first place). But the labor theory of value pointed in a different direction, which is precisely why at this particular moment it became important. For this theme see the following chapter, see Cole, *A History of Socialist Thought,* I, 102 ff.; Beer, *op. cit.,* pp. 147 ff., 188 ff.; Gray, *op. cit.,* pp. 269 ff.; Joseph Schumpeter, *History of Economic Analysis* (New York, 1954), pp. 469 ff.; and Mark Blaug, *Ricardian Economics* (New Haven, Conn., 1958), pp. 140–50 and *passim.*

Chapter 8: British Socialist Economics, 1820–40

1. Ricardo's great work, *On The Principles of Political Economy and Taxation,* appeared in 1817. For the changes introduced in later editions, see Piero Sraffa's introduction to the definitive edition published in 1953 by the Cambridge University Press as Vol. I of the complete *Works.* This preface also gives a brief account of the contemporary debate among Ricardo's followers and his critics on topics such as the theory of value, the real line of division in later years between the orthodox Ricardians and the writers generally known as Ricardian socialists. It was the former—principally J. R. McCulloch, James Mill, and John Stuart Mill—who established Ricardianism as the dominant trend in Britain from about 1820 to 1870. Their interpretation of the doctrine operated with Ricardo's version of the labor theory but made no concessions to socialism (although J. S. Mill in his later years weakened a little on this point). It is worth bearing in mind that one could adhere to the Ricardian value concept without deriving anticapitalist conclusions from it. Ricardo himself had been mainly concerned with the distribution of the social product between landowners, manufacturers and laborers, and with the rate of capital formation on which economic growth depended. Other problems hardly troubled him, and for the rest he treated labor as an instrument of capital. Nor did he ever doubt that private property was the key to economic growth and indeed the foundation of civilized life. It is important to be clear about this, so as not to draw mistaken inferences from utterances such as McCulloch's later statement: "Mr. Ricardo maintains . . . the fundamental principle, that the exchangeable value of commodities or their relative worth, as compared with each other, depends exclusively on the *quantities of labour* necessarily required to produce them, and bring them to market." (J. R. McCulloch, "Notice of the Life and Writings of Mr. Ricardo," in H. W. Spiegel, ed., *The Develop-*

ment of Economic Thought [New York, 1952], pp. 165–66.) For a critique of this interpretation, see Mark Blaug, *Ricardian Economics* (New Haven, Conn., 1958), pp. 33–37.

2. Blaug, *op. cit.,* p. 36, notes that Ricardo did not hold that capital goods are ever produced by labor alone, not even in "that early state to which Adam Smith refers."

3. *Ibid.,* p. 36. For a critique of the classical value concept see Joan Robinson, *Economic Philosophy* (London, 1962), chap. 2. For a more detailed treatment of this topic, see Joseph Schumpeter, *History of Economic Analysis* (New York, 1954), pp. 469 ff. The literature on Ricardo is immense; much of it is worthless, in particular everything written by adherents of the German historical school, who object on principle to the "rationalist" treatment of the subject in terms of "abstract" concepts—as though any sort of theoretical model could be constructed which did not do violence to immediate experience!

The relationship of Marx's fully developed value theory to Ricardo's falls outside our topic. In his early writings, down to 1848, Marx was essentially a Ricardian socialist in so far as he took notice of economics. Subsequently he developed a theoretical approach of his own, which was based on Ricardo's work, but departed from it in important directions. *Capital* has of course been vastly more influential (especially in Germany and Eastern Europe) than the writings of the Ricardian socialists, but we are concerned here with the latter. Moreover, the British debates of the 1820's and 1830's anticipated some of the later Central European discussions.

4. Blaug, *op. cit.,* p. 140.

5. Beer, *op. cit.,* I, 251, believes "Piercy Ravenstone" to have been a pseudonym, while G. D. H. Cole, *A History of Socialist Thought,* Vol. I, *The Forerunners 1789–1850* (London 1955), 219, lists him among the "unknowns." At any rate it is known that in 1821 he published a book under the title *A Few Doubts as to the Correctness of some Opinions generally entertained on the Subjects of Population and Political Economy* and that Ricardo read it and commented upon it in his correspondence with McCulloch, apparently unaware that the author was an Owenite socialist. Ravenstone's only other known work is a tract entitled *Thoughts on the Funding System* (1824). Beer describes him as "essentially a Tory Democrat." Since nothing is known about his life, this description will do as well as any other. Certainly he was not a communist. He belongs to the spiritual progeny of Cobbett but seems to have absorbed the labor theory of value.

6. Patrick Colquhoun, *A Treatise on the Wealth, Power, and Resources of the British Empire* (London, 1814; 2d. ed., 1815), p. 109. For Colquhoun's life and work, see Beer, *op. cit.,* I, 97–98 and *passim;* Blaug, *op. cit.,* pp. 9, 75, 141; and Alexander Gray, *op. cit.,* p. 290.

7. For Gray's writings, see Beer, *op. cit.,* pp. 211 ff.; Alexander Gray, *op. cit.,* pp. 289 ff. Beer treats him as a Ricardian, while Blaug, *op. cit.,*

p. 143, sees no evidence that he ever read Ricardo. Cole views him mainly as a currency reformer. In most histories the probable date of his death is given as 1850, but Alexander Gray has found evidence to show that he became a successful businessman and lived to the ripe age of eighty-four, having apparently retired from public controversy after 1850, when he dropped out of sight.

8. *Lecture on Human Happiness* (1825), p. 20.

9. *Ibid.*, p. 66.

10. For a discussion of Thompson's ethical utilitarianism, see Alexander Gray, *op. cit.*, pp. 269 ff.; and Beer, *op. cit.*, 218 ff. Thompson's writings also include *Appeal of One-Half the Human Race* (1825), a pamphlet on women's rights. The full title of *Labour Rewarded* runs: *Labour Rewarded: The Claims of Labour and Capital Conciliated; Or, How to Secure to Labour the Whole Products of its Exertions. By One of the Idle Classes.* Thompson has been described as "chief of the English Socialist School," and Anton Menger, in his *The Right to the Whole Produce of Labour* (Eng. tr., London, 1899; introduction by H. S. Foxwell) goes so far as to call him "the most eminent founder of scientific socialism." But although a better economist than John Gray, he scarcely deserves such high praise.

11. Cole, *op. cit.*, I, 110–12; Beer, *op. cit.*, 259 ff.; Gray, *op. cit.*, pp. 277 ff. Hodgskin's personal career must be seen against the background of the post-Napoleonic era and his own individualist temper. At the London Mechanics Institution he had helped to found, he became the teacher of a generation of working-class organizers, including such future leaders of the Chartist movement as William Lovett and Henry Hetherington. For a biography of Hodgskin based on original research, see Elie Halévy, *Thomas Hodgskin* (Paris, 1903).

12. *Labour Defended against the Claims of Capital*, p. 80. For a systematic exposition of Hodgskin's views see W. Stark, *The Ideal Foundations of Economic Thought* (London, 1943), pp. 51–103. Blaug, *op. cit.*, p. 143, treats Hodgskin as an errant Ricardian, an interpretation borne out by Hodgskin's remark (in a letter to his friend Francis Place, after reading McCulloch's summary of Ricardo's *Principles* in the *Edinburgh Review*) that "profits are purely and simply a portion of the product of labour which the capitalist, without any right other than that conferred upon him by law, takes for himself." (Quoted by Halévy, *op. cit.*, p. 120.) In 1819 Hodgskin sent Place an outline of a critical study of Ricardo's doctrine (see *ibid.*, pp. 54–72), but the book was never written. A recommendation from James Mill to the editor of the *Morning Chronicle* in 1822 gave him his start in journalism. It is uncertain when Hodgskin turned from political radicalism to socialism, but there is some evidence that Ravenstone's pamphlet gave him a push in this direction. Ravenstone is mentioned in *Popular Political Economy*, p. 77, and it is probably no accident that this was also the period of Hodgskin's involvement in the early labor movement. Remarkably, he was

not influenced by Owen, whose cooperative schemes he regarded with disfavor. For the literature of the period, see G. D. H. Cole and A. W. Filson, eds., *British Working Class Movements: Selected Documents 1789–1875* (London and New York, 1965), *passim*.

13. See A. Bain, *James Mill. A Biography* (London, 1882), p. 364. John Stuart Mill, if less agitated than his father, was then not much more sympathetic to the socialists, although he was personally acquainted with William Thompson and had probably read his books. He seems to have identified socialism with Owenism and to have thought the Owenites less interesting than the French socialists and communists. Of German socialism he knew nothing at all. This emerges clearly enough from his *Principles of Political Economy,* first published in 1848 and considerably revised in 1852, when he modified his criticism of the French socialists and in particular said some kind words about Fourierism. Cole, *op cit.,* I, 308–13.

14. For details, see Beer, *op. cit.,* pp. 236–44; Alexander Gray, *op. cit.,* pp. 283–88; Cole, *op. cit.,* I, 132–39. Biographical details are cited from H. J. Carr's article in *Economica* (November, 1940). John Francis Bray (1809–97) was born in Washington, D.C., the son of an Englishman (an actor who had emigrated to the United States) and an American mother, and taken to England by his father in 1822. He grew up in Leeds, where he became a working compositor, entered the trade-union movement, and in 1837 was made treasurer of the newly formed Leeds Working Men's Association, which had links with Lovett's Chartist organization in London. His book, *Labour's Wrongs and Labour's Remedy, or the Age of Might and the Age of Right,* was published in 1839, at a time when Leeds was the center of Chartism in the north of England and the locale of Feargus O'Connor's *Northern Star.* In 1842 Bray returned to America, where he published a number of socialist writings and took an active part in the American labor movement. He died in 1897 on a farm near Pontiac, Michigan.

15. Cole, *op. cit.,* I, 132 ff. Marx quotes Bray against Proudhon in *Misère de la philosophie,* where he describes him as "an English Communist" and the author of a "remarkable work." This is followed, however, by the suggestion that in Bray's book there may be found "the key to the past, present and future works of M. Proudhon," whose doctrine Marx was about to subject to a fairly searching criticism. The point of Marx's objection is that under capitalism it is illusory to propose (as both Bray and Proudhon had done) that the producers shall exchange the produce of their labor directly and on an equal basis: they cannot do so as individuals, because their labor is effectively socialized by the industrial production process.

16. I. A. Richards, quoted by A. C. Bouquet, *Comparative Religion* (London, 7th rev. ed., 1967), p. 28.

17. For the gradual abandonment of both orthodox Ricardianism and Ricardian socialism, see Schumpeter, *op. cit.,* pp. 476 ff.; and Blaug, *op. cit.,*

pp. 148 ff. It can hardly be thought accidental that the "abstinence theory of profit" made its appearance around 1830, when the manufacturers and their apologists were in urgent need of encouragement. The attack on Ricardo was spearheaded by economists who believed that profits were due to the "abstinence" of the entrepreneur, a line of reasoning naturally popular with their readers. The 1830's were a turning-point in this respect, and not for theoretical reasons alone, although Ricardo's system was vulnerable. In 1836 Nassau Senior replaced the Ricardian triad of land, labor, and capital with "a new division of the factors of production into labor, natural agents, and abstinence. Labor is no longer conceived as an expenditure of human energy measured in time units, but simply as another subjective sacrifice incurred in production, governed by the strength of the disinclination to work." (Blaug, *op. cit.*, p. 155). This doctrine—which might conceivably make sense in an egalitarian community—was solemnly applied to the operation of capitalism! Naturally the manufacturers were delighted. Why reputable economists should have been taken in is less easy to explain, but it is a fact that even socialists allowed themselves to be trapped into a discussion of such propositions, which simply took the existing state of affairs for granted, and then analyzed the greater or lesser "satisfactions" open to individuals, all of whom were treated as equal. In such an atmosphere, socialist theorizing could at a later date make headway only by stressing the "disutility" of being pauperized or unemployed. For a dissection of Mill's value concept, see Blaug, *op. cit.*, pp. 171 ff.; also the same author's *Economic Theory in Retrospect* (London, 1964), pp. 163 ff.

PART THREE

GERMAN SOCIALISM

Chapter 9: The Precursors

1. See Joseph Schumpeter, *History of Economic Analysis* (New York, 1954), pp. 407 ff. So far as Hegel is concerned, it has been established that he came across British economics in 1799, when he read a German translation of James Steuart's *Inquiry into the Principles of Political Economy* (1767); see Georg Lukács, *Der junge Hegel* (Zürich, 1948), pp. 225 ff. The fact was mentioned by Hegel's biographer Karl Rosenkranz, who also noted that Hegel took a lively interest in newspaper reports of British parliamentary proceedings. Around 1803 he must have read Smith, since his name occurs in Hegel's manuscript notes for his lectures at the university of Jena. On this slender foundation of fact Lukács has erected a speculative construction

wherein Hegel appears as a critic of bourgeois society and a direct precursor of Marx. What is rather more relevant is that in his later writings—notably in his *Philosophy of Right* (1821) and in his essay on the British Reform Bill of 1831—Hegel showed himself familiar with contemporary Anglo-French economic and political theory and on the whole inclined to take the conservative side: the cure for social evils such as pauperism (he argued) lies in making the political authority (the state) responsive to those moral principles which had traditionally been upheld by the ancient ruling elites. See Jürgen Habermas, ed., *G. W. F. Hegel: Politische Schriften* (Frankfurt, 1966), especially pp. 277 ff., 361 ff. For Fichte's reaction to the impact of Western liberalism see his *Grundlage des Naturrechts* (1796), *Der geschlossene Handelsstaat* (1800), and his *Reden an die deutsche Nation* (1808)—all in his *Sämmtliche Werke*, ed., J. H. Fichte (Berlin, 1845–46). For a masterly analysis of Fichte's philosophy, see Emil Lask, "Fichtes Idealismus und die Geschichte," in Lask, *Gesammelte Schriften,* ed., Eugen Herrigel (Tübingen, 1923), I, esp. 193 ff.

2. In the strict sense Fichte was never a Romantic, for all his German afflatus. The original inspiration of German Romanticism came from a very different thinker: Johann Gottfried Herder (1744–1803). For a brief but thorough account of his life and work see F. M. Barnard, *Herder's Social and Political Thought* (Oxford, 1965). Carlyle had read Herder and may have been influenced by him, although in the main he was dependent for his understanding of German irrationalism upon Jean Paul and the Romantic novelists. For the rest, he relied on the Schlegels (August Wilhelm and the more eccentric Friedrich), as did Coleridge. This applies in particular to the "organic-mechanical" contrast, which for these writers became synonymous with the distinction between Romanticism and Classicism.

3. For Fichte's philosophy of history, see Lask, *op. cit.,* especially pp. 242 ff. This is the authoritative discussion of the subject, by a philosopher who was himself a distinguished neo-Kantian in pre-1914 Germany. What little Lukács has to say on this topic is derived from Lask, by whom he was profoundly influenced, as indeed were all who came in contact with him. For Herder's role in making the concept of the *Volk*-state available to a later generation of Romantic nationalists, see Barnard, *op. cit.,* pp. 173 ff. Schumpeter, *op. cit.,* pp. 412–13, 459, notes Fichte's influence on Othmar Spann and the "universalist" school in economics. He also stresses the resemblance between Fichte's corporatism and the doctrines advanced by his Catholic contemporary Franz von Baader. But Baader had no political influence, whereas Fichte became the principal inspirer of German nationalism: down to the fateful day in 1933 when the heirs of this tradition amalgamated their party with a plebeian movement that had arisen on Catholic (Austrian and Bavarian) soil—thereby, as it were, bringing the two halves of the reactionary alliance together. This theme does not exhaust the importance of Fichte, but it indicates one particular strand of the anti-liberal tradition in Germany. Some confusion is caused

by the fact that in the later nineteenth century Friedrich List's followers in economics, themselves descendants of men who had been influenced by Fichte's patriotic writings, described themselves as National Liberals rather than Conservatives. National Liberalism—with the accent on National— could easily turn into National Socialism when circumstances permitted.

4. An authoritative introduction to this topic is to be found in Lask, *op. cit.*, pp. 335 ff. For the student who has no German, there exists a comprehensive literature from which it is unnecessary to cite more than a few representative titles, e.g.: *Hegel's Philosophy of Right*, tr. with notes by T. M. Knox (Oxford, 1942); *Hegel's Political Writings*, tr. by T. M. Knox, with an introductory essay by Z. A. Pelczynski (Oxford, 1964); G. R. G. Mure, *An Introduction to Hegel* (Oxford, 1940 ff.); *The Philosophy of History*, tr. by J. Sibree, with a preface by C. J. Friedrich (New York, 1956); J. N. Findlay, *Hegel: A Re-Examination* (London and New York, 1958); Walter Kaufmann, *Hegel—Reinterpretation, Texts and Commentary* (New York, 1965); and Herbert Marcuse, *Reason and Revolution: Hegel and the Rise of Social Theory* (2d ed., London and New York, 1955). For a Thomist critique of German idealism in general and Hegelianism in particular, see Nicholas Lobkowicz, *Theory and Practice: History of a Concept from Aristotle to Marx* (Notre Dame, 1967). For an interesting French study on the relationship of Hegel to Marx, see F. Chatelet, *Logos et Praxis* (Paris, 1962). Mention must also be made of Professor Karl R. Popper's well-known work *The Open Society and its Enemies* (4th ed., London, 1962), whose chapter on Hegel, however, fails to do justice to the topic. Marxist-Leninist literature serves a political purpose and is to be regarded as the codification of an official standpoint, unless produced by writers qualified as "revisionists."

5. Lobkowicz, *op. cit.*, pp. 193 ff. There is a small literature on Cieszkowski, as the reader of Professor Martin Malia's biography of Herzen (*Alexander Herzen and the Birth of Russian Socialism* [Cambridge, Mass., 1961] can discover for himself. The *Prolegomena zur Historiosophie* (1838) represents an important link between Hegel and Marx and more particularly between Hegel and Bakunin. There is indeed no evidence that Marx (who in the 1840's was personally acquainted with Cieszkowski) ever read the book. But Moses Hess did, and Hess for three critical years (1842–45) was Marx's teacher. It was likewise Cieszkowski's book which launched Bakunin on the road to revolutionary anarchism—an outcome that must have appalled the Polish aristocrat. Bakunin was then in Germany studying Hegel's philosophy, and his radical interpretation of Cieszkowski's mystical doctrine that the future can be known was soon to ferment in the heads of Russian students. In far-away Vladimir, the youthful Alexander Herzen—exiled from Moscow for having toyed with the notion of aristocratic conspiracy against the Tsar—read the *Prolegomena* shortly after their appearance and drew from them the assurance that mankind's future could be known and shaped.

A faithful Catholic—his *God and the Palingenesis* (1842) was dedicated to the defense of orthodox Christianity against its detractors among the left-wing Hegelians—Cieszkowski nonetheless had taken the first decisive step from theory to practice, from philosophy as contemplative understanding of the past, to philosophy as speculative construction and *practical determination* of the future. For the coming age could be molded (thanks to Hegel) by "post-theoretical practice": that was Cieszkowski's great discovery in the *Prolegomena*. Absolute knowledge having been attained, "humanity has become mature enough to make its own determinations perfectly identical with the Divine Plan of Providence." Hegel's universal system was the beginning of the end. "Philosophy has now reached so classical a point that it must transcend itself and yield up the universal empire to another." This "other" could only be "practical, social life." Being and thought "must perish in action, art and philosophy in social life, in order to re-emerge and to unfold in the ultimate form of social existence." For his own part, Cieszkowski remained a philosopher, and a Catholic philosopher at that (even though he toyed with the utopian socialism of Fourier). He had nonetheless set the avalanche in motion. Within three years of the *Prolegomena,* the message of revolution was sounded by Moses Hess in another important and neglected piece of writing, *Die europäische Triarchie* (1841).

6. For the above, see among others Guido de Ruggiero, *The History of European Liberalism,* tr. by R. G. Collingwood (Boston, 1959), pp. 211 ff.; H. G. Schenk, *The Aftermath of the Napoleonic Wars* (London, 1947), pp. 65 ff.; Lewis Namier, *1848: The Revolution of the Intellectuals* (Oxford, 1946; 2d ed., 1957), *passim;* E. J. Hobsbawm, *The Age of Revolution* (London, 1962), pp. 109 ff.; Franz Neumann, *The Democratic and the Authoritarian State* (Glencoe, Ill., 1957); Franz Schnabel, *Deutsche Geschichte im Neunzehnten Jahrhundert* (Freiburg, 1949), Vol. II, *passim;* Jürgen Habermas, *Strukturwandel der Öffentlichkeit* (Neuwied, 1962), *passim;* Iring Fetscher, *Rousseaus Politische Philosophie* (Neuwied, 1960), pp. 214 ff. Ruggiero (the first edition of whose work appeared in 1927) presents what might be described as a Tocquevillean account of European society around 1848. He is duly critical of the reign of Louis Philippe but tends to idealize the German situation, going so far as to describe the Prussian reform era after 1807 as "the golden age of Prussian Liberalism" (p. 217). He even turns the arch-conservative Karl vom Stein into a liberal, crediting him with achievements which largely remained on paper (except for the creation of a landless peasantry, which was very efficiently carried through after his fall by the liberal doctrinaires in the Prussian civil service). On this subject see among others Walter M. Simon, *The Failure of the Prussian Reform Movement 1807–1819* (Cornell, 1955). Schenk, who sympathizes with the Romantic conservatives, at least has no illusions about the plight of the hapless Prussian peasantry in the "golden age of liberalism" (see *op. cit.,* pp. 80–83). But then

Italian liberalism had a very similar record in *its* "golden age," so that Ruggiero's enthusiasm for the Prussian reformers is understandable. The net effect of their activities was to discredit liberalism in the eyes of the people, while underpinning the political privileges of the landed gentry by making their economic base invulnerable. The only regions of Germany where the economic position of the peasantry improved after 1800 were those temporarily occupied by the armies of the French Revolution. Elsewhere, the abolition of serfdom was accomplished in such a way as to "compensate" the nobility at the expense of the peasants: a model duly followed by the Russian "reformers" in 1861, with results even more catastrophic in the long run.

7. For the dissolution of the Hegelian school, see the two volumes *Die Hegelsche Rechte,* ed., Hermann Lübbe, and *Die Hegelsche Linke,* ed., Karl Löwith (Stuttgart, 1962). These contain extracts from the writings of the leading Hegelians, whether conservatives or radicals. For our theme it is of course the latter (principally Ruge, Hess, Stirner, Bauer, and Feuerbach) who are significant, but it must not be forgotten that these were rebellious critics rather than interpreters of the master's doctrine. The true Hegelians were prominent among theologians, philosophers, and historians alike. It would be tedious to name them. The point that needs making is that these "orthodox" Hegelians were politically conservative or at most mildly liberal. Moreover, like their master they had no use for Natural Law doctrine and were decidedly critical of Rousseau. To become a revolutionary—and even more so to remain one after the disillusionment of 1848, when liberal democracy proved unattainable—one had to break with Hegel, though one might retain some elements of his thought. This is what Feuerbach did and what made him important, but Feuerbach was remarkable only as a critic of religion. As a thinker he inevitably seemed trivial when compared to Hegel. For Feuerbach see *The Essence of Christianity,* tr. by George Eliot, with an introductory essay by Karl Barth and a foreword by H. Richard Niebuhr (New York, 1957). To a philosopher this is not the most important of his writings, but it is the one that made the greatest stir both at home and abroad.

8. Neumann, *op. cit.,* pp. 22 ff., 160 ff. Legal doctrine in absolutist eighteenth-century Germany had been emptied of its traditional Natural Law content, which justified active or passive resistance to enactments running counter to *lex naturalis.* Kant and his followers recognized no such right, just as Luther (whose spiritual descendants they were) had refused to sanction disobedience to authority—any authority. Kant's doctrine is consistent with any state of affairs under which authority rules by means of general laws rather than arbitrary enactments. In strict theory, a distinction might be drawn between the government and the state, but in practice the two were usually identified. Later German legal philosophy followed in Kant's footsteps: the source of law is the state, and the legitimacy of law follows from its generality. As to their origins, *lex*

naturalis having been cast overboard, the laws might in principle have been regarded as the expression of the "general will," or as the conscious creation of the whole body of citizens. But that would have been democracy and led to unwelcome consequences. Hegel may have been right to distrust his countrymen, but the fact remains that his legal positivism had more in common with that of Hobbes than with the attitude of his Anglo-French contemporaries. The Benthamites naturally held that laws are the creation of civil society, which they identified with bourgeois society. Hegel vested the law-making faculty in the ruler and his bureaucratic advisers, where in fact it was traditionally located so long as absolutism remained intact. Not that the liberals were much wiser: talk of a "government of laws, not of men," concealed the fact that some men always rule, even though they may do so within a legal framework. But at least the liberals had grasped the connection between the supremacy of law and the sovereignty of an elected legislature. Of course, once in existence, this arrangement could be turned against the propertied classes whom they represented.

9. See Marx's letter to Engels of March 25, 1868, where he remarks in passing that the Romantic reaction against the French Revolution, for all its obscurantism and its nostalgia for the past, had cleared the way for the subsequent critique of bourgeois society.

> The second reaction—and it corresponds to the socialist trend, although the scholars in question have no notion of any connection with it—consists in regarding beyond the Middle Ages into the archaic age [*Urzeit*] of every people. Then they are surprised to encounter the most up-to-date in the most ancient [*im Ältesten das Neueste zu finden*], and even Egalitarians to a degree to give Proudhon the shudders. (*Karl Marx-Friedrich Engels: Historisch-Kritische Gesamtausgabe* [Frankfurt and Berlin, 1927–32] [cited hereafter as MEGA], III/4, p. 33.)

Marx's observations, in this very interesting letter, about common ownership among the ancient Germans are evidently one source of Engels' subsequent writings on the subject, and the same applies to his remark that civilization, unless consciously controlled, tends to bring about the physical desolation of those lands (Greece, Persia, Mesopotamia) where the historical process had originally got under way. All this was quite in accordance with the conservative critique of "progress," while "sublating" it in the Marxian manner. But for such a perspective to become possible, Marx himself had to mature and get over his youthful rebellion against the "historical school." In the 1840's no one on the political Left could afford to take a philosophical view of the Romantics and their allies among the philologists and historians: they were the enemy and had to be fought. See Hans Mayer, "Die deutsche Romantik in marxistischer Sicht," in *Zur deutschen Klassik und Romantik* (Stuttgart, 1963), pp.

288 ff. For a more polemical treatment of the subject, in the Leninist manner, see Georg Lukács, *Werke* (Neuwied and Berlin, 1964), VII, 249 ff.

10. Alexis de Tocqueville, *The European Revolution,* ed., John Lukacs (New York, 1959), pp. 7–8, 171–72. In passing it may be observed that, while paying his respects to Burke's "powerful mind," Tocqueville felt constrained to deplore his insularity. "He perceives some of the great future dangers. But the general characteristics, the universality, the portents of the Revolution then beginning, completely escape him. He lives, confined in England, within the old world and he does not comprehend the new and universal meaning of what is happening." (*Ibid.,* p. 163.) This indeed was the wisdom of hindsight, for Tocqueville was writing after having witnessed the European upheaval of 1848–49, but it was true nonetheless. For the original text see *L'Ancien Régime et la Révolution: Fragments et Notes inédites sur la Révolution,* in Tocqueville, *Oeuvres Complètes,* ed., J. P. Mayer (Paris, 1953), II, 340–41.

11. A very good description of these secret fraternities and their rituals is to be found in E. J. Hobsbawm, *Primitive Rebels* (Manchester, 1959; New York, 1963), pp. 150 ff. Briefly it may be said that the labor sects of the 1830–48 period represented a confluence of two distinct trends: an ancient tradition of secrecy inherited from a religious millenarianism largely co-extensive with primitive forms of social revolt (see Norman Cohn, *The Pursuit of the Millennium* [London, 1957], *passim*), and a surge of revolutionary conspiracy in the wake of the great upheaval of 1789. Whether or not some of the democratic brotherhoods were consciously modeled upon the *Illuminati* of the eighteenth century, they certainly adopted Masonic rituals and in some cases overlapped with the more radical lodges. Masons had been prominent in the American and French revolutions, and Masonic sympathies for democratic principles were a factor in the anti-clericalism of French and Italian politics. This, however, was an aspect of bourgeois liberalism. The labor sects of the period, if not modeled upon the lodges, resembled them in their hierarchical structure and in their attachment to elaborate rituals of initiation; but the pace-setters in this field were radical republicans and other neo-Jacobins with contacts among army officers and middle-class officials. Mention has already been made of Buonarroti and the Charbonnerie, and of how the latter constituted a link between the older and the newer forms of revolutionary action, i.e., between Jacobinism and Blanquism or "communism." An enumeration of the numberless fraternities of the period—including the Mazzinian secret societies in Italy, or the Irish Republican Brotherhood (better known as the Fenians) which came into being in the 1850's—would be tedious. The point that needs to be retained is that the revolutionary workers' movement copied their rites, while also conserving some ancient (even medieval) traditions of its own, as in the case of the French *compagnonnages.* Conversely, intellectuals who joined the workers' movement did so typically by way of the secret societies.

12. For literature on this theme, see Julius Braunthal, *History of the International 1864–1914*, Vol. I (London and New York, 1966), pp. 44 ff.; Jacques Droz, *Europe Between Revolutions, 1815–1848* (London, 1967), pp. 94 ff.; Werner Hofmann, *Ideengeschichte der Sozialen Bewegung des 19. und 20. Jahrhunderts* (Berlin, 1962), pp. 74 ff.; Thilo Ramm, *Die Grossen Sozialisten als Rechts- und Sozialphilosophen* (Stuttgart, 1955), pp. 475 ff. Weitling's principal writings are *Die Menschheit, wie sie ist und wie sein sollte* (1838); *Garantien der Harmonie und Freiheit* (1842); and *Das Evangelium eines armen Sünders* (1844). The manuscript of this last work, for which its author had chosen a slightly different title, was confiscated by the Swiss authorities in 1843, a circumstance which has led to some confusion among historians. For the original text and editorial notes on the author and secondary literature, see Thilo Ramm, ed., *Der Frühsozialismus* (Stuttgart, 1955). The conflict between Marx and Weitling in 1846–47 has been described countless times; the classical Social Democratic treatment of the subject is to be found in Franz Mehring's biography *Karl Marx: The Story of his Life* (London, 1936, 1948, 1951), pp. 116 ff. For the genesis of the Communist League, see also Engels' preface to the posthumous third edition (1885) of Marx's 1852 pamphlet, *Enthüllungen über den Kommunistenprozess zu Köln*, in *Marx-Engels Selected Works* (Moscow, 1951) (hereafter cited as MESW), II, 306 ff. There is a detailed account of the topic in Gustav Mayer's standard biography, *Friedrich Engels* (The Hague, 1934), I, 245 ff. See also Boris Nicolaevsky and Otto Maenchen-Helfen, *Karl Marx: Man and Fighter* (London, 1936), pp. 107 ff. It would seem that by the time he came into conflict with Marx, Weitling had been unsettled both by his sudden fame and by his imprisonment in Switzerland, and become somewhat deranged: neither the first nor the last autodidact to lose his bearings in an arena for which his training had not fitted him.

13. Nicolaevsky and Maenchen-Helfen, *op. cit.*, pp. 113–14.

14. Lorenz von Stein's major work went through several editions. The first and most influential appeared in 1842 under the title *Der Socialismus und Communismus des heutigen Frankreichs*. The terms "socialism" and "communism" then (and for many years thereafter) furnished convenient labels for two quite distinct notions: peaceful social reform on the one hand, revolutionary violence (in the Babouvist sense) on the other. The distinction was common to writers of the period and had not been invented by Stein, but he was important in popularizing it among German readers. A later version of this work, an enlarged three-volume affair published in 1850 under the title *Geschichte der socialen Bewegung in Frankreich von 1789 bis auf unsere Tage* (new ed., Munich, 1922), gave an historical account of French socialist movements but also threw out some general hints. Stein is one of the ancestors of modern sociology. In his writings, state and society are clearly distinguished, the economic process appears as the motor of social development, and "civil society" is treated as the material substratum of politics. Stein's theoretical position in 1850 might

thus be described as an amalgam of Comte and Hegel. His preface makes the (Comtean) assumption that it is the task of science to discover the laws governing the dynamic of social development. Classes arise from the functional division between the owners of property and those who do not possess anything but their labor. The social order is thus necessarily based upon inequality. This was standard doctrine among the economists, at least since Smith and Ricardo, and did not in itself constitute an innovation. Where Stein differed from the conventional liberal approach was in introducing the state as a realm of freedom and equality transcending class conflict and preserving the general good. This was part of the Hegelian inheritance, and the point on which he felt bound to differ from the standard liberal treatment of the subject. In 1852–56 Stein published his *Staatswissenschaft* which expounded the principle that "the various orders of society and its classes are linked together in such a fashion as to complement one another." For Marx's real or supposed interest in Stein's work see Shlomo Avineri, *The Social and Political Thought of Karl Marx* (Cambridge, 1968), pp. 53–56. Marx appears to have read Stein's first book on its publication in 1842; he certainly refers to it in the *Holy Family* (1845) and in the *German Ideology* (1846). After he removed to Paris in 1843 he no longer needed Stein, who incidentally was a secret agent of the Prussian government and utilized his contacts in Paris to report to the Prussian Minister of the Interior on the activities of German emigrants; see Gustav Mayer, *Friedrich Engels,* I, 380.

15. For Rodbertus, see Schumpeter, *op. cit.,* pp. 506–7; and Gray, *op. cit.,* pp. 343 ff. Engels' polemic against him is to be found in the East Berlin edition of the *Werke,* IV, 558–68. The posthumously published collection of Rodbertus' writings edited by Wagner and others under the title *Zur Beleuchtung der Socialen Frage* incorporated, among others, the second of his *Sociale Briefe an von Kirchmann,* which established his reputation on its appearance in 1850 (English trans., *Overproduction and Crises* [London, 1898]). It is possible that Marx may have come across the *Sociale Briefe* while at work on his 1859 introduction to a *Critique of Political Economy.* Neither Marx nor Engels appears to have been aware of his earlier (1842) discussion of pauperism and crises. He was after all merely one among the Ricardian socialists of the age, although certainly a pioneer so far as his German conservative readers were concerned. So far as Marx is concerned, one may note Schumpeter's verdict that "Rodbertus' example can at best have taught Marx how not to go about his task and how to avoid the grossest errors." (*Op. cit.,* p. 506.)

16. See Moses Hess to Berthold Auerbach, September 2, 1841, in *Moses Hess, Briefwechsel,* ed. Edmund Silberner (The Hague, 1959), p. 80. Also MEGA I/1/2, pp. 260–61. The authoritative account of Hess' life and work is to be found in Silberner, *Moses Hess. Geschichte seines Lebens* (Leiden, 1966). This massive and immensely learned work is of great value for the understanding of the early socialist movement in Germany. It also

illuminates the social and religious background from which youthful democrats like Hess emerged in the 1830's. Unlike Marx, who came from a well-to-do and cultivated household with aristocratic connections, Hess was an autodidact who had to emancipate himself slowly and painfully from the depressing milieu into which he was born. His subsequent conversion to Zionism induced him to give a somewhat sentimentalized account of his early years, and to pass over in silence the dreadful childhood he spent in the orthodox establishment where he was "beaten black and blue over the Talmud until my fifteenth year." See Silberner, *Moses Hess*, p. 2. On the general subject of socialist attitudes towards the Jewish problem, see Silberner, *Sozialisten zur Judenfrage* (Berlin, 1962), *passim*. There is a useful selection from Hess' writings (including the full text of his famous Zionist pamphlet *Rom und Jerusalem*) in *Moses Hess, Ausgewählte Schriften*, ed., H. Lademacher (Cologne, 1962). This includes extracts from his correspondence, notably some interesting letters to Alexander Herzen. For Marx's controversial essay on the Jewish question, see Nathan Rotenstreich, "For and against Emancipation. The Bruno Bauer Controversy," in *Yearbook* IV of the Leo Baeck Institute (London, 1959).

17. For a scholarly dissection of this theme see Lademacher's preface to *Moses Hess, Ausgewählte Schriften*. For the precise role of Hess in launching the socialist movement, see Hess, "Über die sozialistische Bewegung in Deutschland," in Karl Grün, ed., *Neue Anekdota* (Darmstadt, 1845). (The essay was dated Cologne, May 1844. Reprinted in *Moses Hess Ausgewählte Schriften*.) Grün (1813–87), while less important than Hess, was his principal associate in developing the doctrine of "true socialism" and as such became a favorite target for Marx and Engels from 1846 on. Having been personally acquainted with Cabet, Proudhon, and Considérant, he was able to draw upon first-hand information when in 1845 he published his work *Die Sociale Bewegung in Frankreich und Belgien*. In the Prussian legislature, to which he was elected in 1848, he adhered to the democratic Left.

18. See Lobkowicz, *op. cit.*, pp. 215 ff., for the Left Hegelians in general and Hess in particular. The authorship of the concept of "alienation" is discussed there, pp. 293 ff., and in Robert C. Tucker's well-known study *Philosophy and Myth in Karl Marx* (Cambridge, Mass., 1961). See also Eugene Kamenka, *The Ethical Foundations of Marxism* (London and New York, 1962), *passim;* Erich Thier, "Anthropologie und Eschatologie bei Moses Hess," in Erich Thier, ed., *Karl Marx: Nationalökonomie und Philosophie* (Cologne and Berlin, 1950), pp. 54 ff. For the decisive role of Hess in bringing the Saint-Simonian critique of liberalism to the attention of the youthful Engels, see Mayer, *op. cit.*, I, 100–115. It is not too much to say that in 1842 Hess literally converted Engels to communism—two years before Engels and Marx had entered upon their lifelong partnership. Once this had been formed, Hess with his utopian socialism and his in-

difference to economics was forgotten or treated as an anachronism, but his intervention in the early 1840's was the decisive factor in establishing a link between the French and German radicals. See Sidney Hook, *From Hegel to Marx* (New York, 1950), pp. 188 ff.

19. Hess, "Philosophie der Tat," in Georg Herwegh, ed., *Einundzwanzig Bogen aus der Schweiz* (Zürich, 1843); reprinted in Moses Hess, *Sozialistische Aufsätze 1841–1847*, ed., Theodor Zlocisti (Berlin, 1921); see also *Moses Hess, Ausgewählte Schriften*, pp. 130 ff. In the preface to his unpublished drafts known as the *Paris Manuscripts*, Marx commented favorably upon this essay in which Hess had extended Feuerbach's critique of religion to the political sphere. Hook notes that Marx's friend Köppen at about the same time published an article on "Fichte and the Revolution" in which he extolled Fichte's metaphysical idealism (*op. cit.*, p. 194). Any "philosophy of action" was indeed bound to invoke the Fichtean example, but the concrete examples of revolutionary socialism cited by Hess in 1843 were derived from France: he expressly mentioned Babeuf and Proudhon. Then followed an assertion which must have attracted Marx's special attention: French socialism and German idealism had the same ultimate goal—to set man free from all external constraints, including the material accretions of his own history. This stress upon the substantial identity of the French and German viewpoints distinguished "true socialism" from Marx's later and more realistic attitude, but in 1844 he as yet saw no objection to it.

20. "Philosophie der Tat," in *Moses Hess, Ausgewählte Schriften*, pp. 143–44. See Marx's observations in the 1844 *Paris Manuscripts*, where Feuerbach is invoked to underpin the general principle that spiritual freedom demands for its corollary material self-determination:

A *being* only considers himself independent when he stands on his own feet; and he only stands on his own feet when he owes his *existence* to himself. A man who lives by the grace of another regards himself as a dependent being. But I live completely by the grace of another if I owe him not only the maintenance of my life, but if he has, moreover, *created* my life—if he is the *source* of my life. (Karl Marx, *Economic and Philosophical Manuscripts*, ed., Dirk J. Struik [New York, 1964], p. 144.)

The argument is directed against theology, but it follows up the logic of the antecedent description of man's self-estrangement due to the alienation of labor. "If his own activity is to him related as an unfree activity, then he is related to it as an activity performed in the service, under the dominion, the coercion and the yoke of another man." (*Ibid.*, p. 116). This emphasis upon the intolerable affront thereby done to human dignity reflects Marx's commitment to a fundamental attitude which was to accompany him all his life. What matters in our context is that Hess—in his own, rather more amiable and sentimental fashion—had preceded him in linking atheism with communism as manifestations of the same principle.

21. Hess, "Die europäische Triarchie," in *Moses Hess, Ausgewählte Schriften,* pp. 110–12. The idea of a Western alliance went back to Saint-Simon, but in the Saint-Simonian version it was restricted to France and England and intended to promote liberalism, not socialism. For Hess, as was only natural, German participation was essential.

22. "Über die sozialistische Bewegung in Deutschland," in *ibid.,* p. 175.

23. For Marx's and Engels' onslaught on Hess and Grün in 1846, see *Die deutsche Ideologie,* in MEGA, I/5, pp. 441 ff.; also Marx-Engels, *Werke* (East Berlin, 1959), III, 445 ff. The section dealing with Grün was the work of Engels. Unlike Grün (perhaps the only consistent doctrinaire of "true socialism"), Hess had by 1847 more or less accepted the communist perspective of a proletarian revolution, although he viewed it without enthusiasm. See his article series "Die Folgen einer Revolution des Proletariats," published in the *Deutsche Brüsseler Zeitung* of October-November 1847, a few weeks before Marx was commissioned by the Communist League to write the *Manifesto.* For a lengthy extract, see *Moses Hess Ausgewählte Schriften,* pp. 193 ff. The tone of this article series, with its emphasis upon the class struggle between bourgeoisie and proletariat, contrasts markedly with some of Hess' earlier utterances which provoked Marx's sarcasms in the *German Ideology.* It is evident that by the close of 1847 Hess had come to regard himself as a communist in the "French" sense, albeit in a spirit of resignation and without renouncing his principled commitment to the "religion of love and humanity" which Marx and Engels found so irritating. There was to be a further and even more paradoxical development: when the German Communist League split in 1850 because Marx refused to accept the perspective of an imminent proletarian revolution in Germany, Hess sided with the ultra-radical Willich-Schapper group. Not long thereafter he took a tolerant view of Napoleon III, who in December 1851 had made himself dictator and suppressed parliamentary government in France. The connecting link was evidently the profound aversion for bourgeois liberalism which Hess had come to feel. He went so far as to affirm that it made no great difference whether the dictator was called Napoleon or Blanqui, so long as he made an end of the bourgeoisie and its reign. *Moses Hess Ausgewählte Schriften,* p. 33. In later years Hess reverted to what might be called a social-democratic standpoint and, indeed, became very active in promoting Lassallean ideas, but the immediate aftermath of the 1848–49 revolution found him on what was then the extreme Left. For details of his activities during the revolutionary era, and his later career as an apostle of democratic socialism and/or Jewish Messianism, see Silberner, *Moses Hess,* pp. 271 ff., and *passim.*

Chapter 10: The Marxian Synthesis

1. The biographical data are (or ought to be) familiar, but some of them will bear repetition. Karl Marx (1818–83) was born in Trier, in what was then Prussian territory, three years after the close of the Napoleonic wars. The Marx family, by virtue of the elder Marx's (1777–1838) professional standing as a lawyer and his formal conversion to Christianity around 1816, stemmed from the "assimilated" upper stratum of the Jewish middle class in the Rhineland—a circumstance which incidentally helps to explain Marx's lifelong distaste for Ferdinand Lassalle (1825–64), who had emerged from a less cultivated background in Silesia and lacked the social graces. It was likewise not altogether untypical that the youthful Karl Marx in 1843 should have married Jenny von Westphalen, a childhood friend and the daughter of a liberal-minded aristocrat with vague Saint-Simonian leanings. Marx's school essays in the 1830's are a high-spirited compound of liberal Protestantism, Fichtean idealism, and Byronic romanticism. Having completed his studies at the universities of Bonn and Berlin in 1841 and served a political apprenticeship as editor of the liberal *Rheinische Zeitung* in 1842–43, he found the German atmosphere intolerable and—like Arnold Ruge and likeminded liberal democrats—exiled himself to Paris. Expelled from France in 1845, he went to Brussels, where (together with Engels) he established contact with the leaders of the Communist League. In 1848–49, during the brief German revolution, he returned once more to Cologne as editor of the radical-democratic *Neue Rheinische Zeitung*. From 1849 to the close of his life in 1883, he made London his home. The story of his personal and financial tribulations is familiar, also the fact that for ten years (1853–63) he was the London correspondent of a leading American daily, *The New York Tribune*. In 1864 he became the guiding spirit of the First International, and in later years he and Engels were the principal source of theoretical inspiration for the growing Social Democratic movement in Germany. Only the first volume of *Capital* was completed and published in his lifetime (1867). Later volumes were pieced together from his manuscript by Engels and Karl Kautsky. For the background of the Marx family, see Heinz Monz, *Karl Marx und Trier* (Trier, 1964), *passim*. In the standard biographies by Mehring and Nicolaevsky, some of the dates regarding the birth of Marx's parents and their entry into the Protestant church are incorrectly given.

2. In an account of Marxism (as distinct from the life and work of Karl Marx) more would need to be said about the contribution made by Hess and others. Here one can only direct the reader's attention to the relevant literature: primarily Marx's early writings, which are now available

in most languages. For the beginner there exists a very useful introduction in the shape of two scholarly selections: *Karl Marx—Early Writings,* tr. and ed., T. B. Bottomore, with a preface by Erich Fromm (New York and London, 1964); and *Karl Marx—Selected Writings in Sociology and Social Philosophy,* tr. and ed., T. B. Bottomore and Maximilien Rubel (London and New York, 1956–64).

The voluminous literature on the subject can be approached from the biographical end, where the two standard works are Franz Mehring, *Karl Marx: The Story of his Life* (London, 1936, 1948, 1951), and Boris Nicolaevsky and Otto Maenchen-Helfen, *Karl Marx: Man and Fighter* (London, 1936). The latter work deals mainly with the political side, while Mehring gives the fullest biographical data. Far and away the best analytical study of Marxism as a sociological doctrine is to be found in Karl Korsch, *Karl Marx* (New York, 1963). An extremely learned account of the transformation of Marx's philosophical doctrine into a sterile systematization—from Engels until the final codification under Lenin and Stalin—is provided by Z. A. Jordan's important study *The Evolution of Dialectical Materialism* (London and New York, 1967). This treats the subject critically from an empiricist standpoint, while avoiding the polemical excesses of Professor Karl Popper in *The Open Society* (London, 1962). For a good, short, scholarly dissection of Marx's political philosophy and its Hegelian origins, see Shlomo Avineri, *The Social and Political Thought of Karl Marx* (Cambridge, 1968). This goes at some length into the connection between Marx's philosophy and his economics, a topic slighted by conservative writers like Tucker and Lobkowicz. A brief and scholarly exegesis of Marx's theoretical beginnings may also be found in H. P. Adams, *Karl Marx in his Earlier Writings* (London, 1940, 1965). For a sympathetic but critical biographical essay see Isaiah Berlin, *Karl Marx: His Life and Environment* (Oxford, 1939, 1948, 1965). French and Geman sources are cited below. For an engaging picture of the Marx family circle (which can also serve as an antidote to fanciful psychological speculation on the subject), see Chushichi Tsuzuki's biographical study *The Life of Eleanor Marx, 1855–1898* (Oxford, 1967).

3. See Herbert Marcuse, *Reason and Revolution* (London, 1955), pp. 258 ff.; Sidney Hook, *From Hegel to Marx* (New York, 1950), pp. 56 ff.; Jordan, *op. cit.,* pp. 65 ff.; Korsch, *op. cit.,* pp. 167 ff.; and Gordon Leff, *The Tyranny of Concepts: a Critique of Marxism* (London, 1961). In recent years, a dawning awareness of the difference between the "historical materialism" of Marx and the "dialectical materialism" of Engels has led to a departure from the type of controversy still in vogue around 1957 when Karl Popper published *The Poverty of Historicism,* a work whose uselessness for the understanding of Marx's historical method is rightly emphasized by Leff, *op. cit.,* pp. 77 ff. At the other extreme, Soviet orthodoxy still presents Marx and Engels as the twin originators of a supra-historical doctrine known as "dialectical materialism" which supposedly underlies

their historical materialism. This notion goes back to Plekhanov and Lenin, and consequently retains official status in the Soviet orbit. In Western Europe it is now coming to be recognized even by communist writers that Marx's method was not simply an inverted Hegelianism with the concept of "matter" substituted for that of "spirit." See Louis Althusser, "Contradiction et surdétermination," in *Pour Marx* (Paris, 1966). By contrast, Auguste Cornu's massive three-volume biographical study, *Karl Marx et Friedrich Engels* (Paris: 1955, 1958, 1962) retains the orthodox approach and for all its solidity does not offer a very useful guide to the problem of Marx's emancipation from Hegel. The most enlightening German-language treatment of this difficult subject is to be found in Günther Hillmann's *Marx und Hegel: Von der Spekulation zur Dialektik* (Frankfurt, 1966). See also the same author's edition of Marx's early writings: *Karl Marx Texte zu Methode und Praxis* (Hamburg, 1966–67); Iring Fetscher, *Der Marxismus: Seine Geschichte in Dokumenten,* especially Vol. I (Munich, 1962); Alfred Schmidt, *Der Begriff der Natur in der Lehre von Marx* (Frankfurt, 1962); and Jürgen Habermas, *Theorie und Praxis* (Neuwied, 1963), *passim.* The last-mentioned work, an original and important reconsideration of Hegel's and Schelling's philosophical legacy, makes considerable demands upon the reader.

4. See Hook, *op. cit.,* pp. 28 ff. This is not the place to go into the problem of universals and Hegel's solution of this perennial logical puzzle. It must be enough to say that Marx consistently steers a middle course between Hobbes and Hegel. Theoretical concepts for him have no subsistence prior to their concrete exemplification in empirical reality, but there *are* objective processes at work which have an actual existence within (not behind) the visible, tangible data of immediate experience. "Anything which exists is an exemplification of some universal. That is why it can be understood. But there are no universals without exemplification. That is why universals have meanings which can be communicated. There are no incommunicable meanings." (Hook, *ibid.,* p. 35.)

5. Marx, *Die deutsche Ideologie,* in *Karl Marx-Friedrich Engels: Historisch-Kritische Gesamtausgabe* (Frankfurt and Berlin, 1927–32) (cited hereafter as MEGA), I/5, pp. 10–11. See also Jordan, *op. cit.,* pp. 297 ff.; Korsch, *op. cit.,* pp. 183 ff.; and Bottomore and Rubel, ed., *Selected Writings,* pp. 51 ff. The *Theses on Feuerbach* may be said to constitute the definite point of rupture with the pre-Marxist viewpoint, the latter for our purpose including the "passive" naturalism of Feuerbach for whom the mind was primarily receptive rather than spontaneous; on this point see Marcuse, *op. cit.,* pp. 267–72. For Jordan, the *German Ideology* marks a temporary rupture with Hegel to whom Marx is supposed for some reason to have reverted in 1859, when he wrote his preface to *A Contribution to the Critique of Political Economy.* Jordan attributes the emancipation from Hegel in the 1840's to the influence of French positivism as typified

by Saint-Simon and (indirectly, since Marx had not bothered to read him before 1866) Auguste Comte.

That the *German Ideology* reflects Marx's assimilation of French materialism is undeniable, but the break with Hegel (and Feuerbach) had·already occurred in the *Theses,* where the concept of "practice" (*Praxis*) is upheld against idealist speculation on the one hand and contemplative naturalism on the other. Moreover, Marx (unlike Saint-Simon and Comte) did not elevate "society" to the status of a reality superior to the individuals composing it. To have done so would have meant renouncing the originality of his standpoint, not to mention the German-idealist roots of his thinking. Man and society are an interacting whole, each term implying the other. "The coincidence of the transformation of circumstances and of human activity can only be conceived and rationally understood as revolutionizing practice." (*Third Thesis on Feuerbach.*) For the celebrated *Paris Manuscripts* of 1844, see the standard English-language edition (tr., Martin Milligan; ed., Dirk J. Struik [New York, 1964]), based on the text in MEGA, I/3, as corrected in Marx-Engels, *Kleine ökonomische Studien* (Berlin, 1955). This edition also reprints Engels' "Outlines of a Critique of Political Economy," the essay he published in the *Deutsch-Französische Jahrbücher* of 1844. It was this piece of writing that first brought the two men together. The biographical circumstances are set out in Mehring, *op. cit.*

A brief but extremely competent assessment of Marx's evolution from the quasi-Hegelian standpoint of the 1844 writings to his mature views on social evolution is to be found in the Introduction to Bottomore and Rubel, ed., *Selected Writings;* see also Bottomore, ed., *Karl Marx—Early Writings,* for a different translation and edition of three out of the four *Manuscripts* of 1844, as well as Marx's essays in the *Deutsch-Französische Jahrbücher.* (This edition also supplies a list of authors and works cited by Marx.) Bottomore's introduction to this selection may be read *inter alia* as a critical commentary upon the interpretation of the 1844 *Manuscripts* put forward by other writers, notably Lukács and Marcuse. The subject appears to be inexhaustible. Struik's edition of the *Manuscripts* gives an account of Marx's intellectual progress after 1841, with due emphasis upon the fact that in 1844 Marx was still "the pupil of Hegel and Feuerbach, but already the emancipated pupil who is finding his own way on the shoulders of the great men who preceded him." (*Op. cit.,* p. 31.) For a humanist interpretation of Marx's thought, see Maximilien Rubel, *Karl Marx. Essai de biographie intellectuelle* (Paris, 1957), *passim.* For a somewhat different emphasis see Althusser, *op. cit.,* pp. 23–32, 47 ff., where it is argued that the 1844 *Manuscripts* represent a brief episode in Marx's intellectual development, when—for the first and last time—he attempted to solve a Hegelian problem with the aid of what Althusser describes as "the pseudo-materialism of Feuerbach." It is certainly the case that Marx was a Feuerbachian in 1844, whereas in his student days he had passed through a Fichtean idealist phase before coming across Hegel. Whether it follows that, apart from a brief moment in 1844, he was never in any sense a Hegelian, is another matter. The *Manuscripts* themselves have been exhaustively discussed, and a knowledge of their contents (if not of their esoteric meaning) can by now be taken for granted. For an elucidation of their terminology see the very useful explanatory note supplied by Milligan and Struik, *op. cit.,* pp. 57–60.

6. "Es genügt nicht, dass der Gedanke zur Verwirklichung drängt, die Wirklichkeit muss sich selbst zum Gedanken drängen." Marx, *Zur Kritik der Hegelschen Rechtsphilosophie,* MEGA I/1, 616; Eng. tr., Bottomore, *Early Writings,* p. 54. For a discussion of this theme see Lobkowicz, *op. cit.,* pp. 239 ff. The essential point is that Marx was alone in recognizing the inherent impossibility of all attempts to actualize a "total" philosophy. Absolute knowledge in Hegel's sense was absolute just because it was *not* practical and critical. On the other hand, the relevance of Cieszkowski's or Bauer's "critique" depended on its being grounded in absolute knowledge; hence their position was self-contradictory. Of course Marx did not realize this all at once. In his doctoral dissertation of 1841 he had affirmed that "the *practice* of philosophy is itself theoretical. It is the *critique* which measures the singular existence against the essence, the particular actuality against the Idea." (MEGA I/1, 64.) He was then still under the spell of Bauer. By 1844 he had absorbed the French materialists and correspondingly shifted his ground: one starts not by "measuring actuality against the Idea," but by asking what it is that empirical men—notably those in revolt against the constituted order—actually need and want. This was the sum and substance of Marx's "materialism," a materialism quite compatible with the moral idealism of his youth. For one of the sources of the latter see Schiller, *On the Aesthetic Education of Man* (1795), new ed. and tr. by Elizabeth M. Wilkinson and L. A. Willoughby (Oxford, 1967). For a penetrating study of Hegel's philosophy and its Marxian transmutation, see François Chatelet, *Logos et Praxis. Recherches sur la signification théorique du Marxisme* (Paris, 1962). This is an important work, much superior to Althusser's overrated essays, whose appearance around 1965 caused a minor sensation chiefly because no one had expected a self-confessed former Stalinist and prominent member of the Communist Party to reach the intellectual level normally taken for granted among French *universitaires.*

7. Marx was primarily concerned with the manner in which this process reflected itself in social and economic theorizing from the eighteenth century on, although in *Capital* he went further back. It was only after his death (and then largely under the aegis of Max Weber and his school in Germany) that a corresponding investigation was attempted for the sixteenth and seventeenth centuries, with special reference to the (real or supposed) interaction between the Protestant Reformation and the rise of capitalism in Western Europe and North America. This particular

Fragestellung, or "problematic," had been suggested by Marxism (if not by Marx in person), and whatever one may think of the solutions offered by Weber (and by Tawney in Britain) their approach to the matter took for granted the Marxian concept of "ideology" as "false consciousness," i.e., consciousness unaware of its own historical limitations. For an illuminating discussion of this topic in relation to British seventeenth-century history, see C. B. Macpherson, *The Political Theory of Possessive Individualism* (Oxford, 1962), *passim.* For a more general analysis of European bourgeois civilization since the seventeenth century, see Jürgen Habermas, *Strukturwandel der Öffentlichkeit* (Neuwied, 1962), *passim.*

8. "The outstanding thing in Hegel's Phenomenology . . . is . . . that Hegel conceives the self-creation of man as a process, conceives objectification as loss of the object, as alienation and transcendence of this alienation; that he thus grasps the essence of *labor* and comprehends objective man—true because real man—as the result of man's *own labor."* Marx, *Economic and Philosophic Manuscripts,* MEGA I/3, p. 156; cf. Milligan and Struik, *op. cit.,* p. 177.

9. *Marx-Engels Selected Works* (Moscow, 1958) (hereinafter cited as MESW) I, 362; for the original text see *Werke* (East Berlin, 1961), XIII, 8. The best analysis of this topic is to be found in Korsch, *op. cit.,* 17 ff., where Marx's indebtedness to Smith and Ferguson is duly emphasized. Hegel's approach in the 1820's combined the political authoritarianism of Hobbes with Smithian insights. His description of "civil society" is realistic enough but has a static quality. In the end it amounts to a stoical acceptance of the state of affairs described by the economists, with whose writings he was familiar. See his *Philosophy of Right* (tr. with notes by T. M. Knox [Oxford, 1942]), para. 245, where he refers explicitly to "the example of England" after describing the phenomenon of pauperism and discussing various means of dealing with it; e.g., taxes on the wealthier classes or subsidies from public funds.

In either case, however, the needy would receive subsistence directly, not by means of their work, and this would violate the principle of civil society and the feeling of individual independence and self-respect in its individual members. As an alternative, they might be given subsistence indirectly through being given work, i.e., the opportunity to work. In this event the volume of production would be increased, but the evil consists precisely in an excess of production and in the lack of a proportionate number of consumers.

The "principle of civil society" for Hegel (as for Kant) is violated by the spectacle of paupers maintained from public funds, because "civil society" is made up of independent individuals who are able to maintain themselves and their families by the exercise of some economically useful function. In other words, "civil society" is bourgeois society. Pauperism is an evil that has to be endured, presumably on La Rochefoucauld's principle: "One is always strong enough to support the misery of others."

10. See *Misère de la philosophie,* MEGA I/6, p. 217; cf. *The Poverty of Philosophy* (Moscow, 1956), p. 181. For an elaboration of this point, which is crucial for an understanding of Marx's difference from the "utopians," see his critical reflections on J. F. Bray:

> Mr. Bray does not realize that this egalitarian relationship, this *corrective ideal* which he wants to apply to the world, is nothing but the reflex of the actual world, and that in consequence it is altogether impossible to reconstitute society upon a basis which is merely its own embellished shadow. In the measure that this shade takes on corporeal substance, one perceives that this body, so far from being the dreamed-of transfiguration, is the actual body of society. (My translation after the original, MEGA I/6, p. 157.)

11. For an account of the traditional Marxist approach to this topic, see Korsch, *op. cit.,* pp. 45 ff. The essential point to keep in mind is that what mattered to Marx in his capacity as a theorist (as distinct from his primary moral commitment, which he shared with other socialists of his generation), was not the misery of the working class, but its *place in society.* Anyone might have been moved to alarm or indignation by the wretched condition of the early industrial proletariat, and a great many people were, including philanthropic conservatives like Rodbertus and romantic nationalists like Friedrich List, who became something of a hero to his countrymen on account of his eloquent championship of economic policies (primarily protectionist) designed to further the cause of German national unity. One could also assert that society would fall apart if the "social problem" was not effectively tackled—a favorite theme with socially-minded clergymen. What distinguished Marx was not the passion he put into the denunciation of capitalism, but the fact that he treated bourgeois society as a particular form of social organization which was due to disappear as soon as the working class had acquired a consciousness of its true role: that of being the creator of the great industrial edifice, a Hercules deprived of the fruits of his toil. Of course all this could be disputed, but the dispute turned upon theoretical considerations, not upon vague benevolent feelings which all civilized people might be expected to share.

12. The literature on the subject is immense, but it will be sufficient to note the main sources. On the biographical side there are three: Mehring's *Karl Marx;* Mayer's biography *Friedrich Engels,* I, 245 ff.; and the parallel study by Nicolaevsky and Maenchen-Helfen, *op. cit.,* pp. 122 ff. A brief account of the part played by the Chartists in launching the Society of Fraternal Democrats is to be found in Julius Braunthal, *History of the International 1864–1914,* Vol. I (London and New York, 1966), pp. 62 ff.

For the various editions of the *Manifesto* (in several languages), see the bibliographical note in G. D. H. Cole's *History of Socialist Thought*, Vol. I, *The Forerunners, 1789–1850* (London, 1955), p. 330.

For the original text of the *Manifesto*, see MEGA I/6, pp. 525 ff.; also Engels' *Grundsätze des Kommunismus, ibid.*, pp. 503 ff. This important draft, which Marx utilized when composing the final version, diverges in some respects from the final version jointly signed by the authors. The pamphlet published in February 1848 was swallowed up in the storm of the European upheaval and at first attracted little attention. Later editions include *Das Kommunistische Manifest* (Leipzig, 1872), with a new preface by Marx and Engels, and the fourth German edition of 1890, with a preface by Engels alone—both reproduced in *Werke* (East Berlin), IV, 573 ff.; this edition also includes the preface Marx and Engels composed for the Russian edition in 1882 and Engels' preface to the British edition of 1888.

The first English translation had appeared in Julian Harney's *Red Republican* in 1850 but did not then make much of an impact. Private and unauthorized versions include a Russian translation by Bakunin which made its appearance in 1869; a Polish translation issued in London in 1848; and perhaps an unofficial French translation in 1848, of which no copy seems to have survived and whose very existence is doubtful. Students of the subject are advised to consult Charles Andler's annotated French edition of 1901, and David Ryazanov's "Historical Introduction" to the English translation by Eden and Cedar Paul (London, 1930). In 1948 the British Labour Party marked the centenary of the *Manifesto* by publishing a new English edition with an introduction by Harold Laski.

For the later history of the Communist League see Mehring, *op. cit.*, pp. 200 ff.; Nicolaevsky and Maenchen-Helfen, *op. cit.*, pp. 199 ff.; and Vol. VII of the East German edition of the *Werke*, especially for the text of Marx's and Engels' important *Address of the Central Authority* in March 1850, and for the Société Universelle des Communistes Révolutionnaires of April 1850 (pp. 244 ff., 553–54, 615). See also MESW, I, 106 ff., which gives the text of the March 1850 *Address* but ignores Marx's brief alliance with the Blanquists, which was sealed a month later and quietly wound up toward the end of the year.

13. Nicolaevsky and Maenchen-Helfen, *op. cit.*, p. 167. This was quite in accordance with Marx's analysis of the coming German revolution in the *Manifesto* (whose composition dated from the end of 1847), but it did not go down well with all the members of the League, though at first its working-class leaders stood by Marx in defending the thesis that Germany in 1848–49 was where France had been in 1789, and that the Democrats must be helped (or rather compelled) to take power. The trouble was that the German middle class was not revolutionary in temper, but it was only in 1850 that Marx felt obliged to revise his standpoint on this issue. By then he was unable to prevent a split in the League, whose more

extreme elements, led by Karl Schapper and August Willich, briefly reverted to Weitling's antiquated proletarian utopianism.

14. The *Address* is frequently cited in post-1917 Communist literature and is believed to have had considerable influence on Lenin. On the other hand, Soviet textbooks tend to be silent about the alliance with the Blanquists in 1850. It is true that this did not last long. On the other hand, it did produce a joint declaration, paragraph 1 of which read:

> Le but de l'association est la déchéance de toutes les classes privilégiées, de soumettre ces classes à la dictature des prolétaires en maintenant la révolution en permanence jusqu'à la réalisation du communisme, qui doit être la dernière forme de constitution de la famille humaine.
>
> [The aim of the association is the deposition of all the privileged classes, their submission to the dictatorship of the proletarians, in maintaining the revolution in permanence until the realization of communism, which is to be the final mode of existence of the human family.]

For an analysis of the concept of "proletarian dictatorship" and the respective shares taken by Marx and Blanqui in formulating it, see Harold Draper, "Marx and the Dictatorship of the Proletariat," in *Cahiers de l'Institut de Science Economique Appliquée,* No. 129 (Paris, 1962). The statutes of the Société Universelle bore six signatures: those of Marx, Engels, and Willich representing the German Communist League; J. Vidil and Adam representing the Blanquists; and Harney for the Chartists. See Nicolaevsky and Maenchen-Helfen, *op. cit.,* pp. 208–9. By October 1850 Marx and Engels had become disillusioned with the whole project of an international communist society and notified the Blanquists accordingly. See *Werke* (East Berlin, 1960), VII, 646.

15. For a critical analysis of this part of Marx's theorizing, from the standpoint of a modern Polish sociologist who had assimilated the Marxian method, see Stanislaw Ossowski, *Class Structure in the Social Consciousness* (London, 1963), pp. 69 ff. For a critique delivered from the current liberal standpoint, see Raymond Aron, *Les étapes de la pensée sociologique* (Paris, 1967), pp. 143 ff. Aron goes into Marx's sociology at some length; in particular he makes the valid point that the emancipation of the working class can today no longer be conceived on the model of the bourgeois revolution (*op. cit.,* pp. 192–93). This appears to be also the conclusion reached by those of Marx's present-day French disciples who have adopted a syndicalist position counterposing the working class to the managerial bureaucracy of a state-controlled economy. The *Manifesto* in point of fact anticipates some of Marx's mature formulations, notably in the passage where the British working class is congratulated on having won a peaceful victory in the shape of labor legislation. But in general the emphasis lies upon the dichotomy bourgeoisie-proletariat, with the latter driven to desperation and compelled to act in such a manner as to overturn

the existing social order. "The proletariat, the lowest stratum of our present society, cannot stir, cannot raise itself up, without the whole superincumbent strata of official society being sprung into the air." (MESW, I, p. 44.) On the whole this was to remain Marx's basic attitude until the catastrophic failure of the Paris Commune in 1871 imposed a different approach. But it was left to Engels to spell it out in the 1890's. The subject is strewn with pitfalls for people who imagine that "Marxism" is summed up in the *Manifesto* or some other authoritative document, instead of being a method of approach subject to revision under changed historical circumstances. The communism of 1848 had taken shape in the aftermath of the French Revolution, that is to say, of a *bourgeois* revolution, and as such it later became a model for Lenin in 1917, but after 1850 it lost its relevance for Western Europe and in the end Marx tacitly abandoned it. See George Lichtheim, *Marxism: An Historical and Critical Study* (New York, 1961; 2d ed., 1965), *passim*.

Index

291

European Triarchy, The (Hess), 181
Evangelical Dissenters, 8
Exposition de la doctrine de Saint-Simon, 46, 50, 52, 53, 54

Fabians, 75, 137, 139
Farmers, 116, 117, 119; *see also* Peasants
February Revolution (*1848*), 159
Feminism. *See* Women
Ferguson, Adam, 187
Feuerbach, Ludwig, 154, 156, 163, 170, 171, 172, 178, 179, 180, 182, 184, 188, 189–90, 194, 196, 200
Fichte, J. G., 146, 147, 148, 149–51, 152, 154, 157, 176, 180, 182, 186–91 *passim,* 194, 204
First International (*1864*), 137, 183, 214, 215
Flachat, Eugène, 56
Fourier, François-Marie-Charles, 27, 30–38, 54, 57, 59, 113, 117, 118, 120, 181, 186
Fourierism, 26, 30–38, 49, 68–69, 70–72
Fournel, Henri, 56
France: attempt to introduce democracy in, 17, 137, 210; Bourbon Restoration (*1815–30*) in, 18, 28, 42, 44, 161; February Revolution (*1848*) in, 159; July Monarchy in, 42–43, 45, 61, 63, 68, 71, 206; July Revolution (*1830*) in, 18, 25, 28, 42–43, 50, 145, 158; Paris Commune in, 60, 83, 164, 209; Provisional Government of *1848* in, 62; Second Empire in, 85; socialism in, 7–8, 18; *see also* French Revolution
Fraternal Democrats, 207, 208
Freemasons, 167
French Revolution: bourgeoisie

and, 33; challenge to Christian social order by, 5; Conspiracy of Equals in, 17, 21; and Constitution of *1798,* 22; and Convention of *1793,* 23; and Directory (*1795*), 19, 22; disillusionment with, 13–14; European reaction to, 157, 175, 176, 177; Jacobins in, 19, 20–21, 33, 54, 64; Montagne (*1793–94*) in, 20; and National Convention (*1793*), 64; radical sects in, 3, 6, 22; and Republic (*1795*), 19, 21, 24; and rise of political democracy, 4, 14, 105, 165–66, 210–11, 215

Gauguin, Paul, 69
Geächtete, Der, 166
Germain, Charles, 24
German Ideology (Marx), 183, 190
Germano-Coleridgean school of history, 111–13, 145
Germany: autocracy in, 163–64, 177; *Bürgertum* in, 157–58, 159, 162; industrial revolution in, 158, 161; Jews in, 176–78; liberalism in, 147, 157, 159–60, 161, 162, 163, 164; nationalism in, 147, 148, 150–52, 157, 161; political passivity in, 157, 158–59, 160; reaction of, to French Revolution, 175, 176, 177; *Rechtsstaat,* 159; revolution of *1848* in, 171–72; Romanticism in, 38, 145–49, 150, 151–52, 154, 158, 160; Saint-Simonism in, 59; *Scheinkonstitutionalismus* in, 159; secret workers' societies in, 166–68; socialism in, 10, 145–84; *Weltanschauung* of, 148
Geschlossene Handelsstaat, Der (Fichte), 149